Christmas
at the White House

May your Christmas memories always be filled with love.

Jennifer B. Pickens
Christmas 2009

Christmas
at the White House

JENNIFER BOSWELL PICKENS

FIFE &
DRUM
PRESS

ISBN 978-0-615-28764-5

Library of Congress Control Number 2009907543

Published in 2009 by Fife and Drum Press

FIFE&
DRUM
PRESS

100 Highland Park Village, Suite 200
Dallas, Texas 75205
fifeanddrumpress.com

To my daughters

Abigail Elizabeth and Margaret Manning,

May you never forget the true meaning

of Christmas.

Table of Contents

Foreword

BY LAURA BUSH

I n these pages you will find delightful photographs and reminiscences spanning almost fifty years and parts of two centuries. You will learn about special Christmas traditions of many presidential families, as well as some of the White House traditions that have provided a continuous thread through the years—like the beautiful crèche, magnificent Blue Room tree, and annual one-of-a-kind gingerbread house. You will also discover some of the intriguing personal and national stories that inhabit the building that has served as presidential home, office, and museum for most of our nation's existence.

From the earliest days of our country, occupants of the White House have tried to extend its hospitality to as many people as possible, especially during the holiday season. White House history is packed with accounts of public receptions, gala parties, tours, and open houses, with the "People's House" dressed up in its sparkling best. As the days of horse-drawn carriages have given way to jet planes, television, and the internet, a holiday visit to the White House has become accessible to millions around the world.

Christmas at the White House is celebrated both publicly and privately, and you will find both in this book. While throngs of visitors enjoy the beauty of the splendidly decorated public spaces, each presidential family carries on their own cherished holiday traditions upstairs in the residence. Favorite ornaments hang on the family tree, and small gatherings with friends and family provide a wonderful and sustaining sense of the familiar. I enjoy thinking about the special new traditions and holiday fun that the Obama family—and especially Sasha and Malia—will bring to the White House during their time there.

Of all the indelible memories from our time in Washington, some my family and I will always cherish most are of those beautiful days of celebration. I appreciate the hard work Jennifer Pickens has done to distill many Christmases into this lovely retrospective.

Laura Bush

Preface

I have vivid memories of Christmas as a child growing up in our home in Dallas, Texas. Every Christmas, my mother decked the house with nine full-sized trees—one for almost every room in the house—which she spent days decorating. She covered almost every surface with collections of carolers and snow villages. We also had a nativity in the den where we spent most of our time, reminding us of the true spirit of the season. The decorating would start on Thanksgiving Day. I can still hear the sound of the attic door coming down after the last dinner plate had been tucked safely away and my brother and father had left to go hunting. Down from the attic Mom would bring the first box of decorations, and by the next morning the first of a glittering sea of Christmas cheer would be up. It was the Boswell Christmas ritual.

Downstairs in the front foyer, the Crystal and Silver Tree welcomed all who entered. It was bedecked in sparkling crystal and sterling silver ornaments, many of which my mom had engraved with our names and the years, while others were from my father's days in the silver business. In a nod to nature, the Animal Tree, one of my favorites, stood in a cozy spot in our den. Encircled with a red raffia ribbon, the tree was festooned with dozens of God's wonderful creatures. A large Steiff donkey was placed beside it, and some years an electric train ran beneath it. There was a Snowman Tree in the kitchen accented by knitted items such as mittens, a Fishing Tree in the media room, and a Santa Tree in our sun room.

A giant Traditional Tree towered over us all inside Dad's study. We'd all gather around it on Christmas morning, awed by its grandeur. The tree stood two stories high and included absolutely everything, from delicate ornaments that we made by hand to collections of Dallas Cowboys ornaments, Barbie ornaments, my brother's Star Trek pieces, and others that had all been collected throughout the years. The ornaments on the Traditional Tree were the most special, as they were a way to honor memories of people, places, occasions, and things that mattered to us, no matter how simple.

We each had our own individual tree in our rooms. My brother was welcomed home from college by a Texas Tree, to remind him of his roots. My sister had a Teddy Bear Tree that I was always sneaking in to see. And my mother allowed me to select the theme for my own tree when I was about three: a Pink Tree, since pink was my favorite color. A full-sized pink flocked tree, it was decorated with pink lights, and naturally every ornament on it was pink! It was actually beautiful, and is a tiny tradition that I continue in both of my daughters' rooms today.

As I got older, part of my memories also include Christmas dinners. Mom made savory stuffing, turkey, and traditional Texas pecan pie, and most important, we ended it with conversation. Somehow or another my father would engage us in a political or American history discussion, which often included the whole family and sometimes a family friend who had joined us. These conversations likely sparked my decision to be an American history major in college, and later a political consultant. Our holiday dinnertime conversations are some of my most treasured memories.

In 2004 my husband and I were lucky enough to be invited to a White House Christmas party. I had never been to the White House before, and when we arrived that evening a light snow began to fall. As we stood in line with other guests at the iron gate, I looked up at the American flag waving on top of our nation's house and was overwhelmed with emotion. This was the home where John Adams and Thomas Jefferson had lived, and I was about to step inside! That year, First Lady Laura Bush had chosen a musical Christmas theme, "A Season of Merriment and Melody." It was one of the most beautiful scenes I had ever seen, and as I walked through the amazing displays I could not help but wonder what all of the other Christmas themes had been. When we returned home I searched for a book on White House Christmas decorations to give to family and friends and was dismayed to learn that all of these wonderful traditions had never been thoroughly documented, and books on the subject had never been written.

Researching the book was a great experience, but it did have its challenges. Not every administration documented and took photos of their holiday trimmings each year, so in order to fill in the holes I tracked down information and photos that had appeared in newspapers and magazines, and some came from personal interviews. Some images that are included came by way of the individual artists or museums whose works had appeared in the decorations. Sadly though, often they did not have the photos any longer, or the quality was too poor to reproduce. You can mark the advancement of film technology in this book as the quantity and quality of the photos grows with each year. An explosion of photographs occurs with First Lady Laura Bush; her administration was the first to eventually go fully digital with its photography, and more than any other First Lady before, she went to great efforts to document in detail the decorations of the season during her time at the White House.

Christmas at the White House is the culmination of more than four years of research, and I am very proud to present to you this one-of-a-kind holiday treasure.

Introduction

I hope you will enjoy this compilation of nearly 50 years of Christmas seasons at the White House. Decorations and holiday themes chosen by the nine First Ladies included in this book reveal much about the historic times in which they lived, as well as their individual tastes, personalities, and social and political priorities. I start the book in 1961 with Jacqueline Kennedy, who was the first to choose a decorating theme for the First Residence's Christmas tree. Since then, Christmas at the White House has become one of the most celebrated and anticipated events in the world. Planning and preparations take thousands of hours and involve hundreds of people, from White House engineers and florists to volunteers across the country.

During the early days of our Republic, Christmas was much more simply celebrated. The joining of family and friends for prayer and a festive meal on Christmas day was often the only event that might have taken place, so Christmas was not always celebrated with holiday decor at the White House. Our first President George Washington worked with architect James Hoban to design the White House, but he never spent a Christmas there. He died in 1799, one year before the house was completed. Abigail and John Adams were the first to actually spend Christmas at the White House, as they moved into the residence in November of 1800 while it was still partly under construction. Subsequent First Ladies love to recount how Abigail Adams burned more than 20 cords of wood during the first White House Christmas party trying to keep her guests warm. The house never warmed up, and many left the party early. As the end of the 19th century approached, many of the customs that we associate with the Christian holiday were just beginning in our country. More and more people put up Christmas trees in their homes and decorated them. Children's books featuring Santa Claus and gifts under the tree helped popularize the tradition of holiday decorating. In 1870, Congress passed a law making Christmas a national holiday, and by the end of the 1800s it was considered customary to decorate trees, sing carols, exchange gifts, bake goods, and include many of the traditions associated with Christmas as we know it today. The first recorded presidential Christmas tree decorated for the holidays was during the Harrison Administration on December 25, 1889. President Benjamin Harrison, the 23rd President of the United States, helped trim the tree along with family, friends, and staff members. The tree was placed in the upstairs library, which is today known as part of the private residence. The Victorian-era tree, elegantly trimmed with garlands and lit candles, had gifts mounded underneath. President Harrison exclaimed: "We shall have an old-fashioned Christmas tree for the grandchildren upstairs, and I shall be their Santa Claus myself."

Not all First Families who followed had Christmas trees, but most did. President Theodore Roosevelt, an ardent conservationist, believed that the cutting of trees to decorate homes for personal enjoyment for the Christmas holiday was a wasteful depletion of our nation's forests, and as legend has it, he even forbade his children to have one at the Executive Residence. Much to his dismay, however, his children covertly brought a tree into the White House and decorated it. At the urging of friend and fellow conservationist Gifford Pinchot (the first Chief of the United States Forest Service), Roosevelt later relented and lifted his ban. The Coolidges are known for having many Christmas trees, and even put up three trees inside the Blue Room one year. Franklin D. Roosevelt and his family were famous for their family traditions. Each holiday, President Roosevelt would read Dickens' *A Christmas Carol* surrounded by members of his family, in front of a large tree in the grand ceremonial East Room of the White House. First Lady Mamie Eisenhower, in all her zest for the holidays, set a longstanding record for decking the halls of the Executive Mansion. The Eisenhower Administration had twenty-six trees one year in the White House, reportedly even including one in the laundry room.

In 1961, a young First Lady with small children and a fresh vision for the historic house made significant changes to the way Christmas was celebrated at the White House. Jacqueline Kennedy elected to place the official White House tree in the Blue Room. It was the first time that the White House holiday tree was bestowed with an official decorating theme, and she chose *The Nutcracker Suite*. Since then, the tree has been placed in the Blue Room (with only two exceptions) and has always received a theme from the First Lady. This marked the beginning of what has become a much-loved presidential tradition.

Over the years, Christmas decorations at the White House have become much more elaborate, and as the decorations became more sophisticated and detailed, so did the process. Today the White House typically decides on a theme and plan of execution for the holiday décor by the time the Easter Egg Roll has taken place. Everyone at the White House helps, from the Chief Usher and top executive officers of the residence to the First Lady's Office and florist shop. By summer at the latest, the Executive Residence staff, carpenters, plumbers, electricians and florists have all begun their building, sewing, painting, carving, and more. Once all the materials have arrived and items have been made, the awe-inspiring decorating marathon begins.

Former White House Chief Florist Dottie Temple once described the process: "Like all White House schedules, this one must be met precisely. Some tasks are performed off-site and the materials are brought in, but most are accomplished in the restricted spaces allotted at the White House. In decorating for Christmas, as decorating any other time at the White House, no easy way is guaranteed. As the seat of the government, the White House hosts regular activities despite the hectic holiday season. If a last-minute affair of state takes place, the volunteers just begin when they can, sometimes at three in the morning. Every White House effort proceeds under these circumstances and every practitioner is a picture of patience and master of adaptability."

This special book highlights decades of some of the most beautiful official White House Christmas trees, decorations, themes, and historic traditions, all beautifully captured by 50 years of magnificent photographs taken by talented White House photographers. As you read, be reminded of our nation's great heritage and take special pride in the White House, America's House, which is always most beautiful during the holidays.

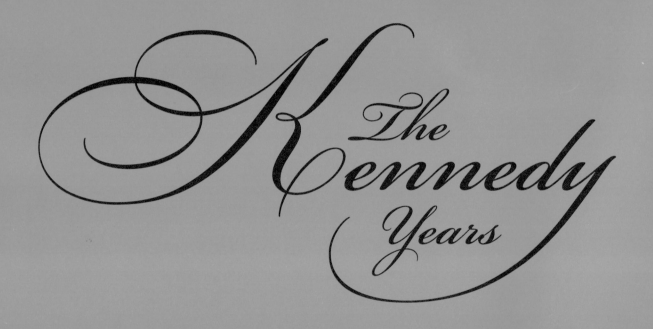

The Kennedy Years

1961-1962

Jacqueline Kennedy

CHRISTMAS, DECORATIONS, AND THE White House go hand in hand, as far as Jacqueline Kennedy was concerned. We all loved to witness her obvious pleasure when she took young visitors to see the decorations, which she had so carefully planned and orchestrated herself, with the help of close friends. Everyone donated exquisite ornaments for the tree. "Ordinary Americans," whatever that means, sent in decorations, too, hoping that they would grace an evergreen branch somewhere on the first two floors.

The White House has always been magical for those who live close to it or those of us who have been lucky enough to have a close relationship with it (such as holding a job within the mansion). But the entire Kennedy family, from Ambassador Joseph P. Kennedy and his wife through all the ranks of children, grandchildren, nieces, nephews, godchildren (there were lots of those, too), went wild with enthusiasm and joy at Christmastime. The Kennedys would take off around Christmas Day for their homes in Florida, but not before everyone connected with the Executive Mansion was exhausted with visits, questions, and more questions. Every year the White House police were specially trained in order to be able to answer the questions of the hordes of visitors to the house. Of course, the most often asked question was, "Where are Caroline and John?" I kept wishing we had two giant dolls representing the children that we could place on little chairs in the corner of the East Room.

There were different trees in unified color schemes (silver and blue, red and gold, all gold, etc.) in different parts of the mansion, and exquisite fresh garlands of Christmas greenery, of-

ten sent by the groundskeepers of George Washington's house at Mount Vernon in Virginia. Children particularly loved the Nutcracker tree, but I loved most of all the magnificent eighteenth-century Neapolitan crèche scene, elaborately staged in the East Room ("America's Grand Ballroom"). The donor, Mrs. Howell Howard, directed the staging of it, and although even more of her Neapolitan crèche figures were displayed on the huge tree in the courtyard of New York's Metropolitan Museum of Art, the debut of the Howard crèche in Washington was dynamite news in the art world. Many editorials pointed out that the crèche highlighted the sacred reason for the celebration of Christmas and that "the religious feeling this crèche has brought to a country fixated on Santa Claus and his toys is an undeniable relief to many."

The main thing I remember about the White House decorations is the awe that they inspired. They looked so inspirational, and from Pennsylvania Avenue you could see the tree lights through the windows if you looked across the grounds toward the North Portico.

Every year at Christmastime I am overcome with nostalgia for the look, the feeling, the sight, and the pine tree fragrances of the White House decorations. I sometimes take some mistletoe, wrap it with red velvet ribbon, and hang it on a few doorknobs of our Washington apartment. It's not the same as the White House mistletoe of course, but the sentiment is certainly there.

Letitia Baldrige

LETITIA BALDRIGE
Social Secretary to the White House and Chief of Staff for Jacqueline Kennedy

The Nutcracker Suite

FOR THE KENNEDYS' INAUGURAL Christmas, Mrs. Kennedy requested that the White House tree be placed at the center of the Blue Room instead of in the East Room, the usual site for the mansion's most decorated tree of each season. Her choice of "The Nutcracker Suite" as the tree's theme was inspired by the Christmas tree that figures so prominently in Tchaikovsky's seasonal ballet classic. It was the start of an enduring White House tradition.

★ ABOVE ★

Some of the ornaments on the "Nutcracker" tree.

★ OPPOSITE ★

President and Mrs. Kennedy pose in front of the White House's first themed Christmas tree, Blue Room, 1961.

JACQUELINE KENNEDY

Jacqueline Bouvier Kennedy brought a sense of subtle elegance to the White House that mirrored her own classic style. At thirty-one, she was First Lady to the youngest President elected to the office and the first Roman Catholic President. From Inauguration Day on, Americans were enthralled with the young First Family.

Bringing much-needed attention to her family's temporary residence, Mrs. Kennedy immediately undertook the task of redecorating the mansion. In her desire to foster public awareness and understanding of the White House's significance as a historic building, she incorporated authentic furnishings and presidential artifacts from past administrations.

Among several holiday customs that Mrs. Kennedy introduced at the White House, the most lasting has been the selection of an annual decorating theme for the official Christmas tree.

* LEFT *

The official tree in the Blue Room.

* OPPOSITE *

Four-year-old Caroline Kennedy gets a long-anticipated look at the enchanting decorations on the Blue Room tree. Her white dress is trimmed in red and embroidered with two gray poodles.

The eighteen-foot balsam fir in the Blue Room was filled with small candle-shaped lights as well as real ginger cookies and candy canes, birds, sugarplum fairies, "dancing" flowers, angels riding crescent moons, alphabet blocks, toy soldiers and musical instruments, tiny mice, small packages, and straw baskets. A stately blue velvet ribbon wrapped the branches from top to bottom, and a large straw star was at the top. Many ornaments had been made by elderly and blind craftsmen from around the country.

The tree was decorated by Paul Leonard and William Strom, interior designers who worked on the various houses of philanthropist Paul Mellon and his wife, Rachel Lambert Mellon, of Upperville, Virginia. Known as "Bunny," Mrs. Mellon was a longtime friend who advised the First Lady on the White House restoration and the selection of antiques and art.

Unlike the well-orchestrated press tours of later years when first ladies would unveil the mansion decorated to perfection, the 1961 event was led by Mrs. Kennedy's press secretary, Pamela Turnure, and the Blue Room tree was still a work in progress. A reporter commented that "the tinsel had not yet been draped and unused decorations lay scattered about the room, awaiting finishing touches." Four-year-old Caroline Kennedy tried to use the occasion to get a glimpse of the tree but was gently whisked away by her father.

Ten other trees, all but two of them undecorated, were placed throughout the rest of the State Floor. A pair of untrimmed cedar trees flanked both the entrance to the Blue Room and the doors leading to the North Portico. Four untrimmed cedars were grouped in pairs in the East Room, and on its four mantels were gold candelabra with red candles. There were also trees upstairs in the family quarters, in the President's office, and even in the kitch-

en, which was decorated by the cooks with kitchen implements and other amusing ornaments. To the White House grounds superintendent, Irvin Williams, this seemed like a "massive" number of trees compared with the two or so that previous administrations had requested in most years.

Fresh wreaths were another innovation this year; made of yew branches by the grounds crew, they hung in the windows of the White House in place of plastic wreaths. Bunches of mistletoe were tied with red ribbon and suspended above the entrances to the East Room and the State Dining Room. Holly festooned George P. A. Healy's famous portrait of Abraham Lincoln in the State Dining Room as well as the chandeliers in the Cross Hall, where bowls of red and white carnations complemented the red carpeting. Ropes of greenery entwined the staircases.

In the words of Miss Turnure, the White House was decorated "in the manner of an American country home," with an emphasis on Christmas greenery. Sparse by today's standards, the decorations even struck some reporters as "less colorful and lavish" than in previous years. Mrs. Kennedy's décor, reflecting her preference for naturalness and understatement, would have seemed the antithesis of the glittering displays of the last Eisenhower Christmas, still a fresh memory.

An increased number of parties and invited guests livened up the mansion. In addition to the traditional reception for the White House staff as well as the open house for staffers' children, Mrs. Kennedy instituted a third type of party in the East Room this year—one for orphaned and abandoned children.

The Children's Tree

I N HER SECOND YEAR AT THE WHITE House, Mrs. Kennedy reused many of her Nutcracker ornaments to create a "children's tree," topped by the same straw star. The sixteen-foot spruce, grown in New England and donated anonymously, was placed in the Grand Foyer, as the Blue Room was under renovation. Fresh garlands, holly, and unadorned trees again filled the State Floor, along with arrangements of red and white carnations, white stock, and baby's breath.

This season Mrs. Kennedy wanted to display a crèche in the East Room that would be a focal point of the Christmas decorations. While searching for a permanent Nativity scene, she arranged for the loan of an eighteenth-century crèche from Loretta Hines Howard, a New York painter and a noted collector of crèche figures. It was Letitia Baldrige, Mrs. Kennedy's chief of staff and White House social secretary, who first approached Mrs. Howard about the loan after seeing an exhibit of figures from her collection. Ms. Baldrige wrote to Mrs. Howard: "Since thousands go through the public rooms every morning, and since the Christmas

★ OPPOSITE ★

As reception guests look on, President and Mrs. Kennedy pose for a photo in front of the 1962 official tree in the Grand Foyer.

★ RIGHT ★

The official tree, a "children's tree" was placed in the Grand Foyer.

decorations at the White House mean symbolically more to our country [than they do elsewhere] we must have a perfectly beautiful crèche." Installed by Mrs. Howard herself, the stunning tableau was a major attraction at 1600 Pennsylvania Avenue.

Mrs. Kennedy wrote Mrs. Howard with her thanks: "The President and I are extremely grateful for the beautiful crèche you have arranged for us in the East Room. Not only is it giving my family enormous pleasure, but it is bringing beauty to the eyes of all the public passing through the East Room. I wish you could hear the comments that are reported to us." A color photograph of the crèche was the illustration for President and Mrs. Kennedy's unsent Christmas card the following year.

Shortly before President Kennedy's term came to a tragic end in November of 1963, Mrs. Kennedy was asked to contribute a brief introduction to "The Story of the Presidents at Christmas," an article written for the December 31 issue of *Look* magazine. Mrs. Kennedy wrote:

★ ABOVE ★

The Kennedys' beloved pony Macaroni pulls Mrs. Kennedy with children Caroline and John. This image became their 1962 Christmas card.

★ RIGHT ★

The Marine Band, the "President's Own," fills the mansion with music in the Grand Foyer.

An ancient tale tells us of the Christmas custom of burning a Yule log in every fireplace and of how, as the log was drawn from the forest, "each wayfarer raised his hat as it passed, for he well knew that it was full of good promises, and that its flame would burn out old wrongs. . . ."

The lights of our trees and homes in this season still signal this most ancient promise of Christmas—the end of all wrongs, the fulfillment of old hopes. This article tells the story of Christmas at the White House. But even though the White House is often a center of national attention—a public building—during the Christmas season it is the home of an American family sharing in the anticipation of the joy of this festival. The world around us is a complicated and troubled place. But through Christmas, we keep unbroken contact with the simple message of redemption and love that God sent into the world so many years ago. . . .

Mrs. Kennedy's message, published in an issue dedicated to the memory of John F. Kennedy, revealed her deep respect for Christmas traditions as well as the unique symbol of the White House as both a public building and a private residence.

★ ABOVE ★

The East Room crèche, flanked by two unadorned cedar trees and portraits of Martha and George Washington.

★ OPPOSITE ★

President and Mrs. Kennedy at a Christmas reception in the Grand Foyer.

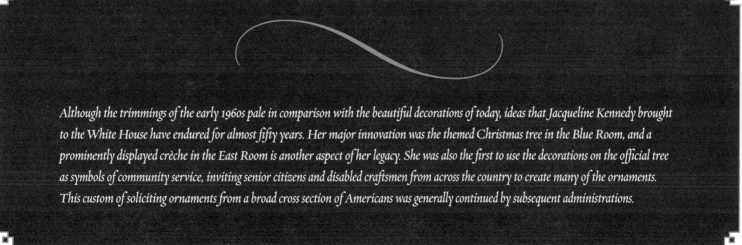

Although the trimmings of the early 1960s pale in comparison with the beautiful decorations of today, ideas that Jacqueline Kennedy brought to the White House have endured for almost fifty years. Her major innovation was the themed Christmas tree in the Blue Room, and a prominently displayed crèche in the East Room is another aspect of her legacy. She was also the first to use the decorations on the official tree as symbols of community service, inviting senior citizens and disabled craftsmen from across the country to create many of the ornaments. This custom of soliciting ornaments from a broad cross section of Americans was generally continued by subsequent administrations.

THE WHITE HOUSE CRÈCHE

(1962–1965)

WHEN JACQUELINE KENNEDY UNVEILED A crèche in the East Room in 1962, she was continuing a custom of several first ladies who had exhibited the season's central religious symbol in this ceremonial chamber.

In 1924, wishing to give deeper meaning to the season, Grace Coolidge set aside the south end of the East Room for a miniature Nativity scene, which she later described in detail:

> *The scene was arranged on a slightly raised dais, covered with green carpeting and surrounded by potted ferns. At the back were placed five evergreen trees, the tallest in the center, the shortest ones at the ends. At the topmost peak of the middle tree gleamed a silvery star with a tiny electric light in the center. Beneath the projecting branches stood a little thatched, covered stable. The rays of the small light fell upon the manger where lay the figure of the Christ child. His mother, Mary, knelt at one side, with Joseph standing by her. In the shadows at the back could be seen a cow, an ass and some sheep. Just outside were the wise men coming to worship, leading their camels. Little wax angels, "the heavenly host," hovered overhead among the trees. And finally there were the shepherd boys tending their flocks of sheep. At one side a mirror simulated a pool of water, reflecting the overhanging branches . . .*

In 1929, Lou Henry Hoover observed Mrs. Coolidge's custom, but on a much smaller scale: she arranged a manger scene under

the tree in the East Room. Mamie Eisenhower was especially fond of Nativity scenes. In 1954 and 1955, she placed a crèche on an electrically lighted miniature stage next to the tree in the East Room. And in 1960, her final Christmas at the White House, the decorations in the East Room included a Nativity scene in three sections that bore the scriptural message "Glory to God in the highest; and on earth peace, goodwill toward men."

What distinguished the 1962 crèche displayed by Mrs. Kennedy was its placement and its artistry. Its installation in a window recess in the center of the east wall, between the portraits of Martha and George Washington, made it both prominent and harmonious with the room's architectural features. Through tasteful lighting, it could be seen from the Cross Hall and as far away as the entry to the State Dining Room.

But the most impressive feature of this Nativity scene was its superior artistic quality. Loaned to the White House by New York artist Loretta Hines Howard, the forty-two-piece Neapolitan crèche exemplified an artistic tradition that reached its pinnacle in eighteenth-century Naples—the tradition of the presepio, a portrayal of the Nativity story with lifelike three-dimensional miniatures. Commissioned by noble fami-

The creche as it is displayed today at the Albright Knox Art Gallery in Buffalo, New York.

lies and sculpted by prominent Italian artists of the time, these crèches portrayed not only traditional biblical characters—the Holy Family, shepherds, the three magi, and heralding angels—but also merchants and tradesmen, peasant vendors, farm animals, and exotic travelers, all elaborately arranged in distinctive settings that were often designed by noted architects.

The heads and shoulders of the human figures were sculpted of terra cotta and polychromed with tempera-based paint in the highly naturalistic style of the Baroque period; the bodies were fashioned of materials such as hemp and wire, with arms and legs of carved wood. The clothing of the figures, sewn by the women of the Neapolitan court, ranged from homespun fabric and sheepskin to silks and brocades to indicate each person's station in life. Finely crafted accessories could include miniature jewelry made with precious metals and gems as well as peddlers' tiny baskets filled with fruits, vegetables, or cheeses fashioned of wax or terra cotta.

Experienced in artistically displaying figures from her collection, Loretta Howard arranged the crèche in the East Room on a three-foot-high table in front of the east wall's center window (which is permanently curtained off, as it faces the East Wing).

She attached the figures, most of which were fifteen to twenty inches high, to moss-covered Styrofoam to create a six-foot-tall pyramid shaped like an evergreen tree. Angels (the largest of the figures) and cherubs hovered at the top; the Holy Family and the Three Kings were at the base, illuminated by tiny white lights. Set against a heavy, dark green velvet backdrop, the tableau was framed by the window's gold brocade curtains with tassel trim. Masses of white azaleas, roses, and carnations completed the scene.

The antique crèche continued to be an annual attraction in the East Room through the 1965 holiday season. Mrs. Howard was actively involved in its setup each year, which took about three days. In 1972, in memory of her friend Helen Northrup Knox, she donated the crèche figures to the Albright-Knox Art Gallery in Buffalo, New York, where they are exhibited annually during the Christmas season.

In 1967 the White House acquired its own Neapolitan crèche as a gift of the Charles Engelhard family.

Unlike the Nativity scenes that have been displayed on the Ellipse over the years as part of the annual Pageant of Peace, those in the East Room have been free of controversy.

The Johnson Years

1963-1968

Lady Bird Johnson

CHRISTMAS HAS ALWAYS BEEN A special time in our family—with the emphasis on extended family. Daddy invited not only his own siblings and their families, but also his staff, especially those who didn't have family near for the holidays. To Daddy, Christmas was always two places, both in Texas—first at his own mother's home and then at the ranch. For the first sixty years of my life, I spent almost every Christmas in Texas. Our White House days were the few exceptions.

Our White House Christmas trees echoed our Texas heritage. They were not department store–themed trees, although I loved visiting those in New York and Washington, but simple Early American, trimmed with popcorn, gingerbread men, dolls, stars, teddy bears, and other childhood toys.

Two special memories stand out for me. On December 9, 1967, Chuck and I were married in a White House ceremony, with bridesmaids in red velvet dresses and U.S. Marines in their blue dress uniforms forming a sword arch. For holiday decorations, we kept the poinsettia trees and some of the wedding glamour. The Blue Room, where we had greeted wedding guests, was transformed within days with a Christmas tree hung with Early American ornaments and glittering silver balls. In place of our wedding altar in the East Room was an elegant antique Italian crèche, featuring not only the Holy Family but a community of people, and given to the White House by the Charles Engelhard family. I have come back many Christmas seasons, bringing my own children to see it.

At Christmas, we always had many parties, which kept our wonderful social secretary, Bess Abell, and all the White House staff busy. We had a party for children from an orphanage and another for members of Congress. We also entertained embassy children, who came wearing their native costumes to show how Christmas is celebrated around the world. At our favorite party—for the White House staff—we handed out large Christmas lithographs that we had signed.

Once the White House was decorated, Mother and Daddy wanted as many people as possible to see it. Mother was always frugal, so ornaments from one year were used the next, as well as new additions such as red swags and red satin baubles from my wedding. We were early recyclers!

In 1968, our final year in the White House, Mother and Daddy decided not to fly to Texas for Christmas Day but to savor our last celebration in Washington. That year much had changed. Chuck was in Vietnam, and our two-month-old, Lucinda, was being pushed in her pram all over the house to see the decorations. Our stockings in the family quarters were decorated with personal symbols: my college, the Marines, and even a cameo of me. As my cousin Becky and I played with our own children in the Blue Room, we knew that this was a time to remember and enjoy, realizing that another family would move in soon.

In looking through Mother's estate, I found a letter from Daddy telling her that he had arranged to pay for the Christmas tree decorations because he wanted her to enjoy them again in the years ahead.

So each year we celebrate with our White House ornaments on the tree at the LBJ Library in Austin.

Lynda Johnson Robb

LYNDA JOHNSON ROBB
Daughter of President and Mrs. Lyndon Johnson

A Period of Mourning

ENTERING THE WHITE HOUSE IN EARLY December under the most sorrowful of circumstances, the Johnsons celebrated their first Christmas at 1600 Pennsylvania Avenue with minimal fanfare, as it followed a month of mourning proclaimed by President Johnson. On the evening of December 22 (the First Lady's birthday), after a candlelight service at the Lincoln Memorial, he lit the National Christmas Tree, the focus of a lighting ceremony on the White House grounds since 1923.

The next day, the black mourning crepe hanging over the doorways and on chandeliers in the White House was replaced with holly, wreaths, mistletoe, and arrangements of red carnations and other fresh flowers. A twelve-foot balsam fir from Vermont, decorated with metallic red, blue, and silver balls and candle-shaped lights, stood against the south wall of the Blue Room. Untrimmed trees were placed in the East Room, Cross Hall, and Grand Foyer, and two cedar trees strung with white lights stood on the North Portico.

Having learned of Mrs. Kennedy's plans to feature the antique crèche in the East Room a second time, the new First Lady invited Mrs. Howard to Washington to set up the scene once again.

On the afternoon of December 23, President Johnson invited members of Congress to an impromptu reception. With fires burning in all the fireplaces and the decorations barely in place, he greeted his guests in the Blue Room with the First Lady by his side. (When the rooms began to fill with smoke, staffers realized that, in their great hurry, they had forgotten to open the flues.)

Later the President gave an informal but well-received speech in the State Dining Room; with no dais at hand, he spontaneously climbed up on a cut-velvet dining room chair and addressed the group. A kissing ball hung from the chandelier.

Mrs. Johnson later said of that evening, "I walked the well-lit hall for the first time with a sense that life was going to go on, that we as a country were going to begin again."

LADY BIRD JOHNSON

Because the Johnsons were hosts at heart, they put their own mark on the holiday season with a December schedule filled with parties. For the first time, dancing took place at every White House state dinner, with an immeasurable amount of true Texas-style energy. Reflecting Mrs. Johnson's passion for nature, which gave rise to her "Keep America Beautiful" campaign, the Christmas décor throughout the Johnson White House tended to feature natural decorations.

* OPPOSITE *

President and Mrs. Johnson and Betty Beale admire the Christmas tree in the Blue Room.

1964
Early American

MRS. JOHNSON ONCE NOTED THAT "Christmas for us—as for most families—has been touched by the continuity of tradition and the mood of the time." To convey a traditional mood, Mrs. Johnson chose an Early American theme for the 1964 official tree, a theme that would prevail, with variations, for the next four holiday seasons. In faithfulness to the style, she strongly believed in decorating the tree with the types of objects that were traditionally used as ornaments, such as cookies, paper flowers, and strings of berries.

Dan Arje, the fashion display director for Bonwit Teller in New York, contributed his time to plan and decorate the eighteen-foot fir, which stood at the center of the Blue Room this year. The 3,000 small ornaments consisted of candy canes and straw stars, toys, flowers, dolls, and realistic-looking ceramic gingerbread cookies in the shapes of sheep, lions, camels, rocking horses, snowmen, and other objects. Strung with popcorn, nuts, and 960 bee lights, the tree was topped by an angel patterned after old Federal designs and custom-made of papier-mâché and antiqued burlap. Surrounding the base of the tree were figures made from burned wood, including a rocking horse, a soldier, and a bugle.

When Mr. Arje purchased the ceramic gingerbread ornaments from Austen Display in New York and revealed their destination to a company employee, Vera Ries, she insisted on baking real gingerbread cookies for

★ ABOVE ★

A close-up of ornaments on the Blue Room tree.

★ OPPOSITE ★

President Johnson adjusts an ornament on the tree during a Christmas party for children, December 16, 1964.

A trumpet player standing under a chandelier filled with santas at a children's party in the State Dining Room

him to take along for the White House tree. Her cookies—big gingerbread hearts studded with almonds—were added to the lower branches after children visiting the Blue Room sometimes tried to eat the ceramic ones. The real cookies were "such a hit with children from three to 83," said Social Secretary Bess Abell, that they were often found with "tiny teeth marks" after young visitors had been present.

A large piñata in the shape of a sunburst and measuring five feet across provided a bit of whimsy. One visitor described it as "a touch of tradition from the old Southwest." The sun's cheery face, framed by a gold mirror and surrounded by tasseled rays, had lav

Outgoing Commerce Secretary John Connor sits with in-coming Commerce Secretary Luther H. Hodge at a table festively decorated with a Christmas tree aboard Air Force One.

A sunburst piñata with lavender eyes, red nose, orange cheeks, and yellow mouth greets visitors in the Grand Foyer. The gilded mirror framed a seasonal display each year of the Johnson administration.

ender eyes, a red nose, orange cheeks, and a yellow mouth, along with accents of red and green. Undecorated evergreens stood in the Grand Foyer, and the columns were entwined with green garlands. Evergreens draped the railing of the Grand Staircase.

The décor of the other rooms conveyed simple elegance. The East Room held four large undecorated trees, along with the Neapolitan crèche, which Mrs. Howard again loaned to the White House. Balsam greenery was plentiful, and mistletoe hung in doorways. Bowls of holly sat on tables under the portraits of presidents and first ladies throughout the mansion.

In the State Dining Room the chandelier and wall sconces were accented with holly, which also filled the vermeil epergnes. Holly mixed with greenery and golden snowflakes decked the mantel. The décor was intended to evoke a sense of nostalgia for the ways in which Americans might have decorated their homes earlier in the century.

★ *1965* ★
Early American
with Traditional Ornaments

MRS. JOHNSON REPRISED HER EARLY American theme in 1965, again assisted by Dan Arje in collaboration with the White House staff. Grown in West Virginia, the eighteen-foot fir was placed in the middle of the Blue Room and decked with 3,000 small ornaments and 960 tiny bee lights. The branches were strung with nuts and candied fruit, carved wooden roses from Hawaii, straw stars, toy soldiers and drums, seedpods and pine cones, and gingerbread cookies in the form of Santa Clauses, snowmen, camels, dolls, milkmaids, and teddy bears. Strings of traditional popcorn and cranberry chains were combined with such creative flourishes as geranium nosegays and petticoat lace. The previous year's figures of burned wood were under the tree, and the Federal angel, made of burlap, again provided the finishing touch on top.

Mistletoe hung over doorways, and greenery and holly garnished mantels and chandeliers. The holly arrangements included blue balls in the Blue Room and red balls in the Red Room. In the Cross Hall, suspended high above the entrance to the Blue Room, was a lavish Della Robbia garland, made with huckleberry twigs, fruits such as apples, lemons, limes, plums, and grapes, pine cones, and lollipops and other candies, all studded with tiny gold Christmas balls.

The crèche that Mrs. Howard of New York had loaned to the White House since 1962 was again displayed in the East Room, this year with a new pale gold, antique satin backdrop.

A pair of evergreen trees decorated with lights flanked the North Portico entrance to the mansion.

★ OPPOSITE ★

A beautiful Della Robbia garland of huckleberry twigs, fruits, pine cones, candies, and tiny gold balls hangs in the Cross Hall above the entrance to the Blue Room.

★ BELOW ★

Lady Bird and President Lyndon B. Johnson pose with a Christmas tree in the private residence.

1966 ★
Early American
with a Contemporary Crèche

THE BLUE ROOM TREE WAS AGAIN trimmed with the previous year's Early American decorations: nuts, popcorn, fruit, wooden roses, and gingerbread cookies of many shapes. (After a holiday party for children, one gingerbread man was discovered with a leg nibbled off.) The Federal angel made of burlap again served as an elegant topper.

This year saw the start of a new tradition; the official White House Christmas tree was selected through a national contest—the first of its kind—sponsored by the National Christmas Tree Growers' Association. Contest winner Howard E. Pierce of Black River Falls, Wisconsin, and his twelve-year-old son Mark made the thousand-mile trip in the family pickup to deliver the tree, a twenty-foot, 600-pound balsam fir. Wrapped in burlap and polyethylene, the tree was maneuvered onto a plywood frame, secured with ropes, and given a spirited send-off by Mark's fellow classmates singing "Oh, Christmas Tree." The local sheriff even hand-lettered a sign for the side of the truck. After the Pierces presented the tree to White House staff, they were given a tour of the State Floor and shown the exact spot where the big fir would stand in the Blue Room. The tree was admired for its density and near-perfect shape, and Mr. Pierce later wrote, "I doubt that the Blue Room has ever hosted a prettier one."

★ RIGHT ★

President and Mrs. Johnson's holiday portrait in the Blue Room.

★ OPPOSITE ★

The contemporary crèche in the East Room.

In front of the east window of the East Room, a new, contemporary-style crèche was set up, funded by Jane and Charles Engelhard Jr. of Far Hills, New Jersey. Mrs. Engelhard was a member of the Committee for the Preservation of the White House, and she and her husband had given gifts to the White House and contributed to renovation projects for the mansion since the days of the Kennedy administration. The unique crèche was displayed under a triptych-like structure of wrought-iron Gothic arches, interwoven with bare branches of laurel and dogwood. Set against a silver blue backdrop overlaid with gold net, it was illuminated with tiny Italian lights. The foot-high figures were fashioned of wood and gilded fabric (either burlap or brocade) by artist Katherine Bryant of Natick, Massachusetts, and consisted of the Holy Family, the three wise men, shepherds, animals, and angels. Flanking the scene were two four-foot angels, which wore collars

★ ABOVE & OPPOSITE ★

President Johnson visits with guests attending a black-tie dinner for members of the Arts Council, Blue Room, December 13, 1966.

of lace from Mrs. Bryant's wedding dress. A gold papier-mâché star studded with crystal prisms was suspended from the center arch. The crèche was designed by the acclaimed design team of "Sister" Parish and Albert Hadley and installed by floral designer Stephen Barany, all of New York.

The Grand Foyer featured "The Twelve Days of Christmas" as a holiday motif. On the intricate gold mirror was a triangle of colorful felt-cut symbols depicting the dozen days and their respective gifts—the twelve drummers drumming at the base of the triangle and the partridge in a pear tree at the apex. A special wreath, inspired by the First Lady's campaign for beautifying America, was also displayed in the foyer. The wreath was made by William Schoettle of New Jersey using the state flowers from all fifty states.

★ 1967 ★
Early American
with Sparkle

FOLLOWING THE DECEMBER 9 WEDDING of Lynda Bird Johnson to Charles Robb in the East Room, much of the décor from the event remained throughout the holiday season. For the official tree, Mrs. Johnson decided to reprise the Early American theme, as it had become this First Family's hallmark.

The Blue Room tree was an Ohio blue spruce, topped by the familiar Federal-style burlap angel and the family's early American trimmings from previous years. Sparkle was added to the mix with shiny silver balls, silver stars, and one-inch round mirrors that cast reflections from the 4,000 tiny lights. Also new this year were ropes of bright-colored felt flowers, wound around the tree like strands of tinsel. Elf figures were nestled at the base of the tree among bare white branches. Dan Arje was again brought in to help design and decorate the tree.

An new element in the Grand Foyer was a large seventeenth-century drummer figure, suspended in front of the gilded mirror. The columns were wrapped with garland adorned with tiny musical instruments. Christmas trees flanked many of the doorways throughout the State Floor, and mantels were covered with a mix of greenery and Christmas balls selected to match the room décor.

The highlight of the 1967 season was the gift of a permanent crèche for the White House that remains a fond favorite today. Donated by Jane and Charles Engelhard, who had funded the interim contemporary-style crèche of the previous year, the Neapolitan crèche was installed in the East Room in the days following the wedding. At the reception for the unveiling of the crèche, Mrs. Johnson said, "This is a lovely Christmas gift to all of the people of this country." Acknowledging Mrs. Engelhard's efforts, she added that the crèche "has indeed been a gift of the heart."

Breaking with family tradition, the Johnsons spent Christmas

★ ABOVE ★

Jane Engelhard, her daughter Annette Reed, and six-year-old granddaughter Beatrix Reed pose with Lady Bird Johnson at the unveiling of the Engelhard family's gift to the White House, December 15, 1967.

★ OPPOSITE ★

The official White House tree, Blue Room.

at the White House that year rather than at the ranch in Texas. With both of her sons-in-law scheduled to depart for military service in Vietnam, Mrs. Johnson later wrote,

> *. . . we opened presents around the tree in our favorite Yellow Oval Room on the second floor of the White House. Like some lovely, fragile bubble, it was a moment to catch, and hold, and remember.*
> *What made it so precious was the feeling that at least one of those in the room would be far away the next Christmas.*
> *Firelight danced on the Christmas tree star—one that had been used by the Roosevelts at Christmastime in the White House.*

1968
Early American
with Good Luck Sunbursts

FOR HER FINAL CHRISTMAS IN THE WHITE House, Mrs. Johnson again called on her friend Dan Arje of New York to assist with the decorations, reminiscent of motifs of the last four years. The mood of holiday cheer was dampened by the fact that both sons-in-law were stationed in Vietnam.

Ornaments of Mrs. Johnson's previous Early American Christmases were used on the white pine in the Blue Room. The Federal angel, made of burlap and sprayed with gold, topped the tree one last time. The 5,000 other ornaments included chains of blue and green felt daisies, strings of popcorn and cranberries, clusters of nuts and pine cones, straw stars, dried seedpods, geranium nosegays, and sugar cookies—shaped like camels, dolls, Santa Clauses, snowmen, and teddy bears and decorated with almonds, glazed fruit, dried cherries (for eyes), and icing. Strings of tiny mirrors reflected the twinkle of 1,300 bee lights. To add something new to the tree, as he did for Mrs. Johnson each year, Mr. Arje designed a set of gold foil ornaments in the shape of sunbursts. "They are for good luck," he told a reporter. "I wanted to wish the Johnsons good luck so I put the sunbursts on the tree."

The rest of the Executive Mansion glowed with familiar elements. The marble columns between the Cross Hall and Grand Foyer were wrapped in garlands of pine boughs and golden leaves, studded with red flowers and miniature golden violins and drums. A six-foot reproduction of an old en-

★ **ABOVE** ★

Dan Arje trims his fifth and final tree for Lady Bird Johnson. Pictured on the ladder is Tom Walsh, a New York decorator.

★ **OPPOSITE** ★

One of the gold foil sunbursts, which Dan Arje added to the Johnsons' last Christmas tree for good luck.

graving of a Christmas drummer, with yellow knee britches, pink plumes in his hat, and his drum strapped to his shoulders, was suspended over the foyer's gold-frame mirror.

The mantels of the State Floor were decorated with mixed greenery and Christmas balls to match each room's décor. Doorways were flanked by native Virginia cedars. Green and variegated holly decorated the chandelier of the State Dining Room, where the dining table was graced by the beautiful bronze-doré Monroe plateau, a spectacularly decorative centerpiece that President Monroe ordered from France in 1817 along with other gilt pieces.

Outside at the North Portico entry, a pair of Norway spruces in wooden tubs were illuminated by white lights. A balsam fir wreath hung above the entrance. The chains of the portico lantern were wrapped with ropes of greenery.

In describing the décor for 1968, a Maryland reporter had this observation:

In the case of the large tree, the trimming is done by a professional display decorator from one of New York's largest department stores

The crèche itself is lighted by one of Broadway's most successful scenic designers. The over-all effect in incorporating their professional talents is to give a touch of stateliness, friendliness even, along with the lordly grandeur that is characteristic of the White House.

There is, of course, a certain awareness that when you are in the White House, you are in the White House.

If you are remotely historically conscious, you are aware the moment you set foot in its door, of the sound of thousands of invisible wings of historic memory beating against your consciousness as you walk through the doors that have figured prominently in each successive administration. The Blue Room. The Green Room. The East Room. Then finally the beautifully sized, and perfectly lighted State Dining Room. The winged ghosts vie for your attention....

As you leave the White House, there is a feeling within you that you have touched history, have brushed up against it. You are richer for it. Christmas, especially, seems to be an appropriate and sentimental time to view the White House. As you leave, you feel a little more confident than when you went in, about the future of this country, and the men who make its history, for the White House has a secret to impart—and that secret is the strength of its continuity.

For her birthday on December 22, President Johnson gave his wife a copy of B. Traven's *The Treasure of the Sierra Madre* along with another special present, as he explained in this note:

My dear—
Upon your return to the White House, arrangements will be made to pay for the Xmas tree decorations so you will own them and enjoy them again in the years ahead....
All my love

In honor of Lady Bird Johnson, many of these decorations are exhibited annually on a Christmas tree at the Lyndon Baines Johnson Library and Museum.

★ ABOVE ★
The Johnsons reviewing a gift in the private residence on Christmas Eve.
★ OPPOSITE ★
The Johnsons gather for a family portrait in the private residence. Left to right: Luci Johnson Nugent with son Lyn, Lady Bird Johnson, President Johnson with Yuki, and Lynda Johnson Robb with daughter Lucinda.
★ OPPOSITE ★
Lynda Johnson Robb shows daughter Lucinda her daddy's stocking, as he was away in Vietnam.

During Mrs. Johnson's tenure at the White House, the press and the public began to take more notice of the mansion's holiday trimmings and the new traditions that were evolving, such as the selection of the Blue Room tree through a national contest and the ceremony of presenting it to the First Lady. Another event that attracted much attention and brought many visitors to 1600 Pennsylvania Avenue was the gift of a museum-quality crèche, which joined the White House collection of art treasures. Through her energy and personal friendship with Jane Engelhard, Lady Bird Johnson is especially remembered for securing a permanent crèche for the East Room, where this true symbol of the season has been displayed by every administration since.

THE OFFICIAL WHITE HOUSE CHRISTMAS TREE

THE SELECTION OF THE OFFICIAL WHITE HOUSE Christmas tree through a national contest is a custom that began during the Johnson administration. Prior to that time, Christmas trees for the Executive Mansion were either purchased or donated, sometimes anonymously.

Since 1966, the National Christmas Tree Association (formerly the National Christmas Tree Growers' Association) has held a national contest for tree farmers to demonstrate their growing, grooming, shearing, and presentation skills. Through state and regional competitions, the best trees from around the nation are chosen, making their growers eligible for this highly competitive national contest that yields a National Grand Champion Christmas Tree Grower. The winning farm earns the honor of delivering a tree to the White House for display in the Blue Room that year.

In the early years of the NCTA contest the winners often had to go outside their own farms—where they grew trees primarily for the average home—to supply a tree tall enough for the White House. When Howard Pierce of Black River Falls, Wisconsin, won the first national contest in 1966 with an eight-foot balsam fir, the White House tree was harvested from the Chequamegon National Forest. The 1974 champion grower, Edward Cole of Mayville, Michigan, delivered a concolor fir that was cut from the front yard of another Mayville resident, Ouina Garner. (This was the year that a Michigan congressman's aide drove into the tree as it lay in the White House driveway; the tree was unscathed, but a protective steel rod at the tip of the tree broke the car's right headlight.) The 1976 winner, Kenneth Guenther, also of Black

* ABOVE *

First champion grower Howard Pierce and his son Mark deliver the White House tree, December 9, 1966. Also pictured are Marta Ross of the First Lady's staff, L. Walter Fix, past president of the National Christmas Tree Growers' Association, and Irvin Williams, superintendent of the White House grounds.

* OPPOSITE *

Scott D. Harmon of Brady Station, Virginia drives a horse-drawn carriage delivering the official White House Christmas tree to the North Portico. The 18-foot Fraser fir was from Mistletoe Meadows tree farm Laurel Springs, North Carolina, 2007.

River Falls, obligingly bought a twenty-one-foot balsam fir from another Wisconsin source for seventy-five dollars.

Today the tree destined for the Blue Room is typically grown on the farm that wins the NCTA grand championship. The White House chief usher visits the winning farm to select a tree for the Blue Room, where it will play the starring role in the mansion's holiday décor. The Blue Room tree has specific require-

★ RIGHT ★

The 2007 official tree on its way to the White House, pulled by Midge Harmon's team of Belgian draft horses Karry and Dempsey, complete with manes braided with green and red "flags" that rose above French braids along the crest of the neck, and tails done up in Scotch knots.

★ OPPOSITE TOP ★

First Lady Nancy Reagan greets the 1986 Grand Champion winners upon their arrival.

★ OPPOSITE BOTTOM ★

National Park Service staff position the magnificent 2008 fir in the Blue Room.

ments. First, it must be at least 18 feet 6 inches tall. If taller, it is cut down to this size. (In 1984, for example, a full two feet had to be sawed off the bottom of the tree.) Cut to this exact height, it will just touch the ceiling after the room's gilded nineteenth-century chandelier is removed and stored, allowing the top of the tree to be attached to the chandelier hook for support. Second, the tree must be straight and perfectly symmetrical, but not too full to interfere with the many ornaments hanging from its branches; and not too wide to fit through the doors. And, of course, it must have a rich color. Depending on its degree of taper, the tree is decorated with 4,500 to 8,000 lights.

Growing such a tree can take between twelve and twenty years. In the words of NCTA spokesman Rick Dungey, "Winning Grand Champion status is very difficult and represents the pinnacle of Christmas tree farming. Each farm family that wins and provides the official White House Christmas tree is proud to represent the entire industry." It is fitting, he adds, that "a real Christmas tree grown by an American farmer, not an imported plastic one" takes center stage each year "in the most famous house in the country." Rarely does a farm win the grand championship more than once; only six growers to date have achieved this feat.

At the discretion of the White House staff, the farm that presents the Blue Room tree may supply trees for other areas of the White House (such as the private residence or state floor) or for Camp David.

Delivering the official tree to 1600 Pennsylvania Avenue was not always the highly anticipated media event of today. Howard Pierce and his son were greeted by a small contingent of White House staffers representing President and Mrs. Johnson, who had not yet returned to Washington from their Thanksgiving holiday in Texas. And in 1976, when Kenneth Guenther arrived from Wisconsin with the official tree, Mrs. Ford was not available so Steve Ford was called out of bed and deputized to receive the tree on his mother's behalf.

Over the years, the delivery of the official White House tree has become an increasingly formal ceremony with much fanfare. In 1994, the television cameras of *CBS This Morning* followed the tree from the time it was cut in Clinton County, Missouri, until it arrived at 1600 Pennsylvania Avenue and was presented to Mrs. Clinton. In recent years it has become customary for the tree to arrive on a festively decorated horse-drawn wagon. Its presentation to the first lady marks the start of the White House holiday season.

To move the tree indoors, a crew from the National Park Service wraps it in a large drop cloth and binds it with rope. After carrying it into the Blue Room, they hoist it into an upright position with the aid of a rope threaded through the chandelier hook. After being shaped to fit, the base of the tree is secured in a custom-built wood and metal tree stand, which consists of a drum within a cylinder that supports the tree and holds about fifteen gallons of water. For additional support, the top of the tree is fastened to the chandelier hook, and the chandelier's electrical box powers the tree's lights, which are strung by the White House electricians. Only then is the tree ready to be trimmed with truckloads of ornaments hung by the volunteers.

After the holiday tours end, the Blue Room tree is taken down and, along with other trees that decorated the White House, shredded or chipped into mulch that is used on the grounds.

The Nixon Years

1969-1973

★ FIRST LADY ★
Patricia Nixon

THE SPIRIT OF CHRISTMAS, WHICH treasures goodwill and generosity, has been expressed in meaningful ways at the White House throughout its history.

Each first family becomes a part of the tapestry of the "President's House" and contributes its own traditions and sentiments to the time in which it is privileged to live there. To my mother and father the White House was always the "People's House," and they opened the door to people from all walks of life. Every guest was a VIP, and thanks also to a dedicated and accomplished White House staff, was treated with the same courtesy as that accorded a head of state!

As First Lady, in addition to promoting volunteerism across America, my mother dedicated much effort to restoration, acquiring many pieces of furniture and art that had once graced the rooms of the Executive Mansion. She was sensitive to all who visited and arranged the first tours specifically designed for the visually and hearing impaired. She had such aids as ramps installed for those in wheelchairs and asked the guards to invite blind visitors to touch the furniture and fabrics.

And, as in homes throughout the land, my mother joyfully oversaw the holiday decorating. She inaugurated the enchanting evening candlelight tours so that people, including those who worked during the day, were able to see the holiday trimmings and envision how the White House looked when it and the Republic were young.

Our family would often come down to the State Floor during these tours and welcome the visitors. Together we would enjoy the beauty and magic of the moment, which would be revisited in remembrance through the years ahead.

For families around the globe, including families of presidents, the Christmas season evokes delightful memories in which giving to others shines. Throughout the eight years that my father served as Vice President, toy companies sent to my sister and me gifts of new toys that we always donated to children in orphanages and hospitals, as my parents wished. The pleasure that Julie and I experienced in thinking how the toys would delight the children far exceeded, I believe, the pleasure of opening gifts under the tree on Christmas morning.

Through the prism of memory, I vividly recall Christmases that my family and I spent at the White House:

The enchanting forty-five-pound gingerbread house, designed by Chef Hans Raffert, that gave great pleasure to the young at heart of all ages.

Extraordinary people such as Chief Usher Rex Scouten, Social Secretary Lucy Winchester, Curator Clement Conger, and many generous volunteers whose talents and industry helped translate vision into beautiful reality.

And I remember how much our family looked forward to gathering upstairs around the Christmas tree decorated with ornaments collected ever since my parents were married. How we enjoyed watching our dogs, King Timahoe, Vicky, and Pasha "open" their own Santa gifts in their inimitable way!

At the Pageant of Peace on the Ellipse in 1969, just before lighting the national Christmas tree, my father spoke of a universal hope of goodwill: the hope of peace. He said, "There is an old saying about Christmas trees. . . . May a Christmas tree be as sturdy as faith, as high as hope, as wide as love. And could I add, may a Christmas tree, our Christmas tree, be as beautiful as peace."

Tricia Nixon Cox

TRICIA NIXON COX
Daughter of President and Mrs. Richard Nixon

★ 1969 ★
American Flower Tree

FOR HER INAUGURAL CHRISTMAS, Pat Nixon had the official tree placed in the Grand Foyer rather than the Blue Room. She suggested this location, she said, "so people going by on Pennsylvania Avenue can see it." She also wanted it to represent all the states, now a frequently observed custom. Working with the First Lady, Henry F. Callahan, executive display director at Saks Fifth Avenue in New York, designed the tree, which he later described as "an American flower Christmas tree." The blue spruce featured 100 eight-inch, pastel-colored velvet and satin balls, made by disabled workers in West Palm Beach, Florida. Each ball was embossed with the name and state flower of one of the fifty states and then embellished with pearls and representative gemstones. "People like to walk around [the tree] and find their state," said Mrs. Nixon proudly.

The tree sparkled with additional glass balls in pastel shades, golden glitter roping, 1,000 tiny electric candles at the tips of the branches, 5,000 bee lights tucked among the boughs, and a gold tinsel star at the top. Saks contributed Mr. Callahan's time and also paid to have the ornaments created.

A profusion of poinsettias filled the State Floor. To avoid a clash of colors, white poinsettias were used in the Red Room while the traditional red variety provided contrast in the Green Room. The Blue Room featured greenery and red candles, with gold and blue balls hanging among the crystals of the chandelier.

PATRICIA NIXON

Patricia Nixon adored Christmas and was known for pulling out all the stops during her years at the White House. She once remarked, "You can't overdo at Christmas time. The more the better, so far as I'm concerned."

She was a true virtuoso when it came to creating holiday magic and panache in America's home. Writing in 1969, a Time Magazine *reporter observed:*

Few presidential couples . . . have gone at the Christmastime merrymaking with quite the gusto of Richard and Pat Nixon. For the holidays they have peopled the place with choirs, Bob Hope, the Apollo 12 astronauts and more than 6,000 other Americans, renowned and unknown. To fuel those guests, the kitchens turned out 25,000 cookies, 1,130 gallons of fruit punch and an identical quantity of eggnog. Nobody in Washington can remember a more festive White House Christmas.

Much like Jacqueline Kennedy, Mrs. Nixon was deeply interested in the history of the White House and greatly expanded its collection of authentic antiques, which increased from one-third to two-thirds of the furnishings during her tenure. Imbuing the mansion with grandeur, she loved to share it with the public through tours and television interviews. She is credited with introducing more holiday customs than any of the first ladies preceding her.

The Cross Hall trimmed for the Yuletide season.

A tabletop display beneath the Grand Staircase features a bright poinsettia surrounded by reindeer figures and festive foliage.

In the State Dining Room masses of holly festooned the chandelier, with red electric candles replacing its usual white ones and a large red velvet bow suspended underneath. Two matching gold wall sconces, removed by Jacqueline Kennedy during her renovation, were back in place and now decorated with holly and red bows. Prominently displayed on a marble-topped console table was a charming gingerbread house made by Hans Raffert, assistant chef at the White House. Impressed by the rich, colorful décor (especially the abundance of red), reporters barely noticed the little gingerbread house, but it would become one of the best-loved and enduring holiday traditions at the White House.

All mantels throughout the mansion were decked with garlands, and fires in all the fireplaces added to the glow. For the first time in more than twenty-five years, boxwood wreaths and candles were hung in all the sixteen windows facing Pennsylvania Avenue. The lighted wreaths in the windows and the Christmas balls on the chandeliers were family traditions that Mrs. Nixon brought with her to the White House.

★ RIGHT ★

The Nixon Family and their daughter Tricia in front of the Official White House tree with the Apollo 12 astronauts and their spouses.

★ BELOW ★

Elegant tables are set for fireside entertaining in the State Dining Room. Carved into the mantel is an inscription ordered by President Teddy Roosevelt, written by John Adams on his second night in the White House: "I pray Heaven to Bestow the Best of Blessings on THIS HOUSE and on All that shall hereafter Inhabit it. May none but honest and Wise Men rule under this roof."

* ABOVE *

The Red Room trimmed for the Nixons' first Yuletide.

* LEFT *

Nina Hyde, fashion editor of The Washington Post, *shows off some of the state flower balls. The balls were designed for the White House tree by Henry Callahan of Saks Fifth Avenue.*

* OPPOSITE *

Tricia Nixon with the gingerbread house.

In the West Hall of the private residence stood a nine-foot-tall blue spruce filled with the Nixons' personal ornaments. These consisted of sentimental decorations made by Julie and Tricia as youngsters as well as a collection of "splendid and sophisticated" ornaments that a friend gave Mrs. Nixon each year. In keeping with another Nixon tradition, there were ornaments bearing the name of each family member. The tree was mounted on a special revolving stand that played "Jingle Bells."

In 1969 Mrs. Nixon launched the popular holiday tradition of the candlelight evening tours. She said she wanted the thousands of Washington sightseers to see the mansion's beautiful public rooms, "so filled with history, and now aglow with the magic and spirit of Christmas."

1970

✶ *Monroe Fans*

FOR THE 1970 SEASON, MRS. NIXON DECIDED to return the official White House tree, a white spruce, to its customary place in the Blue Room. The velvet and satin balls embellished with the fifty state flowers from the previous season were reused. New additions to the tree included fifty-three lace-trimmed gold foil fans, designed in the style of the early nineteenth century, when James Monroe was President—which is why 1970 is called "the year of the Monroe fans." Made by disabled workers in New York, the fans contributed to the color scheme of the room's holiday décor—blue, green, and gold. Also adorning the tree were blue, green, gold, and white satin-finish balls, 8,000 blue and green miniature lights, and hundreds of baubles. Three-tiered swags of gold tinsel were draped around the tree, which was topped by a gold tinsel star. Henry Callahan of Saks again designed the tree. Mrs. Nixon told reporters that, except for the state flower balls, she had personally decided that blue, green, and gold would be a better choice for the Blue Room than the pastel color scheme of the previous year.

In the East Room, chandeliers and sconces held bright red candles. The four mantels were adorned with swags and sprays of miniature ivy and green velvet bows, along with red candles in the Monroe candelabra. On either side of the crèche were seven-foot-tall "trees" of red poinsettias, designed by Henry Callahan and created by arranging more than seventy-five poinsettia plants on a tiered, pyramid-shaped scaffold.

In both the Green and Red Rooms white poinsettias graced the mantels, along with garlands of potted miniature ivy. Mrs. Nixon told a journalist that she loved the aroma of fresh greenery and flowers but "we have to choose things that are going to

✶ **OPPOSITE** ✶

Patricia Nixon unveils the decorated Blue Room tree to the press, December 14, 1970.

✶ **BELOW** ✶

The dollhouse made by a White House carpenter in 1877 for Fanny Hayes as a Christmas gift from her parents, President and Mrs. Rutherford B. Hayes. It was displayed in the Blue Room for the 1970 holiday season.

★ ABOVE ★

Mrs. Nixon presents the 1970 gingerbread house to the press.

★ OPPOSITE ★

Chandeliers and torchères in the Cross Hall, decked with
greenery, pine cones, red bows, and red velvet cardinals.

last for three weeks." She proudly added, "It was my idea to have lots of things in pots that can be watered easily." A dainty miniature Christmas tree stood on the marble-inlaid table in the Red Room. Mistletoe hung over some of the large doorways of the State Floor.

More red poinsettias filled the State Dining Room, where another delectable gingerbread house by Chef Raffert was on display. Large blue spruce wreaths, with red candles in their centers and red bows at the bottom, were again placed in the mansion's sixteen windows facing Pennsylvania Avenue. A fifty-inch blue spruce wreath with a red velvet bow also hung above the front door.

Mrs. Nixon's idea of showcasing Christmas cards and artifacts from past presidencies was another of her holiday innovations. Two wall-mounted display cases in the East Colonnade were constructed to look like a miniature White House door that opened

to reveal Christmas cards sent and received by past presidents and other objects. On view was an 1866 edition of Charles Dickens' "A Christmas Carol," from which President Franklin Roosevelt always read aloud to his family on Christmas Eve. Another was a small red fire engine that in 1930 President Herbert Hoover gave to his executive secretary's son. The boy, along with ten other children, had been present at a small White House party on Christmas Eve in 1929 when a fire broke out in the West Wing. The President's gift was a memento of the occasion

★ ABOVE ★

Mrs. Nixon talking with the press about the White House créche.

★ LEFT ★

The Nixons' dogs in front of their very own tree in the private residence. They also had their own stockings. From left to right: Pasha, a Yorkshire terrier; Vicky, a French poodle; and King Tamahoe, a Irish setter.

Also on display was a large dollhouse that once belonged to Fanny Hayes, the daughter of President Rutherford Hayes. At the request of her parents, it was made by a White House carpenter in 1877 for the ten-year-old's first Christmas at 1600 Pennsylvania Avenue. Known as the Magruder Dollhouse, it was restored before being loaned to the White House, where it was on view at the base of the Blue Room tree. Mrs. Nixon liked the dollhouse so much that she kept it on display for a full year. It can be seen today at the Rutherford B. Hayes Presidential Center.

1971
Gold Foil Angels

ED AND WHITE POINSETTIAS AND lots of red bows, garlands, and pine cones filled the White House in 1971. Philadelphia horticulturist and floral consultant J. Liddon Pennock Jr., who had designed the flower arrangements for Tricia Nixon's wedding in June, lent his expertise in supervising the holiday décor. Henry Callahan was once more in charge of designing the official tree.

The Fraser fir in the Blue Room, reminiscent of the previous year's tree, was adorned with the state flower balls, gold swags, gold fans, and 10,000 gold and white "firefly" lights. The state balls were new, however; they were duplicates of the 1969 balls, which had been retired due to wear and tear. Designed by Helen Murat of West Palm Beach, Florida, they were made by disabled women in the Palm Beach area. Also new to the tree were six-inch gold medallions with an angel at the center; these ornaments were designed by Paula Displays and made by disabled workers in New York. It was Mrs. Nixon's specific request that disabled citizens be given the opportunity to make the ornaments.

★ OPPOSITE ★

Julie Nixon Eisenhower poses with her mother in front of the Blue Room tree.

★ RIGHT ★

An East Room mantel, decorated with topiaries, poinsettias, and miniature ivy draped for a garland effect.

Mother and daughter admire the intricate details of the ginger-bread house, State Dining Room.

The Grand Foyer and Cross Hall were decorated with swags of greenery, pine cones, red bows, and red velvet cardinals. Five-foot trees sparkled with tiny white lights, and each was topped with one of the red birds. The niches of the hallway were filled with seven-foot-high masses of red poinsettias with red velvet bows and more cardinals. The trimmings for the crystal chandeliers were tiered wreaths of greenery, studded with more pine cones, twinkling lights, and red cardinals, to create a bell shape, explained Mrs. Nixon during the press tour.

More wreaths adorned walls, mirrors, and doors. In the State Dining Room, the chandelier and eight wall sconces were entwined with English ivy and variegated holly while garlands of miniature ivy festooned the mantels. A gingerbread house created

★ ABOVE ★

The Nixon family: Edward Cox, Tricia Nixon Cox,
First Lady Pat Nixon, President Nixon, Julie Nixon Eisenhower,
and David Eisenhower in front of the official White House tree.

by Chef Raffert again appeared on the console table that would become its customary spot. Red poinsettias flanked the East Room crèche and adorned the mantels. Also in the East Room was a lavish poinsettia tree, designed by Henry Callahan of Saks Fifth Avenue. It was made by arranging potted poinsettias on a tiered stand. Some were laid on their sides and propped at various angles to create the effect of a single mass. As previously, white poinsettias and a tiny tabletop tree provided holiday accents in the Red Room.

Blue spruce candle-lit wreaths, each accented with a large red velvet bow, were again hung in the mansion's windows. Christmas memorabilia from past presidencies greeted visitors in the East Colonnade for a second year—as they would for Mrs. Nixon's remaining holiday seasons at the White House.

★ 1972 ★
Nature's Bounty

THE CHRISTMAS TRIMMINGS THIS year were inspired by a pair of paintings from the White House collection—*Still Life with Fruit* and *Nature's Bounty*, both by the nineteenth-century artist Severin Roesen. Acquired by Jacqueline Kennedy and hung in the Red Room, the two still lifes, with their lush, vivid fruits, gave Mrs. Nixon the idea of holiday decorations made in the Della Robbia style. She told reporters that she had always liked Della Robbia wreaths, in which fruits are mixed with greenery and pine cones, and for years had given them to friends as Christmas gifts. To execute the concept, she again worked with J. Liddon Pennock of Philadelphia.

A four-foot Della Robbia wreath was suspended in the center of the gilded mirror in the Grand Foyer, and the gilded Monroe pier table displayed an arrangement of apples, pears, grapes, lemons, and limes. Two additional tables in the Cross Hall held similar displays of fruit. More Della Robbia topped the six-foot torchères.

Swags of Della Robbia garland hung gracefully from the tops of the marble columns, which flanked tall pyramid-shaped trees made with tiers of Della Robbia wreaths. The columns themselves, as well as the pilasters, were wrapped with bright red velour and then criss-

★ RIGHT ★

A sconce framed by Della Robbia greenery, reflecting the 1972 theme, "Nature's Bounty."

★ OPPOSITE ★

The Blue Room tree, trimmed with the state flower balls and gold Federal stars.

★ ABOVE ★

The California state ball from the collection of velvet and satin balls representing the fifty states.

★ OPPOSITE TOP ★

The columns and pilasters of the Cross Hall are covered in red velour and criss-crossed with gold braid. Della Robbia wreaths encircle the chandeliers.

★ OPPOSITE BOTTOM ★

The "snow"-topped gingerbread house, with figures of storybook favorites, was placed in the State Dining Room.

crossed with gold braid to form a diamond pattern; centered in each diamond was a gold star. The red velour "clashed too much" with the red carpet in the hall, the First Lady told reporters, so the carpet was taken up and stored for the season. She also pointed out that much of the fruit in the Della Robbia arrangements was real.

The noble fir in the Blue Room was trimmed in 4,000 firefly lights, 3,000 satin-finish balls in shades of gold, pink, red, and blue, the customary velvet and satin state flower balls, 150 gold Federal stars, and strands of gold tinsel.

At the North Portico entrance, two Norwegian blue spruce trees twinkled with firefly lights, and a miniature Christmas tree was visible in the window of Henry Kissinger's office in the West Wing.

★ 1973 ★
Monroe Gold

FOR THIS SEASON, WHICH UNEXPECTEDLY proved to be the Nixons' final White House Christmas, Mrs. Nixon chose an all-things-gold theme in honor of James Monroe, who had renovated the White House in 1817 and purchased gilded clocks and mirrors, gilded furniture for the Blue Room, and gilded tableware. Reflecting this theme, accents of gold lent sparkle to all the public rooms.

As their Christmas gift to staff members, President and Mrs. Nixon gave each a reproduction of a portrait of James Monroe painted by Samuel F. B. Morse, and their official Christmas card had a gold foil border.

Wreaths were scattered throughout the Executive Mansion, positioned around sconces, walls, and doors, all decked with red bows and studded with gold balls. The columns in the Entry Hall were wrapped in gold, and an arch of greenery united the columns and the tall thin trees placed nearby. Red candles were placed in each sconce, chandelier, and candelabrum, with the Monroe pieces displayed on the State Dining Room table.

With the country in the midst of an energy crisis, the White House adopted conservation measures. The Norwegian blue spruces flanking the North Portico entry were not trimmed with lights, and there were no electric candles in the wreaths hanging in the mansion's front windows, as in previous years. The mansion's exterior lighting, installed in 1970 at Mrs. Nixon's request, was switched off.

Instead of the thousands of small lights that were traditionally lit on the National Christmas Tree behind the White House, only one large light at the top was lit, supplemented by four spotlights

★ ABOVE ★

A bird's nest, found in the 1973 Christmas tree, became a home for a bird ornament. Mrs. Nixon saw the nest as a good luck omen.

★ OPPOSITE ★

The White House tree, adorned with gold balls and strings of gold beads.

on the ground.

Inside the mansion a soft, subdued effect was achieved by dimming the interior lighting to "candle power illumination intensity" and burning fires in all the fireplaces.

The Blue Room tree was lit with 2,000 firefly lights, half the number of the previous year. The fabulous state flower balls adorned the Fraser fir, along with many multicolored glass balls of various sizes and strings of gold beads for even more glitz.

The vibrant décor contrasted with the dark mood of the political scene, where events were unfolding that would lead to the President's resignation in the coming year. Yet the First Lady found comfort in a bird's nest that she had discovered in the branches of the eighteen-foot tree. During a press tour she called it "an omen, a sign of very good luck. I've heard it forever that if you get a tree with a nest, it's good luck." She described the gold and white bird ornament that was now cradled in the nest as a "bird of peace" and said that she intended to tell the President about it.

★ TOP ★

The Cross Hall, decorated to highlight the First Lady's "gold" motif.

★ ABOVE ★

The gingerbread house in its customary location in the State Dining Room: on top of a console table with gilded eagle supports.

★ OPPOSITE ★

President and Mrs. Nixon at Camp David.

Many new Christmas customs were established during Pat Nixon's time in the White House. The candlelight tours are still extremely popular, and the unveiling of the gingerbread house in the State Dining Room is one of the most highly anticipated events of the season. The ever—expanding White House Christmas card collection is displayed annually in the East Foyer, and each window facing Pennsylvania Avenue is usually decked with a festive wreath. The huge poinsettia "trees" that Mrs. Nixon liked so much are frequently used throughout the mansion as eye-catching accents. Her fabulous state balls, which would adorn the Blue Room tree for many years to come, are some of the very few ornaments from earlier administrations that remain with the White House, as most have gone to the presidential libraries. Even in years when the state balls are left packed away, the First Lady will often commission new ornaments to represent all fifty states, continuing the tradition inspired by Mrs. Nixon.

The lavish Christmas décor of the Nixon years was an extension of Pat Nixon's pride in the White House and her desire to make it beautiful for everyone who visited. In 1971 she told an interviewer, "I suppose of all the places we've spent Christmas, the White House must be our favorite. There's nowhere else I'd rather be. To be here in this historical house with memories of all the other families who've been here means so much — and to realize that we, in our way, are making a moment of history, too."

THE WHITE HOUSE CRÈCHE

(1967–PRESENT)

THE SEARCH FOR A PERMANENT WHITE HOUSE crèche that would match the quality of the mansion's other art treasures came to an end in 1967 with the gift to Mrs. Johnson of an eighteenth-century Neapolitan crèche from Charles and Jane Engelhard, Jr. of Far Hills, New Jersey. Installed in the same East Room window alcove previously occupied by the crèche loaned by Loretta Howard, it has been displayed in this location every Christmas season since.

After extensive research and two trips to Europe, Jane Engelhard acquired the Baroque-style set of figures from Marisa Piccoli Catello of Naples, whose family had been collecting Nativity figures for more than 300 years. According to Mrs. Engelhard, museums all over the world had their eye on the Catello collection, and the owner would never have parted with the crèche "except that it was for the White House."

The set consisted of thirty-nine pieces. The main figures—the Holy Family, the Three Wise Men, their attendants, shepherds, angels and cherubs, and other personages (such as two men with bagpipes)—ranged in height from twelve to eighteen inches. The magi were depicted riding horses rather than the more familiar camels. Three angels, holding a silver banner with the message "Gloria In Excelsis Deo," and a cherub were suspended over the manger. Three dogs, a goat, a cow, a dove, and accessories such as baskets and melons completed the scene.

For the crèche setting, Tony Award-winning stage designer Donald Oenslager created a multilevel stage with built-in lighting and a proscenium arch in ivory and gold colors to match the architectural details of the East Room. The entire structure, measuring fourteen feet tall and four feet deep, was built so that it could be disassembled for storage each year. Scenery and lighting designer Richard Casler carved the bases for the figures as well as the molding for the proscenium. Describing his design, Mr. Oenslager told a reporter: "It's taken almost as much work as a play, because I'd never done a crèche before. But I've had a marvelous time with it. Because the figures are eighteenth century, I'm making the frame as much like the baroque theatre of that time as possible. The backdrop is dark blue velvet studded with stars and angels, and the whole effect is blue and ivory and gold." Both designers contributed their services for the project.

To formally unveil and accept the gift for the permanent White House collection, Mrs. Johnson hosted a reception for the Engelhard family and guests that included several museum officials who had advised Mrs. Engelhard, along with representatives of Christmas crib societies, such as Angelo Stefanucci of Rome, a crèche collector and the world's foremost presepio authority at the time.

Since the initial installation of the crèche, the setting has been redesigned twice.

In 1978 a new setting was in order when Jane Engelhard purchased ten more figures for the crèche: two angels, two cherubs, a cow, a woman with a basket, a man leading a camel, and a man and

★ OPPOSITE ★

The White House crèche on display in 2007.

woman representing a couple. The new figures, like those in the initial set, were from Marisa Piccoli Catello's collection.

Two years earlier, Mrs. Engelhard had written to First Lady Betty Ford to suggest a revamping of the crèche setting. "I was never very happy about the rococo setting," she wrote. "I did not want to change it at the time because Don Oenslager, who created it, was very proud of his design." But with the designer's death the previous year, Mrs. Engelhard felt the time had come to "simplify the setting." In a memo to Mrs. Ford, White House Social Secretary Maria Downs pointed out that "some fundamental changes" in the crèche were needed, as they would save the chief usher and his staff "multiple manhours and much money." Whenever a holiday event was scheduled in the large, multipurpose East Room (such as an event that required extra floor space or a stage), the crèche had to be completely disassembled and then reassembled for the regular tours. Moreover, frequent handling of the delicate figures was undesirable from the standpoint of good conservation practices. Although Mrs. Ford was enthusiastic about the project, it was not completed until the second year of the Carter administration.

At Mrs. Engelhard's suggestion, Loretta Howard devised a more compact arrangement with the assistance of artist Enrique Espinoza and several staff members of the Metropolitan Museum of Art, including the museum's eminent director of lighting design, LeMar Terry. The new eleven-foot-high vertical setting, a representation of a mountain, was more practical: even with the addi-

tional figures, the crèche now fit entirely into the window recess on the east wall and had a removable front extension. For special events in the East Room, the front section could be easily removed, a protective barrier installed, and the curtains fully drawn in front of the crèche and its figures, which remained undisturbed.

In 1999 the setting for the crèche again received a new look, inspired by the traditional style of eighteenth-century Neapolitan presepio displays. The new aesthetic and architectural elements, which included a village vignette and classical ruins, were constructed of conservationally sound materials, and a new fiber-optic lighting system was installed. Each figure also underwent some restoration. The project received conservation and design assistance from the National Park Service as well as funding from the Charles Engelhard Foundation and the White House Historical Association.

Once the holiday season is over, the tableau is disassembled, and the crèche figures are stored away in a special archival cabinet in a temperature- and humidity-controlled room.

In addition to its religious symbolism, the antique manger scene represents a true labor of love on the part of its donor. Bess Abell, Lady Bird Johnson's social secretary, recalls Jane Engelhard's dedication to finding the perfect crèche for the White House: "She traveled all over to find it, constantly sending us cables with updates on her progress. For her, it was not just a monetary gift. It was a gift of her time, her energy, and, above all, her exquisite taste."

The Ford Years

1974-1976

Betty Ford

ONE OF MY FAVORITE TIMES AS First Lady was the holidays, when the White House is truly at its most beautiful. But of course what makes the holidays so special is being surrounded by family and friends. Joy, love, and a big, happy gathering—that's what I love most about Christmas. It is the season for happiness.

During my three Christmases at the White House, I wanted to share my belief that it is not the ornaments, wreaths, or other decorations that make the holidays so special, but rather being with loved ones and helping people in need. I did not want to change the way my family had always celebrated the holidays just because we were now living in the White House, so I tried to make sure that we kept our same traditions.

I loved my first Christmas at the White House when we had an old-fashioned theme that highlighted patchwork. Susan and I even tried our hand at making a few of the ornaments out of scraps from our sewing basket and some old lace of my mother's. That is a very special memory for me. We always tried to emphasize the old-fashioned, homemade decorations and to inspire the rest of the nation that they could do the same during those difficult financial times. That's why we had folders printed with instructions for making decorations from items found in the home. With my background in the arts, I loved the idea of handicrafts because they express the maker's imagination and creativity without being costly. I wanted the decorations to complement the Executive Mansion, not compete with it.

One of my favorite things about the White House Christmas season was the anticipation of seeing the wonderful gingerbread house that Chef Raffert made each year and watching all the little children who were mesmerized by it. Another was the lovely crèche in the East Room, reminding us what the holidays are all about. And of course we had the beautiful, breathtaking candlelight tours.

What I especially enjoyed were the holiday parties. Jerry and I always thought of the White House as "America's house," and we wanted to bring it to all segments of American society. There was a flurry of social events during the Christmas season, and it was a pleasure and an honor to open the doors to people from all walks of life—performers, athletes, and scientists rubbed elbows with politicians and diplomats. It was such fun to see everyone kicking up their heels and having a good time.

We had a vision of the White House as happy, free, and open, and we did our best to make it that way—not just during the holidays but all year round.

Betty Ford

★ *1974* ★
Handmade Crafts

IN PLANNING HER FIRST CHRISTMAS AT the White House, Mrs. Ford had to deal with the pressures of a shortened time frame, an unanticipated hospital stay, and a climate of austerity. In TV interviews the First Lady said that her family's gifts this year would be "less elaborate," and there was a reduction in the number of official Christmas parties at the White House. Despite budget cuts, President and Mrs. Ford approved of one small extravagance—mistletoe.

Mindful of the nation's poor economy and the need for many citizens to curtail their holiday budgets, Mrs. Ford chose a decorating theme of handmade crafts—especially patchwork, an art form associated with rural America and symbolizing thrift and recycling. With the assistance of patchwork quilt expert Celine Blanchard Mahler, Mrs. Ford created a look that would be easy to replicate in the nation's households and would inspire families to make their own decorations. Instructions for copying the simple, handmade decorations were even prepared for the public.

Maria Downs, who became the Fords' social secretary in 1975, recalls Mrs. Ford's strong interest in Americana: "When she became the First Lady, she decided to showcase

★ RIGHT ★

A patchwork ornament from 1974 on display at the Ford Library.

★ OPPOSITE ★

The First Lady greets the press in front of her patchwork-trimmed tree, December 10, 1974.

BETTY FORD

Following the resignation of President Nixon, Betty Ford was thrust into an unexpected new role. She often found herself in the spotlight because of her health problems as well as her candor and political activism. But she took the challenges in stride. After a little more than a year as First Lady, she was asked whether she felt overwhelmed and trapped in the White House. "It could be considered a goldfish bowl or a gilded cage," she said, "but I made up my mind that I wouldn't let it be that way. I would go ahead and live my life the way I normally would. I've done it. I'm having fun."

Being a gregarious person, Mrs. Ford enjoyed entertaining. While continuing the Christmas customs of her predecessors, she often cast aside conventional White House protocol. Her guest lists included many who were not of the old establishment, and for the first time, unmarried guests could attend state receptions accompanied by someone of their own choosing.

She created a festive and relaxed mood at the White House during the holidays with simple, handcrafted decorations that reflected the kind of old-fashioned Christmas that the Ford family had always celebrated.

everything American at the White House, to highlight the colorful diversity of American crafts, arts, and antiques at White House social gatherings."

The Blue Room tree was a concolor fir, grown in President Ford's home state of Michigan. It was trimmed with 550 different patchwork ornaments, measuring between three and five inches. Consisting of four different shapes and designs (round, pentagonal, "orange peel," and "Christmas lantern"), they were made of two types of fabrics: a cotton print in a variety of calico patchwork patterns and a water-stained blue moiré. The patchwork balls were made by women in North Carolina's Appalachian region, whereas the moiré balls were crafted by senior citizens across the country in coordination with the Quilter's Workshop of Bayside, New York. Patchwork bows and wreaths were made by Bea Starling of the Farm Women's Cooperative Market in Bethesda, Maryland. A 300-foot garland of patchwork-lined blue moiré, designed by Washington florist William Dove to match the wallpaper and curtains in the Blue Room, festooned the branches. Mr. Dove, assisted by interior designer Susan Hutchins of New York, designed the tree.

Mrs. Ford and her daughter, Susan, also made ornaments. The First Lady's ornament, made of scraps of ecru lace from her sewing basket and an old necktie of President Ford's, and then embroidered with her name and the year, was the final item to go on the tree at the press preview.

In a prepared press statement about the decorations, Mrs. Ford said:

I have always loved handicrafts and really became interested in them when I saw quilts being made first-hand in Appalachia. . . . In fact, everything on the tree is hand made from American materials. But people can make these ornaments at home at practically no cost out of scraps of material, milk cartons, shredded newspaper for stuffing and the like. . . I wanted to see how easy it was and made one myself—a lantern. I'm not a sewer, but it was easy and cost me nothing.

In keeping with an early American tradition, the tree was also decorated with fifty handmade toys, donated by a Pennsylvania toymaker. Made of sugar pine without nails, screws, or any other type of metal fastener, the toys included elephants, turtles, mice, alligators, whales, and trucks. Natural-wood baskets filled with nuts and gumdrops added to the homespun look, along with sachets filled with cinnamon, cloves, nutmeg, and other spices traditionally associated with the holidays. Dried statice (California heather) garnished the branches to suggest snow. Ribbon candy also hung on the branches. The tree was illuminated with 3,500

tiny bee lights; they used only 1,000 watts (which was low for that time) and were turned on only for tours and special events in accord with Mrs. Ford's desire to conserve electricity. The lights were reflected in 600 tiny mirrors to intensify the effect.

At the base of the tree were gaily wrapped packages, some decorated with appliquéd scenes made of fabric scraps. Handmade patchwork pillows were also tucked under the tree. The tree skirt was an award-winning patchwork quilt in the Boston Commons pattern with more than 150,000 stitches. The patchwork motif was a decorative element in the other public rooms as well. A turn-of-the-century crazy quilt of moiré and taffeta covered a table in the Red Room, while an ornately stitched cotton and muslin Irish Chain quilt from 1871 was on view in the Green Room. Draped over the grand piano in the East Room was an intricately embroidered satin and silk crazy quilt with fan designs; started in 1865, this variation of a crazy quilt was completed around 1900.

A dozen trumpeting angels created focal points in the niches of the Cross Hall and atop torchères. Designed by Charles Smith of Bill Dove's Flowers and made by volunteer florists, the figures were created with a Styrofoam base covered with aluminum foil and then sprayed gold. The angels' robes were trimmed with fabric in a patchwork print.

The rest of the State Floor was trimmed with natural greenery and red accents. In the windows of the public rooms as well as the north windows of the family quarters, thirty-four wreaths, made of fir, incense cedar, and blue juniper and each adorned with a red bow, were suspended with red moiré fabric.

In the corners of both the State Dining Room and the East Room were twelve-foot topiaries of poinsettias, grown in the White House greenhouse and set in antiqued wooden boxes.

A gingerbread house planned for the State Dining Room was created by Mrs. Mahler from arrowroot cookies, wafers, and candy. But while Secret Service agents were transporting it to the White House from Mrs. Mahler's home in Bayside, New York, the confection was ruined. Chef Raffert made a last-minute substitute, no doubt pleased to see his series of gingerbread houses unbroken.

The "sugared" real fruit used in a centerpiece for the Green Room was actually dusted with salt as an economy measure (salt is not only cheaper than sugar but remains white longer).

For the third year in a row, more than eighty florists from twenty-four states donated their services to make garlands, wreaths, and other floral decorations under the direction of Mr. Dove and Elmer "Rusty" Young, the chief White House florist.

An Old-fashioned Christmas in America

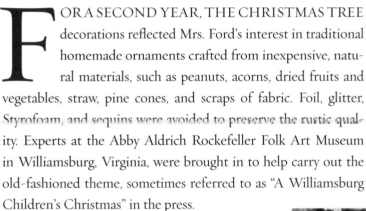

OR A SECOND YEAR, THE CHRISTMAS TREE decorations reflected Mrs. Ford's interest in traditional homemade ornaments crafted from inexpensive, natural materials, such as peanuts, acorns, dried fruits and vegetables, straw, pine cones, and scraps of fabric. Foil, glitter, Styrofoam, and sequins were avoided to preserve the rustic quality. Experts at the Abby Aldrich Rockefeller Folk Art Museum in Williamsburg, Virginia, were brought in to help carry out the old-fashioned theme, sometimes referred to as "A Williamsburg Children's Christmas" in the press.

Seventy Colonial Williamsburg employees and more than one hundred volunteers contributed most of the 3,000 ornaments for the Blue Room tree. Other groups, such as nursing home residents and members of 4-H Clubs and Girl Scout troops, sent additional ornaments. The Douglas fir was trimmed with Pennsylvania Dutch paper cutouts, tiny straw baskets with dried flowers, gingerbread cookies, Italian wafer cookies shaped like snowflakes, crocheted and paper snowflakes and bells, hand-sewn stockings and clothespin figures, wreaths of peanuts, animals fashioned of gingham, felt, and wire, jointed wooden figures, cornhusk dolls, candles with paper ruffs, woodshaving shapes, carved soap figures, chains of paper dolls, strings of popcorn, and tiny white lights. Strands of red peppers were used instead

★ **OPPOSITE** ★

Mrs. Ford unveils the White House tree trimmed with Colonial Williamsburg decorations, December 15, 1975.

★ **BELOW** ★

Traditional, handmade ornaments created by Colonial Williamsburg staff and volunteers for the White House tree.

★ ABOVE & RIGHT ★

*Antique toys from the Abby Aldrich Rockefeller Folk Art
Museum in Williamsburg, Virginia.*

★ OPPOSITE ★

*Mrs. William Schoettle with her needlepoint ornaments that
were displayed on the official White House tree.*

of cranberries, which were considered too messy. A cornhusk angel was at the top. In addition, Mrs. Ford made a red cloth bird for the tree; Susan's creation was a yarn doll. Heinz Bender, the White House pastry chef, made gingerbread cookies that were hung on the tree.

Mrs. Ford hosted a party with punch and cookies at the White House for the 150 volunteers who had helped with the decorations. Jane Hanson, who made eight stuffed doves and several other ornaments and now serves as the music interpreter at Co-

lonial Williamsburg, says of the experience, "It was an honor to make an ornament for the White House. I still have the thank-you note that I received from the Fords."

The museum loaned numerous pieces from its collection to underscore the season's theme. Antique toys were arranged at the base of the tree—cradles, a train, two rocking horses, a wagon, and even a group of dolls seated at a dining table. Ten portraits of children by eighteenth- and nineteenth-century American artists lined the walls of the Blue Room. Three carved wooden carousel

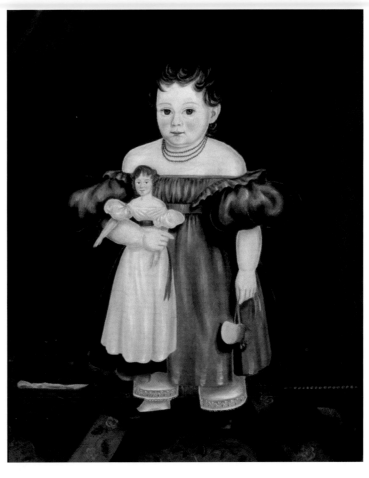

★ **THIS PAGE & OPPOSITE** ★

Oil portraits of children hanging on the walls of the Blue Room carry out the theme
of an "Old-fashioned Christmas in America." Top left: "Sarah Louisa Spencer"
by Henry Walton (1842). Top right: "Boy in Plaid" by an unknown artist
(ca. 1840-1850). Right: "Girl with Doll" by J. Bradley (1836). Above: "Portrait of
Two Children" by Joseph Badger (ca. 1758). Opposite: "Children with Toys" by
William Matthew Prior (ca. 1845).

figures, representing a horse, a giraffe, and a camel and dating from the late 1800s and early 1900s, were positioned in the Cross Hall and the Ground Floor Corridor. Looking down from the landing of the Grand Staircase was a three-foot painted wooden Santa, carved for a toy shop in the 1880s by Samuel A. Robb of New York, a noted carver of cigar-store figures. The Santa was loaned to the White House by the Smithsonian History and Technology Museum (now the National Museum of American History). A boxwood kissing ball hung over the staircase.

* **ABOVE** *

Betty and Susan Ford make ornaments for the tree in the Solarium of the private residence.

* **LEFT** *

A letter from President Ford to Beatrix Rumford on the beautiful Christmas decorations.

* **OPPOSITE** *

Mrs. Ford admires the Christmas tree in the Solarium.

The State Dining Room was filled with colorful arrangements of fruit trees made with miniature apples, pears, lemons, limes, pineapples, and oranges, mixed with evergreens, lotus seedpods, and magnolia leaves gathered from the White House lawn. Surpassing his previous creations, Chef Raffert made a gingerbread house that was three feet tall—enormous for the time.

The Green Room boasted holly-filled bowls and a tabletop tree made of pomegranates paired with magnolia leaves and pods.

In the Red Room, in addition to arrangements of both variegated and green holly, another decoration made its debut—a cranberry topiary made by Christine Heineman of Chestertown, Maryland. It was the first of many cranberry trees that would rest on the Lannuier center table during the holidays. At each window of the White House was a tiny, unadorned wreath.

Mrs. Ford decided to expand on the how-to information of the previous year with a more detailed mailer. Along with instructions for making many of the decorations that appeared on the Blue Room tree that year, it described the role of the Christmas tree in American culture and noted that the first tree to appear at the White House was in 1889 during the term of Benjamin Harrison.

Folk Art Museum director Beatrix T. Rumford, who coordinat-ed all the decorations along with Edna Pennell, expressed the spirit of the décor: "In our increasingly synthetic world, it is reassuring to know that it is still possible to make special things from ordinary ones through the combination of imagination, skillful handcrafting, and time."

Each holiday season the museum sets up a Christmas tree that is decorated with some of Mrs. Ford's original Blue Room orna-ments, along with new handmade ornaments (many of which are based on folk art objects in the museum's collection).

Anticipating the next season, Social Secretary Maria Downs wrote to Mrs. Ford that they would be hard-pressed "to top Wil-liamsburg—we can only hope to come close to it."

The Love that is the Spirit of Christmas

FOR HER LAST WHITE HOUSE CHRISTMAS, Mrs. Ford chose a theme to express the charitable mood of the season—"what Christmas is all about," as she put it. In unveiling the decorations to reporters in the Blue Room, she hung two white cloth doves—embroidered with "Jerry" and "Betty"—on the official tree to symbolize peace and love.

The tree's 2,500 flower ornaments represented the official flowers of the states and territories, a fitting motif in this Bicentennial year. They were created by garden club members, art students, senior citizens, and schoolchildren from across America, using materials such as silk, felt, bamboo, seeds, beads, shells, ribbon, metal, porcelain, and glass. Rounding out the trimmings were small baskets of dried flowers, tiny white lights, and baby's breath. At the top of the tree was a bouquet of forsythia made from paper flowers on natural branches, the creation of first-graders in Ithaca, New York. A birdcage with a pair of porcelain doves was also in the Blue Room.

Throughout the year, the White House had received thousands of gifts from the public to commemorate the nation's Bicentennial. Some of these gifts were displayed at the base of the tree, such as dolls representing Betsy Ross and Paul Revere, hand-sewn quilts, carved birds, and a replica of the aircraft carrier *USS Forrestal* (it was on the deck of this aircraft carrier that President Ford had officially rung in the Bicentennial celebrations on the Fourth of July). Packages colorfully wrapped in red, white and blue also surrounded the twenty-foot balsam fir.

Natural arrangements of bayberry, boxwood, holly, cedar, ju-

★ ABOVE ★

The First Lady examines a handcrafted bird sculpture at the base of the tree, Blue Room.

★ OPPOSITE ★

Packages in colorful red, white and blue wrapping add a patriotic Bicentennial motif to the Christmas tree.

niper, spruce, pyracantha, and wood fern on tables and mantels lent their rough-hewn beauty and Christmas aroma to the public rooms. Wreaths made with noble fir greenery and red velvet bows hung in all the windows on the State Floor. Sconces, chandeliers, and the Grand Staircase were decked with princess pine garlands accented with red braid. The antique Santa Claus of painted wood gazed down on visitors once again from the landing of the Grand Staircase. A giant ball of mistletoe hung over the steps leading to the private quarters.

New York designer Jack Bangs coordinated the decorations, which were intended to be naturalistic. He wanted "to complement the house, not overwhelm it." He was assisted by fifty volunteers from the floral industry as well as Chief Florist Rusty Young and the White House staff.

Phyllis Clasing, a volunteer florist from Skaneateles, New York who helped with this year's decorations, said that the most

wonderful thing about her experience was discovering "the love that goes into the White House Christmas tree." She explained:

The whole tree is decorated with different things people have made and sent. . . . Someone sent all kinds of pine cones. Somebody else made gorgeous magnolia blooms of white reversed velvet and natural foliage. Someone dried Queen Anne's lace and fashioned it in a little cluster. There's life and love in everything on it.

She added that when Mrs. Ford came down to thank the volunteers for their work, "The First Lady was teary-eyed and we were, too."

Some historians have noted that Betty Ford may have faced the most difficult challenge in terms of defining the first lady's role to fit the country's current climate, and that she "seized this moment in history and set a new standard for candor and public service for future first ladies to follow." Her holiday traditions reflected this same resilience of spirit. Betty Ford wanted to keep Americans focused on the true meaning of Christmas during this difficult time, so she took the tinsel out of the White House holiday decorations and restored handcrafted ornaments to the Blue Room tree for a look of authentic Americana.

While keeping certain established customs, such as the candlelight tours, Mrs. Ford initiated the cranberry tree tradition and started the practice of compiling information about the decorations, which later evolved into a favorite White House memento—the holiday tour book. Christmas was one of the many avenues through which Mrs. Ford connected with all Americans. As the Fords' first social secretary, Nancy Lammerding, explained: "Both the President and Mrs. Ford think of the White House as America's house. They want to bring it to all segments of society."

THE GINGERBREAD HOUSE

THE MAGICAL TRADITION OF THE WHITE HOUSE gingerbread house, baked in the White House kitchen and displayed in the State Dining Room, began with the first Christmas of the Nixon administration. Previous gingerbread houses at the mansion had all apparently been sent as gifts. In 1962, for example, the Kennedy children received three gingerbread houses for the family's enjoyment, but they were not on public display at the White House. In 1968, a New Jersey resident sent President and Mrs. Johnson a gingerbread house that was exhibited in the State Dining Room as part of the holiday décor.

But in 1969, with the arrival of German-born Hans Raffert as assistant chef, the unveiling of an annual confection in the State Dining Room became a much-anticipated event. Always displayed on the ornate mahogany console table with gilded eagle supports that was ordered by Teddy Roosevelt, Chef Raffert's gingerbread house was constructed as a simple A-frame, his hallmark design, and then elaborately decorated with cookies, candies, and flourishes of icing. Marzipan figures of Hansel and Gretel (and often the Witch) made regular appearances in the garden, underscoring the Old World tradition of gingerbread houses.

In 1973, a *Time* reporter described the impact of the gingerbread house at one of the holiday parties:

Assistant Chef Hans Raffert fashioned a two-foot-high house out of 16 pounds of gingerbread, mortared it together with six pounds of icing, *shingled it with five pounds of cookies, and decorated it with gumdrops, a pound of hard candy and a dozen peppermint canes. An embassy child stood spellbound before this creation, reached out and broke off a piece of the front and popped it in his mouth.*

Usually weighing about forty pounds, the completely edible concoction also contained four pounds of molasses, one-fourth pound of ginger, one-eighth pound of cinnamon, and, for the icing, thirty-six egg whites and five pounds of confectioner's sugar. At that time, the gingerbread house took twelve hours (including drying time) to create.

Due to the irresistible appeal of the enchanting delicacy, it became necessary to post a guard during children's parties. According to a former presidential aide, "Any available social aide watched over the treasures of the tree, but it took a tough Marine to safeguard the gingerbread house. The White House had

* OPPOSITE *

The 2001 gingerbread house in the State Dining Room, a Roland Mesnier creation, was a replica of the original White House in 1800, home to Abigail & John Adams.

* RIGHT *

Executive Pastry Chef Hans Raffert puts the finishing touches on the 1991 gingerbread house.

learned the hard way that a child's hand is faster than a social aide's eye. Walls had fallen in and chimneys disappeared in the past and . . . kids just seem to have more respect for a Marine." By 1977, the main attraction in the State Dining Room was guarded by two Marines.

Chef Raffert's gingerbread house became a bit grander in the mid-1970s; it now measured three feet tall and two feet wide and weighed about forty-five pounds. By the mid-1980s, it took a week to make and was assembled from twenty pounds of gingerbread dough, six pounds of traditional German cookies, one pound of candy canes, two pounds of hard candies, fifteen pounds of royal icing, and a pound of confectioner's sugar (to imitate snow). The icing was used for decorative designs and as "glue" to hold the walls and roof together. Sometimes, at First Lady Nancy Reagan's request, Chef Raffert would make a second gingerbread house for children in hospitals. When he was promoted to executive chef in 1988, he continued to create his annual showpiece.

The gingerbread houses varied in subtle ways from year to year through the addition of details specific to the current White House family—peppermint candy canes to tempt President Nixon, a little mailbox with Amy Carter's name on it, a front path or a chimney formed with jellybeans as a nod to President Reagan's favorite candy, a marzipan Millie that was sure to please First Lady Barbara Bush. People were always eager to see the personal touches that Chef Raffert gave his creations. His embellishments were always edible, except the wisp of cotton mimicking smoke and occasionally the material used for window panes. For twenty-three years, until his retirement in 1992, he made the tasty-looking confection.

The torch then passed to Executive Pastry Chef Roland Mesnier, who turned the gingerbread house into the sensation that it is today. Departing from his predecessor's A-frame design, Chef Mesnier devised and built ever more ambitious, architecturally detailed structures, each a clever interpretation of the year's decorating theme. And like Chef Raffert, Chef Mesnier personalized each piece of confectionary art with miniature versions of the first family's pets and other motifs specific to the mansion's current residents.

For his first effort, Chef Mesnier created not one gingerbread house but an entire gingerbread village! Then for another eleven years he produced amazing and unique structures, ranging from scale replicas of the White House to historic homes, Washington monuments, Santa's workshop, and a castle. His creations, many weighing more than 300 pounds, were made of completely edible ingredients—primarily gingerbread, chocolate, and marzipan, with no cardboard whatsoever. Even the shims and supports were made of gingerbread. He and his assistants would bake the gingerbread dough in 30-by-35-inch pans, then use a band saw to precision-cut the gingerbread into pieces that they would mortar together with chocolate icing. Tiny figures and other details were modeled out of marzipan. Something of a tinkerer, Chef Mesnier came up with a technique for making "gingerbread veneer," a very thin-cut piece of gingerbread that could be bent for making intricate shapes. A perfectionist as well, he often worked from real blueprints created by the engineers in the Usher's Office.

Although the annual project was the pastry team's most difficult of the year, requiring some 200 hours of design and construction work, Chef Mesnier tackled it with enthusiasm: "Building the gingerbread house made me feel like a kid again," he says. Among his masterpieces, the "House of Socks" from 1993 remains his favorite. Another memorable creation was the castle of 1998. Consisting of 100 pounds of dough and 40 pounds of chocolate, it was also the only one of his gingerbread houses that had to occupy the dining table (due to its size) instead of the console table—and the only one that almost met with disaster. As it was being moved into place, the main tower began to sway while the press watched with bated breath, anticipating the story of the season. When the chef quickly reached out and stabilized the structure, he heard sighs of relief, tinged with a little disappointment, he suspects.

At the request of First Lady Laura Bush, each gingerbread house between 2001 and 2008 was a different replica of the White House, featuring different views and of course different details. During this period Roland Mesnier was succeeded by Executive Pastry Chef Thaddeus DuBois and, more recently, by Executive Pastry Chef Bill Yosses. In 2007 and 2008 Chef Yosses made the gingerbread houses coated entirely with white chocolate; each weighing 400 to 500 pounds. The 2008 gingerbread house was the heaviest ever made.

Children and adults alike can look forward to more White House Christmases marked by one of the most popular rituals of the season— the creation of a fabulous gingerbread house that never fails to surprise and delight.

The Carter Years

1977-1980

Rosalynn Carter

Christmas has always been a special time for our family to do something together. At home in Plains, we would go to our farm and cut down a choice red cedar tree. When our children were small, they would make the decorations—simple things like paper chains, strings of popcorn, pine cones painted in different colors, and tinsel from sliced tinfoil wrap. Then we would all gather and trim the tree with these handmade ornaments. As the children grew older, our additional decorations became more sophisticated, including electric lights with manufactured glass bulbs that we bought at local stores. Our total collection would be saved and carefully unpacked and hung on the tree each year, sentimental reminders of happy holidays long past.

When we came to the White House, we enjoyed sharing our own family traditions and values with the American people. The White House is truly a home that belongs to all Americans. Each year I looked forward to planning the decorations for the holidays. They were times to celebrate the talents of our fellow citizens, recall fond memories of earlier holidays, and reflect on the meaning of the season.

Our first Christmas in the White House was especially memorable. While First Lady in Georgia, I asked the Georgia Association of Retarded Citizens to decorate our tree in the Governor's Mansion. The results were wonderful. So in the spring of 1977, I contacted the National Association of Retarded Citizens and asked if they could help me decorate the official White House Christmas tree, which stands in the Blue Room and is seen by thousands of visitors during the holiday season. More than 1,500 children and adults working in 200 schools and workshops all across our country made ornaments.

That very special tree was a testament to the creativity, ability, and spirit of the mentally retarded people who had fashioned each of the handmade decorations. And the materials they used reflected the diversity of our great nation—redwood from California, seashells from North Carolina, corn kernels from Iowa, and of course peanuts from Georgia! The tree was a symbol and a celebration of the many ways that individuals from all backgrounds and ability levels contribute to our country. It was truly an expression of one of the most important messages of the season.

Showcasing the talents of our citizens, both past and present, was the central theme of our Christmas decorations throughout all our years in the White House. Intricately fashioned Victorian toys on the Veitch fir in the Blue Room in 1978 evoked memories of Christmases past and gave a magical feel to our celebration that year. Students from the Corcoran School of Art in Washington, D.C., decorated the White House Christmas tree, a Douglas fir, in 1979. Inspired by American Colonial folk art, these talented young people created fabulous ornaments that recalled our past and reflected the promise of our future. Another Douglas fir graced the Blue Room in 1980 and provided the focal point for an old-fashioned Christmas. All its decorations were also handmade reproductions of nineteenth-century dolls, hats, fans, and other Victoriana. Once again volunteers played a major role, as they had done every year, in decorating all the state rooms in the White House with seasonal greenery and flowers, yet another wonderful testament to the spirit of the season.

Every Christmas in the White House was special, and each became a treasured memory.

Rosalynn Carter

1977
Classic American Christmas with Handmade Crafts

A CLASSIC AMERICAN CHRISTMAS was created at the mansion for 1977. More than 2,000 handcrafted ornaments for the White House tree came from members of the National Association for Retarded Citizens at the invitation of Mrs. Carter, who was active in mental health reform. The project involved 200 workshops and 1,500 individuals representing local and state chapters of the organization. The result was more than 2,000 ornaments. Mrs. Carter wanted the tree to reflect the home states of the individuals who made the ornaments and to demonstrate how much the mentally disabled have to share.

The branches of the Blue Room's Noble fir were hung with such items as cornhusk dolls from Indiana, seashell ornaments from Delaware, pine cones from Colorado, bird nests of Texas moss, nut pods from Hawaii, redwood items from California, medallions made from Mardi Gras beads, a manger of Popsicle sticks, cotton-spool trains, silvered eggshells, a God's Eye (a weaving made with two crossed sticks), red stockings, seed-pod flowers, rope wreaths with red bows, smiling Santa faces made of yarn, felt angels, and garlands of peanuts from Georgia. Amy's favorite was a worm made from purple pipe cleaners.

The use of mostly native materials for tinsel and trim

ROSALYNN CARTER

Rosalynn Carter entered the White House after being Georgia's First Lady for four years, which prepared her for the task of managing the countless social and cultural events that she and President Carter hosted at the Executive Mansion.

During her tenure at the White House, she sought to convey the true sentiment of the season. "Commercialism has cost the nation much of its Christmas spirit," she said. "It's very, very important to realize what Christmas is and what it stands for . . . we sometimes lose track of that. Christmas is a family affair and more—to show your friends and neighbors you care for them. It is what our lives mean." She especially wanted the Carters' young daughter, Amy, only in grade school at the time, to have fond memories of her holidays at the mansion.

Although the details of the holiday décor were executed by White House staff, President and Mrs. Carter actively participated in the planning; decisions about decorations, themes, guests, and budgets were always shared. Gretchen Poston, the Carters' social secretary, later told an interviewer, "The President was as involved as anybody."

★ OPPOSITE ★

President and Mrs. Carter and daughter Amy in front of the White House Christmas tree.

was meant to remind people of objects that they or their children had made for their own trees. Mrs. Carter announced that some of the decorations would be donated to Children's Hospital.

New York designer Mark Hampton, who helped coordinate the decorations, said that the effect was intended to be "homey, simple and traditional." He added, "It should look like a great house and not a public building."

The rest of the State Floor received the careful attention of Mr. Hampton, the White House staff, and approximately ninety volunteers from various garden clubs. Masses of poinsettias were everywhere—more than 300; baskets of poinsettias hung in the windows, and tiered pyramids were placed in the halls. The mansion was also festooned with holly, heather, branches of pink quince blossoms, mistletoe, and 300 yards of evergreen rope.

At holiday balls, buffets, receptions, and teas, the Carters entertained 5,000 guests; in addition, they invited 9,000 visitors to special candlelight tours. As part of the holiday fare, White House

pastry chef Heinz Bender baked seventy-five fruitcakes. Although the Carters had restored the pre-Kennedy custom of serving nothing stronger than wine in the public rooms, the chef made no alterations to his usual recipe, which included rum, bourbon, and sherry—he knew that the First Lady's mother, "Miss Allie," always borrowed enough whiskey to make her annual Christmas Lane Cake. Chef Raffert's classic gingerbread house, guarded by two Marines, occupied its customary place in the State Dining Room.

A holiday surprise that year was a strange present that was sent to the White House for Amy—a red, white, and blue chain saw—after a young friend of Amy's told a reporter that the President's daughter wanted a chain saw for Christmas because "she likes the way they work." Within days, this Associated Press story appeared in newspapers across the country:

A manufacturer, eager to please, rushed Amy her very own chain saw,
a bright red, white and blue model that any young woodsman would be
glad to use on the stately White House trees

★ OPPOSITE ★
The First Lady shows the mansion's "Classic American" Christmas tree to reporters, Blue Room, December 13, 1977.

★ RIGHT ★
The gingerbread house.

★ BELOW ★
Handmade ornaments give the tree a traditional, homespun look.

Meanwhile, calls have been pouring into the White House from eager Christmas shoppers who want to know what, other than a chain saw, Amy wants for Christmas.

Mary Hoyt, a White House spokeswoman, said chain saws are out . "I think Amy might have said train set, not chain saw," Mrs. Hoyt said. But before the White House is deluged with train sets, Mrs. Hoyt says, the Carters want well-meaning gift buyers to know that the President and Mrs. Carter would rather such gifts be sent to needy children and not to their daughter.

Despite Mrs. Hoyt's announcement, a number of additional chain saws arrived at the White House for Amy. The Carters returned them all except one that had come from a factory whose workers had individually signed the attached card. It was kept for the future Carter Presidential Library—to join gifts to the Carters from various heads of state.

1978
Victorian Antique Toys

IN THE COURSE OF REDECORATING THE third floor's Solarium earlier in the year, Mrs. Carter discovered a hand-colored steel engraving that depicted visitors arriving in horse-drawn carriages at the North Portico of the White House. The nineteenth-century print not only inspired the Victorian theme for the 1978 decorations but was selected by President and Mrs. Carter for their 1978 Christmas card. For the next two years they continued to use other historic scenes of the White House on their official holiday card.

Mrs. Carter set the stage for the Yuletide mood with this message, printed in a holiday program for White House visitors:

Jimmy, Amy and I invite you to let your imagination take you back to Christmas celebrations of years ago. This year, we trimmed our tree with antique toys . . . We hope they will bring back special memories for you and will give our younger visitors a glimpse of life in the days of their grandmothers and grandfathers.

Her holiday tour booklet, the first of its kind for the White House, contained pictures and descriptions of some of the Victorian toys on display in the Blue Room as well as information about the Christmas tree itself. Her booklet was such an excellent idea that a similar booklet has been prepared by every first lady since Rosalynn Carter.

The Blue Room tree, a Veitch fir with dark green needles and a silvery blue undertone, was truly an

* OPPOSITE *

Antique toys give the White House tree a Victorian look in the Blue Room. The 2,800 toys were on loan from the Margaret Woodbury Strong Museum in Rochester, New York.

* BELOW *

A holiday wreath frames the Presidential Seal over the door to the Blue Room.

antique enthusiast's dream. The branches were filled with more than 2,800 antique toys, all on loan from the Margaret Woodbury Strong Museum in Rochester, New York, and arranged with the help of museum representatives. There were dolls from many different countries, toy soldiers, circus clowns, miniature furniture, and animals of every sort—zebras, sheep, puppies, and teddy bears with accessories. On top was an antique Santa Claus in his cherry-red robe. The theme of Victorian Americana was carried out through ceramics, quilts, and decorative folk art. One special toy was an original stuffed Mickey Mouse doll, which was celebrating its fiftieth birthday and was highlighted in Mrs. Carter's holiday program. Each item on the tree was at least fifty years old.

Ornaments were tied with bows of red, green, or gold yarn, a feature of Christmas tree decorations during the late nineteenth century. Interspersed throughout the tree were American and German greeting cards from the period 1900 to 1920.

In lieu of wrapped presents, the base of the tree was surrounded by forty larger toys dating from about 1875 to 1900, in-

★ ABOVE ★
The First Lady displays Victorian-era decorations on the Christmas tree, December 12, 1978.
★ OPPOSITE LEFT ★
The 1978 gingerbread house with a Victorian-era mailbox.
★ OPPOSITE RIGHT★
A tabletop arrangement of pine cones and greenery enhances the portrait of President Dwight D. Eisenhower by J. Anthony Wills.

cluding a doll "mansion" with its original wallpaper and draperies, a cast-iron train, a rooster pull-toy, wicker doll furniture, a horse-drawn carriage, an Uncle Sam bank, a rocking horse with a tail and mane of real horsehair, Snow White and the Seven Dwarfs, and numerous other venerable pieces of the Victorian period. An original teddy bear made by Margarete Steiff of Germany and other stuffed bears were also on display, coinciding with an exhibit that had recently opened at the Smithsonian Institution's National Museum of History and Technology to commemorate the seventy-fifth anniversary of the teddy bear. As the new Strong Museum was not yet open to the public, the White House display of selected pieces from the collection was a much-heralded event. The museum toys were valued at $93,000 at the time.

Mrs. Carter and Amy came down to hang a few of the decorations, and President Carter gave it a final inspection. Pleased with the tree's Victorian finery, the First Lady said, "It reminds me of when I was a little girl. It brings back a lot of happy memories."

Another highlight of this season was the Engelhard family's

donation of ten additional figures to the White House crèche in the East Room.

Decorations across the State Floor created a look from yesteryear with a mood of warmth and naturalness. Greenery, pine cones, and an abundance of bright red poinsettias filled the room, along with tall, unadorned cedar and fir trees. As in Victorian homes, many candles were used throughout the mansion. Red candles in hurricane lamps, surrounded by natural greenery with magnolias, were displayed on mantels, and the usual white candles of chandeliers were fitted with red cylinders. The upper walls in the State Dining Room and East Room were draped with over 1,500 feet of white pine, juniper, cedar, and pine roping. Large wreaths of greenery with red ribbon hung in the windows. Potted pink, red, and white cyclamen as well as paperwhite narcissus reflected the popularity of conservatories during the Victorian period.

The décor was the work of Rusty Young, chief White House florist, and more than forty volunteer florists from eight states.

★ 1979 ★
American Folk Art

PLANNING FOR CHRISTMAS OF 1979 began in March, with work intensifying throughout the summer. Gretchen Poston, White House social secretary, told a reporter that people often heard her cheerfully "caroling in July." But when the holiday season actually arrived, just weeks after the onset of the Iran hostage crisis, the mood at the White House turned somber. The National Christmas Tree on the Ellipse was kept dark except for the star cluster atop the tree. President Carter gave Amy the honor of pulling the switch that lit up fifty smaller trees, one symbolizing each hostage. Rosalynn Carter said, "It's a special time of year. Christmas is still Jesus' birthday—a time to come together, to count our blessings and pray for the hostages." She also announced that holiday parties would be more subdued.

Mrs. Carter selected American folk art as the theme, with decorations made in the Colonial style by contemporary artisans. She wanted "ornaments that represented the handwork of young artists of the country, a fresh, different presence," said Gretchen Poston.

Mrs. Carter enlisted a design team of ten fine arts students from Washington's Corcoran School of Art (now the Corcoran College of Art and Design) to make over 500 ornaments in mixed media—needlework, ceramics, and carved balsa wood. Figures of rocking horses, angels, sailboats, fish, posies, dried flowers, and even a miniature White House were placed on the Blue Room's Douglas fir. Many ornaments were characteristic of the period— such as miniature weathervanes, trade signs, and dolls—and were created in subdued colors or antiqued to appear old. One thousand artificial red apples and gold Christmas balls served as unify-

★ **OPPOSITE** ★

Ornaments made by students at the Corcoran School of Art in Washington, D.C..

★ **ABOVE** ★

The official White House Christmas tree, decked with more than 600 handmade ornaments, Blue Room.

ing elements.

Ceramics students from the school made life-size ceramic objects, which were displayed in Plexiglas boxes at the base of the tree. These included a large ski boot, ballet slippers, a teddy bear, cameras, and an authentic-looking duffle bag, all symbolizing the tradition of giving. Atop the tree was an embroidered gold eagle in a circle. For a second year, Mrs. Carter prepared a holiday tour booklet highlighting the Blue Room tree and its handcrafted ornaments.

The décor for the rest of the mansion was simple and understated. Green wreaths with bright red velvet bows hung in the windows; mistletoe hung over doorways. In addition to green and white poinsettias, fir trees dotted with red and yellow apples filled the Grand Foyer and Cross Hall. Mantels were topped with arrangements of more red and yellow apples with mixed greenery.

Dottie Temple, former chief florist at the White House, recalls the pitfalls of using fresh fruit as a decorative element:

Even with careful preseason planning, things can go wrong. During one Carter Christmas, we decided to use a healthy quantity of fresh fruit in the green arrangements. The fruit pyramids on the tables in

★ ABOVE ★
State Dining Room, trimmed for the holidays in preparation for the Congressional Ball.
★ OPPOSITE ★
The gingerbread house, with Amy's own mailbox and miniature rocking horses in the front yard.

the State Dining Room, with their luscious apples, lemons, limes, and kumquats, were stunning. The first few days they were on display, they were fine. Then Washington had one of its unpredictable mid-December heat waves, and the fruit flies took over the large room. We had to redo everything in permanent fruit. Needless to say, from that day on, fruit has generally been used only for special events of short duration.

Chef Hans Raffert added some special touches to his annual masterpiece this year—solar collector windows made of aluminum foil and a miniature mailbox with Amy's name on it. (The solar motif referred to President Carter's advocacy of solar energy and his installation of solar panels on the White House roof in the summer of 1979.) It was the tenth of Chef Raffert's gingerbread creations.

1980
An Old-Fashioned Victorian Christmas

NOSTALGIA FILLED THE AIR DURING the 1980 holiday season, as the Carters began saying their farewells. The décor was also nostalgic, turning the clock back to an America of the nineteenth century.

For her last White House Yuletide, Mrs. Carter sought the decorating talents of Louis Nichole, a young furniture maker in Hartford, Connecticut, who was just beginning to make a name for himself with his feminine "Old World" decorative accessories—such as paper roses, frilly pillows, delicate porcelain dolls in lacy dresses, and Christmas wreaths made with nosegays and old silks and satins. To create a nineteenth-century "heirloom" look, he chose a color palette of ecru, the color of old lace, and dusty rose, a shade inspired by the Sterling Silver variety of tea rose. As social secretary Gretchen Poston explained to reporters, "The inside of the rose is cream and the edges faded pink." She described the theme as "one of high, romantic, Victorian fashion but contemporary in composition."

The Douglas fir in the Blue Room was trimmed with reproductions of Victorian porcelain dolls dressed in exquisite handmade gowns. Other ornaments consisted of stick-mounted doll heads of bisque and hand-painted porcelain; miniature Victorian-era hats, parasols, and fans; nosegays of lace, velvet ribbons, rosebuds, and baby's breath; more than 1,000 silky, rose-colored tassels (instead of icicles); and thousands of balls covered in "antique" striped tapestry (lisserie), fancy braid, and vintage laces resembling crochet, all accented by miniature white lights. In later

★ ABOVE ★

A close-up of an ornament by Louis Nichole for the Blue Room tree.

★ OPPOSITE ★

The old-fashioned "roses and lace" Christmas tree. Victorian-style dolls in lace gowns and a palette of ecru and dusty rose gave the tree its unique look.

years, the tree came to be called the "roses and lace" tree.

Around the base of the tree was an array of old-fashioned toys in shades of muted pink and rose—rocking horses, giant jack-in-the-boxes, a marionette, clowns and jesters, miniature stick horses and doll carriages, and a replica of a Christmas street scene with three Victorian-style dollhouses, all with miniature furnishings. Bandboxes, placed under the tree as gifts, were painted a dusty rose and covered in rich fabrics, lace, and ribbons to match the ball ornaments.

Mr. Nichole and his extended family, all living together in a four-room apartment, worked on the decorations for over a year. Because of the size of the tree, the designer created large ornaments that would fit the tree's scale—the dolls were three feet tall, and the balls were six and eight inches. For the delicate lace of the

dolls' dresses, he cut up the Nottingham lace tablecloths and linens that he had designed for a special White House event in the fall. To make the balls for the tree, his mother glued 20,000 pieces of fabric to the foam balls; his father filled the apartment with a maze of cardboard compartments for storing the balls (as the quantity of balls grew, they spilled over into his two aunts' apartments on other floors of the house). The brick dollhouse alone, which was built with more than 10,000 real miniature bricks, laid and mortared with traditional techniques, took 140 hours to complete. His father made the bandboxes, which were later covered on-site by the volunteer florists. To give the decorations the antique look that had become his signature, he applied thinned tar, egg whites, and gesso to the materials.

The designer and his family turned out 350 dolls and eight

Victorian dollhouses for the State Floor as well as more than 4,000 other ornaments and decorations. "No one ever complained," he recalls. "Occasionally my mama's friends and my ten aunts would come over and help, and no one seemed to care that we didn't have room to sit in the dining room or the living room. Everyone sat at the kitchen table and made ball after ball after ball. As long as we had food and conversation, our family was always happy."

As an extra flourish in carrying out the season's theme, Mr. Nichole designed a party dress for Amy—a satin gown with lace and velvet ribbon, fashioned after the gown of a doll hanging on the tree and likewise made from the recycled lace tablecloths. He also coached her in the proper way to carry the train.

The rest of the State Floor was decorated in the same hues. Wreaths of mixed greenery with large dusty rose velvet bows

Boxwood, ligustrum, and cedar trees, festooned with dusty rose moiré taffeta, line the Cross Hall, along with ligustrum topiaries in the niches. The hall leads to the East Room, where the crèche is on display.

Chef Raffert's 1980 creation.

★ LEFT ★

A poinsettia tree.

★ OPPOSITE ★

The First Lady displays a ball gown made especially for her daughter Amy. It was designed by Louis Nichole after one of the Victorian dolls on the tree and handmade from Nottingham lace tablecloths.

and moiré taffeta hung in the windows, complemented by masses of pink and white poinsettias. Boxwood, cedar, and ligustrum trees, trimmed with miniature lights and dusty rose moiré taffeta swags and bows, filled the Cross Hall. The Presidential Seal above the door to the Blue Room was framed by a wreath of greenery trimmed with rose-colored velvet ribbon and a moiré taffeta bow.

The centerpieces in the State Dining Room were hatboxes filled with bouquets of silk flowers and set on lace tablecloths designed by Mr. Nichole. At a dinner honoring the Cabinet and senior staff, the table decorations included containers filled with Sterling Silver roses and little decorated boxes of chocolate truffles for the guests.

The old-fashioned Yuletide was celebrated with White House holiday parties that included readings from Dickens' "A Christmas Carol," hayrides, roasted chestnuts and grog, and carolers from Washington schools and churches. By the end of the season, the new pastry chef, Roland Mesnier, had made approximately 250 fruitcakes and 12,000 cookies. (When Chef Mesnier was hired, Chef Raffert had informed him that his duties would *not* include making the annual gingerbread house.)

For the second year in a row, the National Christmas Tree on the Ellipse remained unlighted except for a brief period of 417 seconds—one for each day the Americans had been held hostage in Iran.

At the same time that Rosalynn Carter cast aside certain conventions and transformed the professional and political roles of the First Lady, she preferred a traditional old-fashioned look when it came to decorating for the holidays—a décor that would not detract from the season's true spirit.

Wanting to open the White House to as many people as possible, she not only continued the candlelight tours but expanded them, issuing special invitations to groups of elderly and disabled citizens. With true Southern hospitality, she made a constant effort to enhance every visitor's experience at the White House, especially during the holidays. The Christmas season, she once said, is "one of the happiest times and the best times for people to come see the White House—[it's] always beautiful." In providing a tour booklet about the mansion's Christmas decorations as one of her many projects, she started an annual tradition that has evolved into a prized keepsake. Every visitor who takes a holiday tour of the White House today comes home with a little bit of Rosalynn Carter's legacy.

★ ABOVE ★ *One of the popular candlelight tours, a White House tradition established by First Lady Patricia Nixon. December 27, 1973.*

★ *Traditions* ★

CANDLELIGHT TOURS

AMONG RESIDENCES OF HEADS OF STATE, THE White House is the only one that is open to the public on a regular basis and free of charge. Until restrictions were imposed in 2001 due to security concerns, as many as 1.5 million people would visit the White House each year, making it the world's most visited house.

Of course, the best time to tour the Executive Mansion is in December, when its halls are decked with Christmas finery, so the holiday tours have long been an annual ritual for many. An estimated 125,000 to 160,000 people visit the White House during the season, chiefly the last two weeks of December.

The candlelight tour, started by First Lady Patricia Nixon, quickly became the most popular of these tours. On Christmas Eve

of 1969, President and Mrs. Nixon announced that the White House would be open to the public on December 29 and 30 from 7 to 9 p.m. These self-guided evening tours were "a big hit," Mrs. Nixon later told the press, and a tradition was born. The tours gave visitors an opportunity to see the mansion not only in its holiday grandeur but after dark, when the state rooms were rarely seen by the public.

The following year saw the addition of Christmas music, performed by the Marine Band and various choirs. The public candlelight tours were held on December 28 and 29, followed by a special candlelight tour on December 30 for staffers and their families. Mrs. Nixon had learned that certain government units which performed essential services for the White House—such as the White House police, Secret Service agents, Army Signal Corps members, and others—were operating under a quota system that determined which employees would attend the holiday staff parties. The Nixons remedied this situation by not only scheduling an extra candlelight tour for the excluded staffers and their families but also sending them engraved invitations to view the White House in all its splendor. To enhance the ambience and allay any nervousness among the tourists, Mrs. Nixon asked the U.S. Secret Service Tour Officers who acted as guides to wear gray slacks and navy blazers instead of uniforms and to keep their pistols concealed.

In a 1971 interview, Mrs. Nixon explained her idea of the candlelight tours:

We've always tried to make Christmas special and different. At the White House we enjoy giving surprises, too. Because we want to share the house with as many people as possible, we've started a tradition of candlelight tours through the state rooms. So many people are here in Washington at Christmastime and the men are free in the evenings, so this gives them an opportunity to enjoy the White House as well. The chandeliers are turned low, fires [are] flickering, and there's music. We hear people breaking into song, up in our rooms. That's so nice, to know they're enjoying it.

Announcing the 1973 candlelight tours, a *Time* article noted, "The staff will dim the electric lights in the public rooms of the mansion. In their place, dozens of candles will be lit. Oak fires will be kindled in the eight fireplaces, and the President and his family will open the doors and invite the public in." In evoking atmosphere, the article overstates the number of fireplaces that were used. As Julie Nixon Eisenhower writes, "Fires burned in the Red, Green, and Blue rooms, and the chandeliers and wall sconces were turned so low they appeared to be candles."

Lining the East Colonnade with tall candlesticks topped by candles—sometimes red, sometimes white—in clear glass chimneys is another custom that began during Mrs. Nixon's tenure. Crafted by the White House carpenters, the handsome candlesticks were made of teakwood that is believed to be part of the ten-ton shipment of teak given to President Dwight Eisenhower as a gift from the Burmese government.

Over the years, the experience of seeing the White House in subdued light changed little from one administration to the next; although the custom of burning fires in the parlors ceased after the Reagan administration, and use of the teakwood candlesticks was discontinued sometime during the Clinton administration.

By the 1990s the candlelight tours were scheduled between 5 and 7 p.m. on three consecutive evenings in late December, usually right after Christmas. No reservations were needed; people simply showed up at the East Gate, and anyone in line by 7 p.m. would be admitted, all on a first-come, first-served basis. (A regular daytime tour required a same-day ticket that was free.) The throngs of visitors would sometimes have to endure rain, snow, or bitter cold, and the wait was so long that the Clinton administration posted this warning on the White House website: "Candlelight tours are often very crowded, the wait may be long, and the weather will probably be cold, so please dress appropriately." In 1998, when a candlelight tour meant a three-hour wait in the cold, a National Park Service ranger estimated that 4,000 to 6,000 undeterred visitors would pass through the White House in a single evening.

Visitors taking the candlelight tour would follow the same self-guided route as that for the daytime tours, entering by the East Wing, passing through the East Garden Room, and then walking down the pleasant East Colonnade, with holiday wreaths hanging in all the windows. Visitors would then walk through the East Foyer, with its display of official White House Christmas cards, and then along the Ground Floor Corridor, where portraits of former first ladies were illuminated by more candles on pier tables. From the corridor visitors could peek into the Library and Vermeil Room before walking upstairs to the State Floor. The next stop on the tour was usually the East Room, with its magnificent crèche, followed by the parlors—the Green Room, the Blue Room with its stately evergreen lavishly trimmed and roped off, and then the Red Room. The soft glow of the dimmed chandeliers and wall sconces created a dramatic effect in all the public rooms. Finally, tourists would walk into the State Dining Room, then along the Cross Hall to the Grand Foyer and exit through the North Portico. As with the regular tours, U.S. Secret Service Tour Officers were stationed in the rooms to answer questions.

The post-2001 security rules have greatly reduced the number of visitors who tour the White House nowadays, but both regular and candlelight tours are still available to those who contact their congressional representative's office in advance. In 2008, as many as 1,200 people had reservations for the candlelight tour on each of three evenings. A total of 60,000 people—including guests attending invitation-only parties—were expected to visit the White House during the holiday period.

To compensate for this restricted access, First Lady Laura Bush and the White House staff launched the Barney Cam in 2002. The video tour of the mansion's decorations, starring the presidential terrier, attracted such a devoted following that the White House produced a new edition each subsequent year of the Bush administration.

The Reagan Years

1981-1988

Nancy Reagan

I LOVE CHRISTMAS. I ALWAYS HAVE. Not only is it a beautiful time of year, but it seems to bring out the kindest, gentlest qualities in everyone. And Christmas in the White House is unlike any other Christmas celebration. Every room is filled with the warm spirit of the holiday season, with trees, wreaths, candles, and thousands and thousands of twinkling lights. Visitors from all over the world come to experience the magic of Christmas—it is America's House, after all.

The White House staff spends most of the year planning the decorations. And, believe me, it's a little strange to be asked for Christmas ideas around St. Patrick's Day! In the days before Christmas, the staff and dozens of volunteers work together to get everything ready. In one of our early years, I invited the young people of Second Genesis, a drug treatment center, to join us. This became a tradition for us, and they returned again and again to help trim the trees.

Each year the White House decorations are a little different, and the themes have been as varied as the families who have lived there. My husband and I loved a traditional, old-fashioned Christmas, and the decorations throughout the White House reflected that. There were beautifully trimmed trees everywhere, with American folk art ornaments, miniature toys, teddy bears, and antique dolls. I was especially fond of some darling little papier-mâché urchin carolers one year, and there was a wonderful toy train, with its little teddy bear conductor, circling the official White House Christmas tree in the Blue Room. Some years were devoted to special themes. We had a musical Christmas one year, with decorations that featured favorite Christmas songs and carols, and another year we had a Mother Goose theme. We wanted visiting children to have a magical experience at the White House, and it was so much fun to watch their faces light up with joy.

I'm a great believer in tradition, and there were some special White House customs that were very important to me. The White House crèche, displayed every year since 1967, was always given a place of honor. And a favorite of ours was the magnificent gingerbread house created every year in the White House kitchen—customized for Ronnie with the addition of jelly beans, of course!

Our own tree upstairs in the private residence was always old-fashioned and very simple. We strung popcorn and decorated the tree with our family ornaments, many of which were made by our children when they were little. Each member of the family had their own little white porcelain angel ornament with their name on it. I still have those little angels, and they're given places of honor on my tree every year.

While it is beautiful year round, the White House at Christmas is filled with special feelings of love, peace, and goodwill. It was a privilege and an honor for me to have been a part of it, and I will carry the spirit of those Christmas celebrations with me forever.

Nancy Reagan

An Old-Fashioned American Christmas

WASTING NO TIME, MRS. REAGAN and her staff began planning for her inaugural Christmas months in advance. White House social secretary Mabel "Muffie" H. Brandon sent out a memo in July about Christmas plans so that every last detail could be determined, including the question of whether the official tree would be in the Blue Room or the Grand Foyer. An old-fashioned American Christmas in theme and spirit was chosen, along with the time-honored holiday palette of red and green, accented with white and gold. The old-fashioned ornaments reflected the personal taste of the First Lady, who stated, "I don't like a white tree with purple balls." Mrs. Brandon informed the White House staff: "The basic concept . . . is an old-fashioned American Christmas. Balls and big bands are out; choirs and minstrels are in. Good fellowship will be more important than opulence."

★ **OPPOSITE** ★

President and Mrs. Reagan by the Blue Room tree.

★ **RIGHT** ★

One of the "Peaceable Kingdom" wood sculptures by Eleanor Meadowcroft of Salem, Massachusetts that graced the bottom of the official tree.

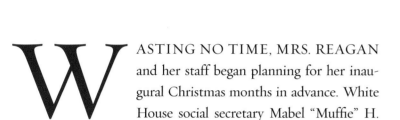

NANCY REAGAN

Grace under fire came naturally to Nancy Reagan, having been First Lady of California for nearly eight years. So although the Reagans came to Washington in the face of economic malaise, it was apparent that the new First Lady and onetime actress would give the White House a glamour and sophistication that matched her own.

From her first Christmas at 1600 Pennsylvania Avenue, she elevated the decorations to a new level of splendor, and at the same time promoted public awareness of social issues of the time. Often seen in a stylish, festive tartan plaid wool skirt during seasonal interviews, she relished her role as the mansion's hostess showing the décor to the press. "Christmas is my favorite season," she said. "I still believe in Santa Claus."

The Douglas fir in the Blue Room was decorated with 800 animal ornaments crafted by eight artists selected by the American Folk Art Museum in New York. The items were made chiefly of tin, fabric, and wood and patterned after the naïve folk art style of Edward Hicks' famous painting "The Peaceable Kingdom." Created with popular early-day techniques such as rosemaling, stenciling, and decoupage, the animals included pigs, ducks, roosters, and other barnyard animals: lions and lambs, elephants, and fish, and creatures of fancy—all hung on branches sprinkled with white crocheted snowflakes and gleaming with tiny white lights. Larger wooden animals formed a procession around the base of the tree. At its top was the archangel Gabriel, copied by Pennsylvania tinsmith David Claggett from a nineteenth-century weathervane in the museum's collection.

★ ABOVE ★

Nancy Reagan decorating the Christmas tree in the Blue Room, December 3, 1981.

★ BELOW ★

"Peaceable Kingdom" wood sculptures by Eleanor Meadowcroft of Salem, Massachusetts.

★ OPPOSITE ★

Mrs. Reagan chats with volunteers by the handmade Victorian dollhouse.

Another Gabriel, also a miniature version of a nineteenth-century weathervane, adorned the tree. This ornament marked the first in the series of official White House ornaments issued each year by the White House Historical Association.

The tree was also trimmed with old-fashioned foil paper cones adorned with lace and ribbon, little reed baskets filled with herbs and potpourri, gold paper chains, strings of popcorn, and bright-colored origami animals, birds, flowers, and Christmas symbols created by artisans from the Friends of the Origami Center of America and one of its co-founders, paper-folding expert Michael Shall. Mrs. Reagan resurrected the 100 cherished state flower balls commissioned by Pat Nixon, along with multicolored glass balls dating back to the Eisenhower administration.

The State Floor evoked a magical quality, with fifteen Christmas trees and a proliferation of red and white poinsettias. This was more than the usual number of trees, and the First Lady requested trees with layered branches to show the decorations and artificial snow to the best advantage.

Adding to the merry mix in the Cross Hall was a handmade Victorian dollhouse—complete with electricity. Created over a four-year period by Aline Gray, a Philadelphia decorator, the three-story, twelve-room dollhouse boasted furniture to scale, needlepoint rugs, chandeliers, and even nine tiny oil paintings, such as a portrait of George Washington copied from Rembrandt Peale's famous likeness. Its little Christmas tree was made of real greenery and decorated with amethysts, gold beads, and a string of pearls. Also in the Cross Hall were six Christmas trees adorned with real (but unlit) candles.

The East Room featured topiaries made of apples, artfully arranged in silver ice buckets and topped with a pineapple. The historic Monroe plateau in the State Dining Room was garnished with holly and greenery.

Mantels throughout the public rooms were lush with magnolia leaves, shiny red fruit, plump red candles in hurricane lanterns, and red ribbon. Some of the magnolia leaves were even taken from trimmings from the White House's own trees. White narcissus

served as centerpieces in the Red and Green Rooms, with more narcissus, cyclamen, and pink poinsettias in the Grand Foyer.

Hanging in the Grand Foyer was a kissing ball of mistletoe, beneath which President Reagan was said to have "caught" Mrs. Reagan. But he found some of the other floral arrangements less agreeable because of his sensitivity to pollen. When White House Chief Florist Dottie Temple took the Reagans around the State Floor for their first look at the decorations, the President was so overcome with sneezing that the plants had to be relocated to areas where he rarely spent time.

The East Foyer was decked with forty golden wreaths made from seashells collected by a class of New Jersey fifth-graders. The Colonial tradition of shell wreaths fit perfectly with the Early American Christmas theme. The East Colonnade windows were filled with wreaths and long red bows, and at the end of the corridor was a display of Christmas cards of previous administrations, a tradition started by Pat Nixon.

★ *1982* ★
An All-American,
Old-Fashioned Christmas

T HE DECORATIONS FOR MRS. REAGAN'S first Christmas at the White House were so well-received that she decided to keep changes to a minimum the second time around. In her welcome letter to the 1982 tour guide, she wrote: "I love an old-fashioned theme—with a crèche, a gingerbread house, candlelight, natural wreaths with large red bows at each window, the smell of Scotch pine filling the halls and, best of all, the wonderful fir tree." Beloved media personality Willard Scott, dressed as Santa Claus, helped show the press the holiday décor and hand out recipe cards and monkey bread.

The Blue Room tree, a Fraser fir between twenty and twenty-five years old, was decorated not only by the regular group of White House staff and volunteers but also volunteers from Second Genesis, a residential program in the greater Washington area for recovering drug addicts. Having launched her "Just Say No" campaign, the First Lady invited the program's participants to come to the White House to help with crafting many of the thousands of origami ornaments—silver and gold metallic snowflakes—for the tree. The workers spent six weeks at the Old Executive Office Building next door to the White House and then ultimately hung their creations on the tree. In a thank-you note to Mrs. Reagan, the organization's executive director and deputy executive director wrote, "The residents of Second Genesis who had the good fortune to participate in decorating the White House Christmas

★ OPPOSITE ★

First Lady Nancy Reagan.

★ BELOW ★

The White House Christmas tree, sporting silver and gold paper ornaments.

tree are still expressing their awe and delight at having been asked to assist you in this happy task. . . . Those who worked with you last Friday will carry with them always the memory that the very gracious First Lady of the Land took the time to show them her concern and her love."

The tree also held old-fashioned foil paper cones with lace and ribbon, the Nixon state ball ornaments, and hundreds of glass balls from the Eisenhower years. In describing the concept for the tree, Muffie Brandon wrote, "We wish the Christmas tree to be an old-fashioned family tree. There will be some tinsel ropes, but no hanging tinsel, and we will certainly use beautiful lights, but we wish it not to look in any way commercial, but like a glorious testimony to traditional American family Christmas." In total, approximately 2,000 ornaments sparkled alongside 5,000 lights. Atop the tree

★ ABOVE ★

Nancy Reagan joins the volunteers in decorating the Blue Room tree, December 10, 1982. The bird ornament at her fingertips is the official 1982 White House Christmas ornament, a replica of a dove of peace weather vane atop Mount Vernon.

★ ABOVE ★

Chef Hans Raffert with his gingerbread house.

was a porcelain angel dressed in red velvet and lace. Nearly two feet tall, it was made by White House florist Nancy Clarke.

A second White House Historical Association Christmas ornament hung on the tree this year—a reproduction of the Dove of Peace weather vane atop the cupola of George and Martha Washington's Mount Vernon home.

Traditional holiday décor filled the public rooms. Red and white poinsettias were placed throughout, and each window framed a large wreath of greenery sporting a single bright red bow. Fir trees decorated with clip-on candles, papier-mâché angels (replicas of those in the East Room crèche), and almost 100 pounds of unshelled walnuts wrapped in lace stood in the two niches of the Cross Hall. From the railing of the Grand Staircase hung a wreath encircling a porcelain angel dressed in gold and red fabrics.

★ ABOVE ★

A decked-out buffet table awaits White House guests.

★ ABOVE ★

Mrs. Reagan with volunteers from Second Genesis, a rehabilitation program championed by the First Lady throughout her White House tenure.

1983 ★

An Old-Fashioned American Christmas

ALTHOUGH SHE RECEIVED MANY suggestions for the 1983 theme (including a "George Washington" tree to celebrate his 250th birthday), Mrs. Reagan so loved the charm of the old-fashioned Christmas theme that she called for another encore, this time with an emphasis on children. As in 1978, the Margaret Woodbury Strong Museum in Rochester, New York, loaned antique toys from its impressive collection. Hundreds of items were on display—not simply in the Blue Room but in the other public rooms as well.

The noble fir in the Blue Room was trimmed with more than 1,200 antique toys and artifacts: miniature dolls, horse-drawn trolleys and carts, paper toy soldiers, tinplate carriages, trains, cast-iron banks, and dollhouse furniture of wood, wicker, and tinplate. Surrounding the base of the tree was a circus parade, also on loan from the Strong Museum. Made by A. Schoenhut, one of the country's most prominent toy makers between 1872 and 1935, the set consisted of two bandwagons, two cage wagons, a chariot, and more than 100 figures representing circus performers and animals. Atop two pier tables in the Blue Room were Humpty Dumpty Circus sets, also made by the Schoenhut company.

Second Genesis again participated in the decorating process and created 500 foil ornaments in varying colors and shapes, reminiscent of those found on trees in the early 1900s. As she had for the past two years, Mrs. Reagan included the 100 Nixon state

★ ABOVE ★

Heirloom dolls made in France between 1870 and 1895 are displayed in the Cross Hall. The doll on the right was made in Paris by Bru Jne & Cie (ca. 1880).

★ OPPOSITE ★

Mrs. Reagan sits on Santa's (President Reagan's) lap at a Christmas Eve party at the Wick residence in Washington, D.C., December 24, 1983.

★ LEFT & OPPOSITE ★

Antique dolls and other toys, on loan from the Margaret Woodbury Strong Museum in Rochester, New York.

★ BELOW ★

An elaborate 100-piece circus parade surrounds the tree. The tree stand is painted to look like a toy drum.

★ ABOVE ★

The White House Christmas tree, decorated with antique toys.

★ OPPOSITE ★

Humpty Dumpty Circus sets (ca. 1925), by A. Schoenhut and Company of Philadelphia, below the portrait of James Monroe in the Blue Room. The wooden figures depict the ringmaster, lady acrobats, clowns, tigers, and elephants.

balls and the glass balls from the Eisenhower era.

On display in the East Room, the Cross Hall, and the Grand Foyer were four types of antique dolls loaned by the museum: Lenci dolls, French fashion dolls, dolls with china heads, and mechanical dolls. These priceless collectibles were placed in Plexiglas boxes on pier tables and surrounded by greenery and red hurricane candles. Mirrors, doorways, and other architectural features were accented with bright red bows and greenery.

The Italian-made Lenci dolls, which dated back to 1919, were placed in the East Room. The hand-painted felt characters included children, milkmaids, ladies of fashion, and such known personalities as silent film idol Rudolph Valentino. Although the French

* ABOVE *
Steiff bears strike playful poses on a wreath in the Cross Hall.

* LEFT *
The 1983 gingerbread house. In addition to Hansel and Gretel and the Witch, Chef Raffert included Santa in his sleigh and a wishing well filled with jellybeans.

* OPPOSITE *
President and Mrs. Reagan decorate the Christmas tree in the private residence, December 24, 1983.

dolls were originally designed as playthings for children, they were also used by French designers to display women's fashion options; their popularity peaked between 1865 and 1885. The china-head dolls, though made primarily in Germany, were also manufactured in Austria and France. The mechanical dolls included two made by Gaston Decamps, head of the Parisian firm Roullet and Decamps, one of the most creative and successful manufacturers of automata (key-wound figures).

In the Cross Hall, on the railing of the Grand Staircase, Steiff bears frolicked on a holiday wreath.

★ *1984* ★
A Snowy Winter Wonderland

T HIS YEAR'S DECORATIONS WERE inspired by a "Brandywine Christmas," a popular annual exhibition at the Brandywine River Museum in Chadds Ford, Pennsylvania. Around 1974, museum volunteers began using natural materials to create Christmas tree ornaments in the shape of miniature animals, angels, and stars—which they dubbed "critters." Visitors fell in love with them, and the menagerie multiplied. Their fame spread so far that Ted Graber, a Beverly Hills interior designer who had redecorated the Reagans' private quarters in 1981, suggested the interesting ornaments for the White House tree. Mrs. Reagan was so taken with some samples that she chose these ornaments over ten other proposed options.

Working from June to November, more than sixty volunteers from the museum crafted approximately 2,800 ornaments for the Blue Room tree, a blue spruce. The ornaments included 600 animals in the shape of rabbits, lions, reindeer, owls, and other assorted wildlife figures, as well as 150 angels and 100 stars. All-natural materials indigenous to the Chadds Ford region were used in their construction—pine cones, seedpods, acorns and other nuts, milkweed, cockscomb, bark, and teasel, embellished with ground mica for sparkle. (Every year since, the Brandywine River Museum has been decorated

★ OPPOSITE ★

President and Mrs. Reagan celebrate in front of the official White House Christmas tree.

★ BELOW ★

Ornaments made by Brandywine River Museum volunteers.

★ RIGHT ★
*President Reagan and the First Lady peer
through the branches, East Room.*

with similar ornaments that the volunteers continue to make and also sell to the public.)

Once again the volunteers from Second Genesis lent a hand by making additional ornaments. To complete the look of a snowy winter wonderland, hundreds of crystal icicles and miniature white lights were mixed with baby's breath (to simulate fallen snow), dusty miller, euonymus, paulownia, and lunaria.

Museum volunteers also created life-size geese and a Santa with reindeer for the Blue Room. The geese were constructed of grasses, and their nests were decorated with dried ornamental grains and vines. Santa, made of teasel and cockscomb, had a dried apple for a head and milkweed fuzz for hair and eyebrows. His boots were fashioned from pods of sweet bay magnolias. With movable joints, he could either sit or stand. The reindeer were created from four martynia pods and—for Rudolph's nose—a berry.

Presenting the Blue Room tree to the press and holding her new puppy "Lucky," Mrs. Reagan stated, "I think this year is pret-

tier than the year before." She then confessed: "I say that every year."

The First Lady also used the occasion to publicize the need for organ donation. She had heard about a child named Amie Garrison from Clarksville, Indiana, who was seriously ill and awaiting a liver transplant. The five-year-old had expressed a wish to hang her favorite ornament—a Santa Claus riding a tricycle—on the White House Christmas tree. Mrs. Reagan invited Amie to the White House so that she could add her Santa ornament to the tree in the Blue Room.

Six flocked trees in the East Room were trimmed in baby's breath, glass icicles, and white lights. The Cross Hall was filled with red and white poinsettias as well as other trees decorated with papier-mâché angels. Whimsical papier-mâché figures representing urchin carolers and dressed in shabby wool clothing stood on mantels and tables in the East Room, Cross Hall, and Grand Foyer .

★ ABOVE ★

President and Mrs. Reagan and Lucky on Christmas Eve in the private residence.

★ OPPOSITE ★

The gingerbread house with illuminated windows and a jellybean chimney. Chef Raffert made the windows of gelatin leaves and stained them with red, blue, and green food coloring as a nod to the White House parlors.

An Old-Fashioned, Turn-of-the-Century Christmas

Mrs. Reagan stands with actor Larry Hagman, dressed as Santa, during the press tour of the Christmas decorations, December 9, 1985.

The Fraser fir, trimmed with 1,500 ornaments made from last year's Christmas cards.

CHRISTMAS AT THE WHITE HOUSE in 1985 was reminiscent of Mrs. Reagan's previous themes. The State Floor was again transformed into a magical winter wonderland with more flocked trees, but the highlight of décor was the abundance of dolls and bears interspersed throughout the mansion.

The Blue Room tree was a Fraser fir trimmed with 1,500 ornaments made from the approximately 40,000 Christmas cards that the Reagans had received the previous year. These decorations, along with 500 gold foil snowflakes, were made by the White House floral staff and volunteers from Second Genesis. Also adorning the tree were the 100 state balls, the hand-blown glass ornaments from the White House collection, and miniature white lights.

Surrounding the base of the tree were two wooden trains and a depot. The five-car trains came complete with engine, coal car, two passenger cars, and a caboose, all constructed by White House craftsmen. Stuffed bears dressed as passengers and engineers were placed in the cars. Side tables in the room displayed additional teddy bears.

A teddy bear motif was chosen to coincide with what many presumed to be an anniversary of the teddy bear. As former White

★ ABOVE ★

★ ABOVE ★

*Mrs. Reagan examines the Christmas decorations during
the press preview.*

★ OPPOSITE ★

*Toy trains filled with teddy bears circle the base of the tree.
Teddy bears and building blocks make for a whimsical vignette,
Blue Room.*

House Chief Florist Dottie Temple recalls:

> *For our tribute to "old Teddy," we trimmed the tree with hun-
> dreds of Steiff teddy bears and antique toys. . . .We covered the small
> trees with more teddy bears dressed in Colonial-type garb handmade by
> my assistant, Nancy Clarke. Even the wreaths throughout the Man-
> sion had teddy bears hanging from them. The bears appeared to have
> invaded the White House. As it had turned out, our celebration was a
> bit premature, but we happily took credit for leading the way in our
> nation's tribute to cute little bears.*

The Steiff bears added a note of whimsy to the otherwise
formal State Dining Room. Here the White House floral staff
fashioned cone-shaped boxwood topiaries for the pier tables and
studded the foliage with shiny red wax apples and bears in red
clothing that appeared to be climbing the "tree."

Upon entering the East Garden Room on the ground floor,
visitors were greeted by a large topiary made of pink and white
poinsettias. The East Colonnade was lined with wreaths accented with large bows of green ribbon instead of the customary red.
Potted white poinsettia plants lined the hallway. For the candlelight tours, the long corridor glowed with light from white wax

Flocked trees create a wintry effect
in the East Room.

candles in tall teakwood candle stands, that were made by White House craftsmen. Also on display in the East Foyer was the collection of White House Christmas cards, along with the original art commissioned for President and Mrs. Reagan's 1985 card—a watercolor by Thomas William Jones titled "The Blue Room at Christmas." The Reagans were so taken by the artist's talent that his work appeared on their official Christmas card for the remainder of their White House years.

Special dolls, designed and created by the White House floral staff, graced mantels and pier tables. The dolls were posed to depict turn-of-the-century winter scenes like sledding, ice-skating, snowman building, and sleigh riding. The dolls' faces were made of heavy cotton material and were hand-painted for a rosy-cheeked effect; their clothing was made from fabric scraps and vintage clothes.

Throughout the State Floor festive greenery, red ribbon, red bows, and white candles were in abundance. Large wreaths, suspended by red ribbon and trimmed with red berries, pine cones, and decorative cardinals, hung in the Cross Hall. The niches of the historic hall contained trees trimmed with gold "doll" snowflakes, gold-wrapped walnuts, gold glass balls, papier-mâché angels, and white wax candles. Six 16-foot flocked blue spruce trees in the East Room were decorated with paper snowflakes, made by Second Genesis volunteers, as well as icicles, tinsel, and tiny white lights.

Mixed greenery and red tulips, white narcissus, and amaryllis adorned the Red and Green Rooms. Ivy topiaries with strings of glass beads and bead sprays further enhanced the rooms' décor.

1986
A Mother Goose Christmas

THE NURSERY RHYMES OF MOTHER Goose and other children's classics provided the decorating theme this year for the Blue Room. Fifteen soft-sculpture scenes, crafted by the White House carpenters and arranged around the base of the tree, depicted such favorite characters as: Mary and her Little Lamb, the Three Little Kittens, Tweedledee and Tweedledum, the Three Blind Mice, Old King Cole, Wee Willie Winkie, Jack and Jill, Little Jack Horner, Old Mother Hubbard, Peter the Pumpkin Eater, and Jack Be Nimble. On the side tables in the Blue Room were Jack Sprat with his wife and the Old Woman Who Lived in a Shoe.

To underscore the Mother Goose theme, the tree's branches were decorated with 100 soft-sculpture miniature geese, with a soft-sculpture angel at the top, all made by the White House floral staff and Second Genesis volunteers. Other ornaments on the tree included 750 wooden cookie cutouts, made by White House carpenters in the shape of Santas, bells, and angels and then decorated by the Second Genesis volunteers. Also appearing on the branches were the gold foil snowflakes and Christmas card ornaments

* OPPOSITE *

Nancy Reagan at a taping session for the NBC television special "Christmas in Washington," East Room, December 8, 1986.

* BELOW *

Yankee Doodle adorned the mantel in the State Dining Room.

★ ABOVE ★

Little Miss Muffett on a mantel in the State Dining
Room.

★ OPPOSITE LEFT ★

President and Mrs. Reagan stand in front of the Blue
Room tree.

★ OPPOSITE RIGHT ★

Nancy Reagan and television personality Ed McMahon
dressed as Santa greet the press, December 8, 1986. A
marzipan version of First Pet Rex stands in the front
yard of Chef Raffert's gingerbread house, flanked by fruit
topiaries embellished with gold mesh.

from previous years, the state balls and hand-blown balls from the White House collection, and thousands of miniature white lights.

With the assistance of volunteers from the floral industry, more Mother Goose figures were installed around the State Floor. The pier tables in the Grand Foyer and Cross Hall featured soft sculptures of Little Miss Muffet, Georgie Porgie, and Mother Goose and her gander. Yankee Doodle, the Crooked Man, Humpty Dumpty, and Hey Diddle Diddle figures stood on the mantel in the East Room.

Also in the East Room were six eighteen-foot blue spruce trees, flocked and trimmed with silver snowflakes, silver-streaked clear glass ornaments, icicles, tinsel, and white mini-lights. Trees placed in the niches of the Cross Hall were decked with gold doily snowflakes, gold glass balls, papier-mâché angels, small white wax candles, and gold-wrapped walnuts.

The State Dining Room was bursting with color. Centerpieces featured topiaries made of ivy grown by the National Park Service and decorated with fruit. The Lincoln portrait was draped with a garland of mixed Christmas greenery, red ribbon, and fruit wrapped in gold mesh.

Large cone-shaped displays of pink and white poinsettias stood in the East Garden Room. In each window of the East Colonnade a wreath was suspended by green ribbon, and potted white poinsettias lined the walkway. Another arrangement of pink and white poinsettias stood in the East Foyer, along with a display of official White House Christmas cards. Also on exhibit was the watercolor commissioned for the 1986 card, Thomas William Jones's rendition of the East Room, a room that had not yet been depicted on a White House Christmas card.

Two sixteen-foot blue spruces with lights stood outside the North Portico entrance. Chains holding the early twentieth-century lantern, which famously hangs under the porch, were draped with greenery trimmed with holly and red bows. Each window facing Pennsylvania Avenue sported a wreath of mixed greenery and a bright red bow.

A Musical Christmas

THIS YEAR'S MUSICAL THEME WAS carried out not only in the Christmas decorations but also in the music that echoed through the White House's historic halls when various choirs performed during the public tours, a long-standing holiday tradition.

The song "Toyland" set the mood for the Blue Room. The Fraser fir was trimmed with 350 assorted wooden toys—such as tricycles and trucks—made by the White House carpenters and decorated by Second Genesis volunteers. An array of miniature musical instruments, ornaments shaped like musical notes, and sheets of music rolled and tied with ribbons also hung from its boughs. Gold foil snowflakes, cookie cutouts, and ornaments made from Christmas cards were reused from prior years, along with the state balls and hand-blown glass ornaments from the White House collection. A pier table in the parlor displayed a vignette of Santa, Mrs. Claus, and their elves preparing toys.

The East Room was filled with even more trees than in past years. Eight blue spruces, some as tall as twenty-one feet, were flocked and decorated with white lights, silver snowflakes, icicles, and tinsel. For the room's four mantels, the White House staff created vignettes from the songs "Rudolph, the Red-Nosed Reindeer," "Frosty the Snowman," "Parade of the Wooden Soldiers," and "Suzy Snowflake." The musical vignettes in the Cross Hall and the Entrance Hall consisted of "I Saw Mommy Kissing Santa Claus," "All I Want for Christmas Is My Two Front Teeth," and "Santa Claus Is Coming to Town."

Musical vignettes deck the mantels of the East Room. Below: "Parade of the Wooden Soldiers." Opposite: "Rudolph, the Red-Nosed Reindeer."

In the niches of the Cross Hall were trees decorated with gold glass balls, snowflakes made of gold doilies, papier-mâché angels, walnuts wrapped in gold foil, and white candles. Traditional greenery throughout the State Floor was adorned with red bows, red berries, pine cones, tiny gold musical instruments, and a dusting of artificial snow.

The tables in the State Dining Room were topped with boxwood topiaries sporting red cord and gold beads, while floral arrangements in the Red and Green Rooms consisted of greenery, amaryllis, paperwhites, and tulips.

★ TOP ★

A volunteer decorates with tinsel in the East Room.

★ ABOVE LEFT ★

The traditional display of White House Christmas cards, East Foyer.

★ ABOVE RIGHT ★

The 1987 gingerbread house, another of Chef Raffert's grand creations.

★ OPPOSITE TOP ★

The Cross Hall, with a view of the crèche in the East Room.

★ OPPOSITE BOTTOM ★

National Park Service staff and volunteers decorate the East Room.

The East Foyer and East Colonnade were reminiscent of the previous holiday season, with such trimmings as wreaths with green bows, potted white poinsettias, and the pink and white poinsettia "tree." A wreath of Christmas greenery with a bright red bow was hung in each window of the mansion.

★ ABOVE ★

The Christmas tree, trimmed with musical-themed ornaments.

★ OPPOSITE ★

The East Colonnade, decked with poinsettias, wreaths, and the historic teakwood candlesticks.

1988
An Old-Fashioned Christmas

OR THE REAGANS' FINAL YULETIDE at the White House, the First Lady chose to return to the Old-Fashioned Christmas theme that she had chosen for four previous seasons. As she felt "very sentimental" about this particular Christmas, the décor included a large sampling of the Reagans' seven seasons at 1600 Pennsylvania Avenue.

To give the balsam fir in the Blue Room an old-fashioned look, White House staffers created 300 wooden candles, 100 hot-air balloons of papier-mâché, and 75 yarn dolls. Volunteers from one of Mrs. Reagan's favorite organizations, Second Genesis, painted the ornaments and helped decorate the tree for the final time. Other trimmings included icicles made of gold beads, 120 red balls wrapped in gold mesh, assorted toy ornaments, the decorative items made previously by Second Genesis volunteers, the Nixon state ball ornaments and glass balls from the White House collection, and thousands of tiny white lights. Encircling the base of the tree was a motorized toy train filled with stuffed bears, ringed by another group of larger

* OPPOSITE *

The 1988 Blue Room tree, decorated with wooden candles and papier-mâché hot-air balloons for an old-fashioned look.

* BELOW *

The Reagans take a tour of the holiday decorations upon their return from Camp David.

Scenes of ice skating in a winter wonderland in the East Room.

Mrs. Reagan gives her final press tour of the Christmas decorations with comedian Rich Little as Santa Claus, December 12, 1988.

President and Mrs. Reagan stand together in the historic Blue Room.

stuffed bears.

Pier tables in the Blue Room displayed more teddy bears, one group with alphabet blocks and the other with a hot-air balloon.

In the parlors and the State Dining Room, arrangements of greenery were again accented with red and gold. Holly, fresh red and white tulips, paperwhite narcissus, and amaryllis were placed in the Red and Green Rooms while tables in the State Dining Room gleamed with boxwood topiary spheres adorned with red cording, small packages, satin roses, and gold foil fans.

The winter wonderland in the East Room was more spectacular than ever. Eight blue spruce trees, all flocked and ranging in height from fourteen to twenty-one feet, were decorated with tiny white lights and silver snowflakes, icicles, and tinsel. Old-fashioned scenes of ice skaters were displayed in the manner of decorative fire screens that were popular in the seventeenth and

eighteenth centuries. The floor under the trees and the displays was covered with fluffy artificial snow. To complete the look, snowy woodland wildlife scenes were arranged on the mantels, and the room's gilded mirrors were draped with garlands of mixed greenery dusted with artificial snow.

The effect was perhaps best described by White House Pastry Chef Roland Mesnier: "I felt as if I needed to put a coat on the first time I walked through the room. I actually got a chill! It was just like walking through a winter park." He said it was his favorite Christmas at the White House.

Anita McBride, a veteran of sixteen White House Christmases, fondly recalls Mrs. Reagan's penchant for flocked trees. "That was one of my greatest memories of working in the Reagan administration—that Mrs. Reagan loved those flocked trees, with all the 'snow.' It was truly a winter wonderland, absolutely stunning!"

As First Lady, Mrs. Reagan elevated the White House Christmas décor to a new level, one worthy of a Hollywood extravaganza. Recalling the 1988 season, White House historian William Seale said, "The last Reagan Christmas reminded me of the old movies. It was beautiful and the most loved by the public." The Reagans, he added, "knew how to succeed—they wanted it done and done right, and they would plan it out and execute it perfectly."

Nancy Reagan liked to see holiday finery in every nook and cranny of the State Floor. During her tenure, the White House staff brought in more trees than in past years, and Christmas vignettes were displayed on every available surface. She frequently described the decorations as "magical," an indication of her warm feelings about the Christmas season at the White House.

A lasting legacy of the Reagan administration is "Christmas around the World," an annual exhibit at the Ronald Reagan Presidential Library and Museum. The exhibit features a selection of fully decorated trees representative of the twenty-six countries that the President or First Lady visited during their White House years.

THE CRANBERRY TREE

ONE OF THE MOST INCONSPICUOUS BUT charming holiday traditions at the Executive Mansion is the annual cranberry "tree" in the Red Room. A focal point of the parlor's holiday décor, the lovely crimson topiary stands two feet tall on the most important piece of American Empire furniture in the White House collection: a marble-inlaid center table made around 1810 by the renowned furniture maker Charles-Honoré Lannuier.

The origins of the White House cranberry tree can be traced to 1975, when Christine Heineman of Chestertown, Maryland, arrived at the mansion with a Styrofoam cone, sphagnum moss, fresh cranberries, and her talents as a floral designer. One of the many White House volunteers who assisted with various types of flower arrangements, Mrs. Heineman made the topiary in one afternoon, and her techniques are still used today in creating the Red Room's hallmark centerpiece.

For the past twenty-five years, the chief responsibility for making the cranberry topiary has fallen to Myrtle Elmore of Upperville, Virginia, a volunteer who has been helping trim 1600 Pennsylvania Avenue for the holidays since her daughter worked for First Lady Nancy Reagan in the 1980s. Mrs. Elmore proudly remembers the first one she made, having learned the technique from Chief Florist Nancy Clarke. "Red was a favorite color of Mrs. Reagan's," said Mrs. Elmore, "so she particularly liked the cranberry tree."

Each year Mrs. Elmore purchases enough fresh cranberries to make two trees, preferring the darker berries. A second tree is necessary as a replacement because cranberries at room temperature begin to soften after a time. She and White House florists and other volunteers then spend nearly two days making the topiaries, working around the clock at the off-site facility in Maryland where many of the mansion's decorations are assembled and stored each year.

To make a topiary, Mrs. Elmore covers a cone-shaped piece of Styrofoam with preserved green moss. She inserts a piece of florist wire into the stem end of each cranberry, dabs it with glue, and then inserts the other end of the wire into the cone. She starts at the bottom and works in courses around and up the cone until she reaches the top. It can take more than 200 cranberries to cover the cone completely, she says, and the size of the cranberries will determine how long the job takes. As soon as both trees are finished, they are sprayed with an acrylic lacquer to extend their shelf life. One of the topiaries goes straight to its honored spot in the Red Room and the other to the cooler in the White House flower shop, where it is refrigerated until it is needed as a replacement.

The cranberry tree is figured prominently in Cindi Holt's oil painting of the Red Room that President and Mrs. George W. Bush commissioned for their official 2004 Christmas card.

★ ABOVE ★

A close-up view of the cranberry tree.

★ OPPOSITE ★

Cranberry tree, Red Room, December 1999.

The Bush Years

1989-1992

Barbara Bush

OUR FOUR CHRISTMASES AT THE White House were so special for George and me as well as for our whole family.

The theme for our first holiday in the White House, "A Storybook Christmas," was very personal for me. Ever since I was a young girl, I have loved to read, and through the years books have entertained me, comforted me, inspired me, and taught me a great deal about the world and its people. Seeing replicas of my favorite book characters decorating the White House brought back happy memories.

Deciding that year's theme was easy. I had founded the Barbara Bush Foundation for Family Literacy because I truly believe that if every man, woman, and child could read, write, and comprehend, we would be so much closer to solving many of the problems facing our nation. That is why I became committed to promoting literacy when George was in office and why I continue to do so today.

Our second year in the White House we highlighted one of America's most beloved ballets, "The Nutcracker." I marveled at the beautiful snow covering the trees, mantles, and tables on the State Floor—I truly felt as if I were in a winter wonderland instead of at the White House. Our grandchildren, who were very young at the time, also loved the snow, but for a different reason: snowball fights.

We enjoyed celebrating "A Needlepoint Christmas" in 1991. Much time and patience goes into needlepoint work, so I was very grateful to the many people who made the ornaments for the magnificent Blue Room tree. Now in "retirement," George and I decorate our Houston home with needlepoint ornaments I have made through the years. Every Christmas, as I hang these on our tree and along our staircase, I fondly remember the 1991 holiday season.

"Gift Givers" was the perfect theme for our last year in the White House. During George's years in office, he tirelessly encouraged every American to be a "point of light" by giving back to the community and helping those in need. From volunteers ringing the bells for the Salvation Army to those donating clothes and toys for needy children, the generous spirit of Americans certainly shines the brightest during the Christmas season.

The best part of Christmas at the White House was the people. Each year the same small army of volunteers would work tirelessly for a week to decorate the White House. These dedicated and talented individuals, along with the great White House florists, carpenters, and other staff, did a fabulous job each year, and George and I will always appreciate their efforts.

Our Decembers were filled with receptions where we enjoyed meeting new people and seeing our family and so many friends. The entertainment during these receptions was especially wonderful as soloists, carolers, and string quartets performed the sounds of the season. My favorite memory from my four Christmases as First Lady was sitting upstairs in the private quarters reading a book and listening to the beautiful music on the State Floor below. It was simply magical.

George and I are grateful to have had the opportunity to experience Christmas at the White House, a place like no other. We send you our best wishes for many joyful Christmases filled with your family and much love.

Barbara Bush

★1989★
A Storybook Christmas

OR HER INAUGURAL CHRISTMAS, MRS.
Bush selected a theme that was inspired by her concern
for family literacy. After a long period of working with
literacy programs as a volunteer, she had established a
foundation to fight illiteracy in the spring of this year, and her literacy campaign became the signature of her tenure as First Lady. In
her Christmas tour booklet for 1989, she wrote: "The huge official
tree in the Blue Room carries a special message this year in honor
of our concern for building a more literate America. Under the tree
are books for readers of all ages, and we hope they will inspire you to
have a very merry and well-read Christmas with your own families."

The official White House tree, a Fraser fir, arrived at the gate
to the North Portico in the customary Clydesdale-drawn carriage.
But first dog Millie, the famous English Springer Spaniel, who accompanied the First Lady to the presentation ceremony, became
nervous about the horses and had
to be picked up when the tree was
unloaded. Mrs. Bush noted, "Millie
cannot steal this show, please."

BARBARA BUSH

*Celebrating Christmas in grand style was an
activity that Barbara Bush took in stride. Prior to
entering the White House, she had acquired experience in entertaining as the wife of a diplomat and
then in the Vice President's residence for eight years.
Soon after her husband's inauguration, planning
for Christmas began. "I thought Nancy Clarke
and Gary Walters were kidding when they came
to talk to me about the Christmas theme in February," Mrs. Bush wrote in her memoir. "But the
decorations are all made in house, and the ribbons
and other materials have to be ordered early." She*
*managed the festivities
with ease and a sense of
fun, qualities that read-
ily endeared her to the
public.*

★ RIGHT ★

*A display on a side table in the Blue Room
announces the 1989 theme.*

★ OPPOSITE ★

*The Blue Room tree, decorated with a story-
book theme.*

The Blue Room tree came to life with eighty handmade dolls with hand-painted faces, all representing favorite fictional characters. Created by the White House floral staff under the direction of Chief Florist Nancy Clarke, the dolls depicted Babar the Elephant, Scarlett O'Hara with her wide-brimmed hat, the Velveteen Rabbit, Mary Poppins, Pokey the Puppy, the Mad Hatter, Pinocchio, the Tin Man, Oliver Twist, Scrooge, Little Red Riding Hood, and many others. Also hanging from the branches were miniature books, painted wooden letters and numbers, and the traditional state balls and hand-blown glass ornaments from the White House collection. Wrapped in red bows, 200 children's books were arranged at the base of the tree. A vignette in the south window of the Blue Room depicted a family of soft-sculptured figures reading "'Twas the Night before Christmas."

The rest of the State Floor was transformed into the proverbial winter wonderland. The Cross Hall and Grand Foyer were filled with sixteen trees trimmed with tiny white lights, artificial snow, icicles, and tinsel. Large red poinsettia arrangements lined hallways,

★ ABOVE & OPPOSITE ★

Handmade dolls representing favorite storybook characters.

★ OPPOSITE BOTTOM ★

Children's books at the base of the tree underscore the First Lady's literacy campaign.

★ ABOVE ★

Chef Raffert with his twentieth gingerbread house for the East Room.

★ OPPOSITE ★

The Cross Hall and Grand Foyer glisten with white lights, flocked trees, and bright red accents.

and all the doorways were framed by garlands and wreaths with bright red bows.

The Red Room was decorated with white poinsettias, holly, and fresh flowers, along with the annual cranberry tree. The Green Room was filled with pink poinsettias, fresh flowers such as tulips and amaryllis, and a small topiary studded with gold musical instruments. Two large blue spruces in the East Room were trimmed with red ribbon and realistic-looking grapes, pears, apples, oranges, pomegranates, and more. In the State Dining Room boxwood topiaries and other decorations made extensive use of lollipops, peppermints, candy canes, cookies, and other goodies.

To stress the importance of books, Mrs. Bush read stories aloud at special parties for homeless children and delighted them

by distributing holiday gift bags. She told reporters, "There's sort of a little message in our Christmas—a family-oriented reading-to-your-children message."

Due to inclement weather, President and Mrs. Bush had to cancel plans for a weekend at Camp David, which gave them a firsthand opportunity to witness staff and volunteers trimming the mansion for the holidays. When the Bushes caught the decorating team enjoying a mock snowball fight with the artificial snow, the presidential couple ended up inviting everyone upstairs to see the family tree and its trimmings, which she attributed to "elves." Later, in her memoir, she wrote: "Bad weather gave us one of the nicest experiences we had in George's four years as President—watching the Christmas decorations go up."

The Nutcracker Suite

S TIRRING MEMORIES OF THE FIRST themed Christmas at the White House, Mrs. Bush reprised Jacqueline Kennedy's "Nutcracker" theme for the 1990 season.

Described by Mrs. Bush as "where magic can be most truly felt," the Blue Room was filled with decorations made by the White House staff to capture the mood of Tchaikovsky's holiday classic. The official tree, a Fraser fir, was trimmed with forty-five porcelain dolls representing dancers from the ballet, toy soldiers sporting red jackets, and fifty pairs of beaded ballet slippers, including a pair autographed by members of the Bolshoi Ballet and given to the First Lady the previous summer. As usual, the state balls of velvet, lace, and ribbon and the hand-blown glass balls from the White House collection found their places on the tree. A nutcracker figure stood beneath the tree on a blanket of "snow," along with wrapped presents. A castle made of plastic pipe portrayed the Marzipan Castle in the Land of Sweets. Standing guard in the Blue Room were several giant toy soldiers, complete with red jackets and black hats. During the holidays Mrs. Bush hosted a White House performance of "The Nutcracker" by the Washington Ballet.

At the official unveiling of the decorations, Mrs. Bush gave the press corps a surprise treat when, for the first time in any reporter's memory, she invited them upstairs to see the family tree. It was trimmed with the Bushes' personal ornaments, some of them

★ BELOW ★

The White House Christmas tree, decorated with "Nutcracker" ornaments.

★ OPPOSITE ★

A close-up of the "Nutcracker" ornaments on the Blue Room tree.

★ ABOVE ★

White House Pastry Chef Roland Mesnier and his assistants, Marlene Roudebush (center) and Franette McCulloch, assemble a holiday centerpiece of hand-blown sugar. The confection was made for a Christmas brunch hosted by the Bushes in the private residence.

★ LEFT ★

First Pet Millie, dressed as Santa, takes the reins of the sleigh. The tennis rackets signify one of the First Lady's favorite outdoor activities.

★ OPPOSITE TOP ★

The Red Room at Christmastime.

★ OPPOSITE BOTTOM ★

White House Chief Florist Nancy Clarke assembles a nutcracker figure in the Family Dining Room.

dating back more than four decades. A total of forty-seven trees, 54,000 lights, and miles of ribbon were part of the mansion's lavish decorations.

Visitors would enter through the East Wing on the ground floor and stroll down the beautiful East Colonnade, filled with red poinsettias and wreaths in each window. After passing the display of official White House Christmas cards dating back to 1953, they would climb the stairs to the State Floor, decorated in a classic palette of red and green. Flocked trees with tiny white lights lined the hallways, and bright red poinsettias, red bows, and wreaths dotted every corner. "The heart of the season," Mrs. Bush noted in her

★ ABOVE ★

The State Dining Room.

★ LEFT ★

Hans Raffert's annual gingerbread house.

★ OPPOSITE ★

The 1990 family Christmas tree at Camp David, with
"George & Barbara" spelled out in block letters around the base.

welcome letter in the 1990 Christmas program, "can be found in the East Room, where a magnificent wood and terra cotta crèche from 18th-century Italy reminds us of Christmas' enduring message of hope."

The Red Room was filled with fresh red and white flowers, white poinsettias, and the cranberry tree, always a focal point. More fresh flowers and pink poinsettias were placed in the Green Room.

In the State Dining Room Chef Raffert created a gingerbread house with President and Mrs. Bush in mind: its front yard had figures of children and a doghouse with a miniature Millie.

A Needlepoint Christmas

WHEN A NEEDLEPOINT CLUB FROM St. Martin's Episcopal Church in Houston gave President and Mrs. Bush a needlepoint crèche in 1989, the personal gift was simply meant to show warm feelings for two fellow members of the congregation. Presented to the First Lady in Houston and then transported to the White House on Air Force One, the forty-five piece crèche joined the family's Christmas decorations upstairs in the private residence. Along with traditional nativity figures, the scene included a few whimsical touches: an armadillo; the Bushes' spaniel Millie; the longhorn steer Bevo, mascot of the University of Texas; a black sheep named Saintly; and a Wise Man wearing a crown made from the cap of a Crown Royal bottle. This labor-intensive gift, which Mrs. Bush pronounced "the most beautiful thing you ever laid eyes on," inspired the 1991 needlepoint theme. The Bushes had admired this crèche made by the Saintly Stitchers, as the club was called, so much that shortly after President Bush was elected President, the Saintly Stitchers got to work.

★ RIGHT ★

The First Lady's own needlepoint ornament, a version of Millie.

★ OPPOSITE ★

First Pet Millie guards the entrance to the Blue Room from the Cross Hall.

The Saintly Stitchers worked for about eighteen months, along with White House staff and other volunteers, to create the 1,370 needlepoint ornaments for the noble fir in the Blue Room and the other public rooms. The many animals, toys, angels, Santa Clauses, gingerbread men, snowflakes, stars, rocking horses, candy canes, fruit, and other objects were based on 106 patterns created by Nancy Clarke, chief florist at the White House. Three of the ornaments were made by Mrs. Bush herself: Raggedy Ann and Andy and First Dog Millie. Even friends and family participated. Her daughter, Dorothy Bush LeBlond, made a horse while her ten-year-old granddaughter Barbara Bush made a star. Several figures bore a resemblance to the First Lady—such as a six-inch, white-haired angel blowing a horn and wearing a three-stranded pearl necklace

★ ABOVE ★

First Lady Barbara Bush examines the figures of the needlepoint crèche made by the Saintly Stitchers in the private residence, December 1989. This crèche inspired the 1991 needlepoint theme.

★ LEFT ★

The First Lady's own needlepoint ornament—a Raggedy Andy doll.

★ OPPOSITE TOP ★

Needlepoint structures created by the Saintly Stitchers are displayed in the private residence of the White House.

★ OPPOSITE BOTTOM ★

A Noah's Ark scene with needlepoint animals in the Blue Room.

An exquisite edible centerpiece created by Executive Pastry Chef Roland Mesnier
for a holiday brunch in the private residence, 1991. The ornament ball and its
ribbon were made completely of hand-blown sugar.

Mrs. Bush stands with Executive Chef Hans Raffert and his final
gingerbread creation.

★ ABOVE ★

Members of the Bush family admire the decorations in the Blue Room. Sam LeBlond and Walker Bush (below) watch the train make its way through the needlepoint village.

★ RIGHT ★

The First Lady's own needlepoint ornament—Raggedy Ann.

★ RIGHT ★

The official Blue Room tree, complete with a needlepoint village and train beneath the branches.

(an obvious reference to Mrs. Bush and her famous pearls). During a preview tour for the media, Mrs. Bush noted, with sly humor, "There are a lot of white-haired, fat, pearled ones."

At the base of the tree was a needlepoint village consisting of eighty-two turn-of-the-century houses, churches, and other structures, nestled in artificial snow. An electric train loaded with freight (including a miniature tree) traveled between destinations marked "Houston" and "Washington, D.C."

★ ABOVE ★
Granddaughter Marshall and President Bush, holding grandson Walker, inspect the Christmas cookies on the tree in the Oval Office.

★ RIGHT ★
Bush grandchildren Ellie and Sam LeBlond play in the artificial snow as the White House is being decorated for the holidays.

★ OPPOSITE TOP ★
Larger-than-life nutcrackers stand in the East Garden Room.

★ OPPOSITE BOTTOM ★
Mrs. Bush at the arrival ceremony of the White House Christmas tree.

Arranged on a pier table in the Blue Room was a ninety-two-piece Noah's Ark, including forty-four pairs of animals—elephants, monkeys, alligators, and quail (in honor of Vice President and Mrs. Quayle), to name a few. Whereas the menagerie was all in needlepoint, the wooden ark was constructed by White House carpenters. The Bushes' personal eighty-piece crèche from 1989 was prominently placed in the south window. Mrs. Bush called the Blue Room "a needlepoint world of enchantment."

Needlepoint structures, such as churches, shops, and houses, were stitched from seventy-nine patterns displayed on pier tables

★ ABOVE ★

President Bush reads Christmas stories to his grandchildren during the holidays at Camp David.

★ LEFT ★

Millie watches over a needlepoint church, part of a tabletop decoration in the Green Room.

★ OPPOSITE ★

President Bush walks toward the South Portico, waving to people on the Truman Balcony, December 10, 1991.

and mantels in the other two parlors. It was estimated that 500 nee-dlepointers—members of Saintly Stitchers, the White House staff, and volunteers from around the country—devoted 150,000 hours to the project, apart from the 1,600 hours that forty volunteer flo-rists contributed over a six-day period to install the decorations.

Twenty-five trees were placed throughout the White House, nineteen of them in the Grand Foyer and the Cross Hall. Gar-lands of greenery and bright red bows wrapped around doorways and lined the East Colonnade. Four blue spruce trees in the East Room were trimmed in red and gold ribbon, gold glass pine cones, glass balls, and strings of gold beads. The mantels were adorned with red candles encased in large hurricane globes surrounded by

mixed greenery. A Santa Claus in a sleigh, constructed by White House craftsmen and adorned with mixed greenery, sat on the large center table. More greenery festooned President Lincoln's portrait. Throughout President Bush's four years in office he maintained his own tradition in the Oval Office: a Christmas tree always filled with individually-wrapped gingerbread cookies, made by a family friend, that he joyfully gave to all that entered the office.

The gingerbread house in the State Dining Room again in-cluded figures of Millie and small children. It was Chef Raffert's twenty-third and last confectionary house for the mansion before his retirement.

1992
Gift Givers

FOR MRS. BUSH'S FINAL CHRISTMAS AT THE White House, she chose to highlight the tradition of gift-giving throughout history and the many legendary figures who are said to visit children on a particular winter night to bring them fruit, confections, or toys.

Gift givers such as the Three Wise Men, the Bishop of Myra (or Saint Nicholas, as he came to be called), Kris Kringle, Papa Noel, the Snow Maid, Tsai Sen Yeh, and others symbolizing the season's spirit of generosity were represented by dolls dressed in elaborate costumes and displayed on the grand fir in the Blue Room. At the pinnacle of the tree was a large crimson-robed Santa Claus, who is believed to be a composite personality that evolved from various cultures. All eighty-eight figures on the tree were created by White House staff.

Red bows, red and gold balls, and white electric candles shone throughout the branches. An illustrated book featuring legendary gift givers and other familiar Christmas figures was displayed on four side tables in the room. Other Yuletide customs related to giving gifts, such as hanging stockings from a chimney or placing a wooden shoe at the door, were woven into the décor as motifs.

To mark the 200th anniversary of the start of construction on the White House, this year's official White House ornament commemorated the laying of the cornerstone on October 13, 1792. A nineteenth-century lithograph of the mansion, after a watercolor

★ OPPOSITE ★

Dolls representing legendary gift givers hang from the tree branches. The tree topper is a crimson-robed Santa.

★ BELOW ★

With Millie at her side, Mrs. Bush admires the 1992 official White House Christmas tree.

★ ABOVE ★

Chef Mesnier and crew assemble the final pieces of the ginger-bread village in the kitchen.

by Augustus Kollner, was reproduced on a ceramic oval to form one side of the ornament. The reverse side was inscribed with the text of the cornerstone.

Thirty trees were placed throughout the White House amid a color scheme of traditional golds and reds. Garlands draped over the Lincoln portrait in the State Dining Room were accented with red and gold paisley-patterned ribbons. On the dining table was a Santa figure in a gift-laden sleigh, pulled by reindeer and flanked by two topiaries studded with gold balls and ribbons.

The gingerbread house made its customary appearance in the State Dining Room, and this year marked the debut of Executive

★ ABOVE ★

President and Mrs. Bush take their photo with Santa in front of the official White House Christmas tree.

Pastry Chef Roland Mesnier. Given free rein by Mrs. Bush to use his creativity, Chef Mesnier turned out the first of many masterpieces: an elaborate Santa's Village with elves sledding through white frosting and miniature versions of Millie and her puppy Ranger. According to Chef Mesnier, "Millie is the only truly presidential dog to have lived in the White House. She was presidential to the core. She never barked and always followed Mrs. Bush everywhere she went, perfectly a few steps behind; she would lie down beside her when Mrs. Bush sat down and would immediately get up and follow her."

In the East Garden Room a tree was trimmed with the previ-

ous year's popular needlepoint ornaments. Pier tables along the Ground Floor Corridor also displayed a small village of needle-point houses dusted with "snow." At Mrs. Bush's request, the family tree in the private residence was placed in front of a window in the Yellow Oval Room so that it would be visible to all those attending the Christmas Pageant of Peace on the Ellipse, just south of the White House.

Outside the White House, seven-foot trees trimmed in white lights stood at the South Portico and on the Truman Balcony. The North Entrance was flanked by sixteen-foot blue spruce trees. Three Della Robbia wreaths were hung on each level of the residence.

★ ABOVE ★

Santa in his sleigh on the banquet table in the State Dining Room.

★ OPPOSITE ★

Mrs. Bush, with her grandchildren Sam and Ellie LeBlond, places the star atop the National Christmas Tree, November 30, 1990.

Recalling her White House years, Mrs. Bush said one of the things she loved most about living in the Executive Mansion was "to come home to find your Christmas tree all decorated." The First Lady also enjoyed other rituals of the season, as she described:

First of all, forty people, all volunteers, come from around the country at the beginning of December and spend a week decorating. They put up the wreaths, the trees, the thousands of lights. They climb up on ladders and dump big boxes of plastic snow. We even have great snow fights! . . . Christmas in the White House is honestly a dream. All day long there are tourists. All day long, singing groups come in. Sometimes I open the door and hear these fabulous choirs. And sometimes we go downstairs to listen, and the tourists faint. There is a congressional ball, and we have a diplomatic reception. And we have a children's party and a party for the household staff, and they bring their children, and it is so cute you can't believe it. Every night there is carol singing, and my grandchildren all come down to sing and have fun. It's a wonderful, wonderful time.

Mrs. Bush will be remembered for holiday themes that had personable, comforting elements—like lots of "snow," greenery, and bright red bows—while injecting a bit of novelty and surprise. More important, in making literacy a theme, she was the first to use the holiday decorations to call attention to important current issues.

The George Bush Presidential Library and Museum annually exhibits a Christmas tree decorated with many of the ornaments from Mrs. Bush's White House years.

THE HOLIDAY TOUR BOOKLET

EACH VISITOR WHO IS LUCKY ENOUGH TO TAKE a holiday tour of the White House receives a keepsake—the official holiday tour booklet. Prefaced by a welcome message from the President and First Lady, the pages describe the decorations in each room on the tour route, sometimes with details about the historical furnishings.

In 1974 Betty Ford distributed printed information about the mansion's seasonal decorations for the first time. Anyone who wanted to make patchwork ornaments similar to those hanging on the Blue Room tree that year could write for complete instructions with patterns. The next year saw a more polished brochure—an accordion-fold mailer prepared with the help of the Colonial Williamsburg staff. It was printed in red and green ink on various colors of paper, such as cream, yellow, orange, and blue. Entitled "A White House Christmas 1975," it contained some historical tidbits about the holiday but remained primarily a how-to folder, with patterns and instructions for making several simple ornaments: a corn husk doll, a clothespin cardinal, a snowflake carved from soap, and more. The brochure closed with a short Christmas greeting from Mrs. Ford: "The President and I wish you a Merry Christmas."

Rosalynn Carter developed a holiday tour guide in 1978 that set the standard in general appearance and content for all the booklets of her successors. Her first booklet, approximately the size of a folded sheet of office paper, was titled "The White House Christmas Tree 1978." Its cover was illustrated with a silhouette representing President Benjamin Harrison decorating the first Christmas tree at the White House. The brown ink and ecru cover stock gave the publication a turn-of-the-century look that matched the year's decorating theme. The four pages of the simple saddle-stitched booklet were devoted to a welcome message from Mrs. Carter, descriptions of selected toys displayed on the Blue Room tree, and information about the museum that had loaned the decorations and the grower who had supplied the tree. Photographs accompanied the descriptions of the decorations.

A WHITE HOUSE CHRISTMAS 1975

A NUTSHELL HISTORY OF THE AMERICAN CHRISTMAS TREE

THE WHITE HOUSE
CHRISTMAS TREE
1979

Christmas at the White House
1981

Holidays at the White House 1995

a WHITE HOUSE CHRISTMAS

1991

1985

Christmas at the WHITE HOUSE

Christmas at the White House 1984

Christmas at the White House 1982

The Nutcracker

HOLIDAYS AT THE WHITE HOUSE 1996

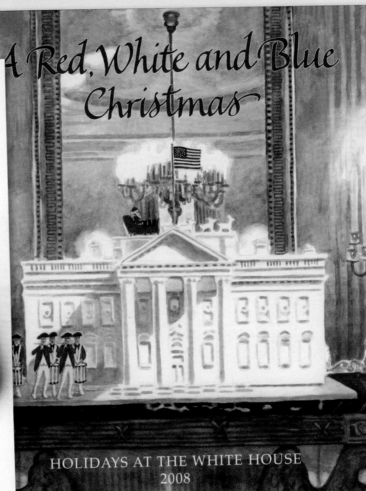

A Red, White and Blue Christmas

HOLIDAYS AT THE WHITE HOUSE 2008

Holiday Reflection

The White House 2000

A Season of Merriment and Melody

Holidays at The White House 2004

santa's workshop

HOLIDAYS AT THE WHITE HOUSE 1997

CHRISTMAS AT THE WHITE HOUSE 2007

Holiday in the National Parks

For a few years, the booklet remained largely the same in appearance, although line drawings replaced photographs as the mode of illustration. Nancy Reagan's 1981 booklet devoted the last page to a list of musical groups that performed at the White House during the holidays. It measured six inches wide by nine inches tall, a size that stayed constant for several years. In 1983 the booklet expanded to eight pages, and in 1984 it became a two-color publication, using combinations of red (her signature color), green, and ivory paper and red and green ink—a design of all the remaining Reagan booklets. By 1985 the booklet's contents became more detailed, and the text was organized as it is today—by room. In 1987 and 1988, the usual title "Christmas at the White House" was replaced with a title matching the season's decorating theme. The booklets had expanded to twelve pages but were slightly smaller: a little more than five inches wide by eight inches tall.

Barbara Bush's holiday booklets were very similar to Mrs. Reagan's. President Bush's signature was added to the welcome message, and the list of musical performers grew longer, now requiring two full pages. The titles of Mrs. Bush's booklets varied between "A White House Christmas" or "Christmas: The White House" with the specific year.

With Hillary Clinton, the booklet underwent a number of changes. Photographs were sprinkled throughout the pages once more, and the size and design varied widely from year to year to reflect the holiday theme. The 1993 booklet, titled "Holidays at the White House," listed the craft artists instead of the musical performers, and the booklet's production team was credited for the first time. Whereas previous booklets usually began with the Blue Room tree because of its importance, the 1993 text was organized to match the tour route, a structure used in subsequent years. The 1995 booklet was the first to use four-color printing, which permitted a full-color photograph on the inside front cover of President and Mrs. Clinton and Chelsea. A Clinton family portrait was a feature of Mrs. Clinton's booklets for the remainder of her tenure. Beginning in 1996, the season's theme became the title of the booklet, and "Holidays at the White House" was treated as a subtitle. Decorative fonts and other elements of book and magazine design appeared, giving the booklets a more sophisticated and permanent look. Their length ranged from eight to twelve pages, and their shapes varied from square (8½ by 8½ inches) to an eye-catching vertical (7 by 11 inches). For the first time, the booklets were printed on recycled paper.

Laura Bush had all eight of her holiday booklets printed on the same paper stock and in a uniform size (7 by 8 inches), so they could be saved as a set. The decorative theme was again used consistently as the title, with various subtitles (usually "Holidays at the White House" but with "The White House" and "Christmas at the White House" on two occasions, along with the specific year). The similarity of style among the booklets was achieved through colorful, often whimsical illustrations, all by different illustrators of children's books. Enhanced with stories about historical figures and events, the text was clearly written to appeal to younger visitors; the 2002 booklet even included a "Presidential Pets Matching Game." Ranging from eight to sixteen pages in the length, the booklets devoted the last page to information about the White House Visitor Center, which has taken on a more important role since 2001.

The holiday tour booklets are not only mementos of a fabulous experience—they have also become collectors' items.

The Clinton Years

1993-2000

Hillary Clinton

EVERY FIRST FAMILY ADDS ITS UNIQUE mark to holiday celebrations at the White House. As you will read, Bill, Chelsea, and I embraced the traditions of many families who lived there before us and also started some of our own.

Choosing a holiday theme, as I describe in *An Invitation to the White House*, was the first thing I did to prepare for the holidays at the White House. The holiday theme was closely guarded—we joked that it was the First Lady's "state secret"—and never fully revealed until the White House was completely decorated and the festivities were ready to begin.

As you will read, we transformed the White House into "Santa's Workshop," "Winter Wonderland," and "The Nutcracker Suite," which had special meaning for our family because Chelsea had performed in this holiday favorite for many years.

Christmas was always a special time for visitors who lined up to see the decorations. Our greatest joy came from sharing the holiday spirit with children from local schools who were a captive audience in the East Room when Bill would read "'Twas the Night before Christmas." This was not only a Clinton family tradition—since we used to read the same story to Chelsea—but also a 200-year-old American ritual of filling the White House with children during the holidays.

Everyone who visited during the holidays was excited to see the ornaments, the giant gingerbread creation that the White House pastry chef created each holiday season, and most of all, they were lucky enough to have their photos taken with Buddy and Socks.

As much as we love Christmas traditions, we also wanted to make sure Americans of all faiths felt welcome at the White House during the holiday season. Over the eight days of Hanukkah, a menorah was placed in the West Wing lobby and the Oval Office to honor the Jewish religious holiday. We also hosted a Ramadan event to mark the end of the holy month of fasting and prayer for Muslims and to generate a wider understanding of Islam in our country.

The final days before Christmas were a time we cherished each of our eight years in the White House. Bill, Chelsea, and I began our own private celebrations with traditions passed down from our parents and ones that had evolved with us as a family. Relatives and friends came over to cook with us, sing carols, and enjoy Christmas Eve dinner before attending church services. And even while he was President, Bill often joined other last-minute shoppers at local stores on Christmas Eve.

Christmas morning was our time to open presents, recount how we had eaten too much the night before, and share our gratitude for the bounty of love and support that blessed our family and community.

I hope you will enjoy reading the magical stories and traditions in the pages that follow.

We send you our best wishes for many joyful Christmases filled with your family and much love.

Hillary Rodham Clinton

1993
Angels

SEVERAL MONTHS AFTER THE inauguration, Mrs. Clinton was surprised to learn from Chief Usher Gary Walters and Social Secretary Ann Stock that it was time to start planning for Christmas: "Being the type who's relieved if my own tree is up and decorated by Christmas Eve, I was shocked to hear this," she said. "But . . . we began meeting about mistletoe and holly just after Washington's cherry blossoms had started to fade." Still, work on the decorations did not gear up until the summer.

It was the Year of the American Craft, so for this holiday the First Lady asked Michael Monroe, curator of the Smithsonian Institution's Renwick Gallery, to assemble works of the nation's leading craft artists for display throughout the White House. More than seventy pieces, made of fiber, ceramics, glass, metal, and wood were put on view on pier tables, mantels, and desks as part of a permanent White House crafts collection, resulting in a striking contemporary look. As one visitor observed, "It certainly puts a different spin on the 18th-century White House."

Three thousand artists across the country were invited to contribute handmade ornaments depicting angels, which Mrs. Clinton had selected as the seasonal theme. The White House received 7,500 items in

HILLARY CLINTON

Having served as Arkansas' First Lady for twelve years before entering the White House, Hillary Clinton was undaunted by the challenge of orchestrating spectacular seasonal displays, Washington, D.C.–style. She opened the doors of the White House to a wider public than ever before, and with a deep appreciation for former first ladies and their role as "custodian" of the nation's most splendid residence, Mrs. Clinton worked actively to make the White House a showcase for art treasures and historic furnishings.

★ OPPOSITE ★

The entrance to the West Wing. The presence of the two Marines indicates that the President is in the Oval Office.

★ LEFT ★

"JAZZmin," a sax-toting angel ornament made from black ash and wood shavings, by Jenalee R. Frazier.

a broad range of styles, and these were used to decorate not only the Fraser fir in the Blue Room but trees and wreaths throughout the State Floor. "Some are quite elegant and rather magnificent. Some are funky and down to earth," she told the press. "They run the whole gamut."

And she was right! There were two angels dressed as President Clinton (playing a saxophone and sporting a halo); versions of a winged Socks, the Clintons' cat; a voluptuous Mae West with wings; and a ceramic diner called Angel's. A green velvet tree skirt was quilted by artisans from each state, occupied territory and possession, and the District of Columbia; the fifty-seven panels were embellished with local motifs, such as Arkansas apple blossoms, Florida marine life, and Ohio buckeyes. Each quilter also contributed a fabric heart that was hung on the tree, along with the traditional state balls from the Nixon administration, gold glass balls, and strings of gold beads. The tree's branches gleamed

★ ABOVE ★

President and Mrs. Clinton view one of the American crafts on display in the Ground Floor Corridor.

★ OPPOSITE ★

Socks sits on the hand-quilted tree skirt that would be displayed each year of the Clinton Administration. Its fifty-seven panels depict motifs from all the states, the District of Columbia, and occupied territories and possessions.

★ OPPOSITE ★

Angel of sandblasted, layered glass by Valerie Surjan of Rancho Cordova, California.

with 7,150 white lights.

Twenty-one additional trees stood in other areas of the White House, absent the flocking seen in recent seasons. One of the six largest, displayed in the Diplomatic Reception Room on the ground floor, was the "wheat tree;" it was adorned with ornaments crafted from wheat straw or wheat kernels and accented with red bows, red balls, and tiny white lights. A children's tree in the East Wing entrance was trimmed with ornaments from selected schools of the Blue Ribbons School Program, sponsored by the Department of Education.

Six large blue spruce trees stood in the East Room, wrapped in burgundy and gold ribbon and decked with gold glass balls and strings of gold beads. The mantels and mirrors were decorated with greenery and wreaths, also with burgundy and gold ribbon.

In the Grand Foyer and Cross Hall, garlands of greenery with red and gold ribbon were draped over the arches and entryways. A kissing ball of boxwood and mistletoe hung from the ceiling between the columns.

In the State Dining Room, gold and paisley ribbons were intertwined with garlands and topiaries. But what stole the show was Chef Roland Mesnier's "House of Socks," a replica of the White

The 1993 official White House Christmas tree, decorated with angel ornaments made by 3,000 American artists.

★ OPPOSITE TOP ★

First Cat Socks gingerly looks on at his many likenesses in the annual gingerbread creation made by Chef Mesnier. This year, a White House replica called the "House of Socks" was the chef's favorite.

★ OPPOSITE BOTTOM ★

A view of the wreaths along the West Colonnade.

House, architecturally accurate and to scale. The special gingerbread house featured a marzipan Socks in twenty-one imaginative poses—hauling Santa's sleigh, ice-skating, playing a "Soxaphone," even posing as a Secret Service agent. The "very large cookie," as some reporters described it, weighed between 80 and 100 pounds and measured 50 inches long, 30 inches wide, and about 35 inches high. It took more than 150 hours to build.

As in prior seasons, the East Foyer greeted visitors with a display of earlier presidential Christmas cards. But the official White House card for 1993 had a new twist—it was the first one with a photograph of the presidential couple. The Clintons' holiday portrait was taken by award-winning New York photographer Neal Slavin.

The Twelve Days of Christmas

ALTHOUGH SHADES OF BURGUNDY and gold again prevailed throughout the State Floor, Mrs. Clinton swapped the contemporary look of 1993 for a Victorian atmosphere. She chose the classic 200-year-old English carol "The Twelve Days of Christmas" as the theme. Designers from Polo/Ralph Lauren Creative Services donated their time and talents toward decorating the mansion, along with nearly fifty volunteers.

The Colorado blue spruce in the Blue Room came from none other than Clinton County, Missouri. In keeping with the theme, its branches were trimmed with drummers, French hens, milkmaids, turtledoves, and, of course, partridges in pear trees, all made by students from around the nation—at university art departments, design schools, and primary and secondary National Blue Ribbon institutions. In a welcome letter in the holiday tour booklet, the Clintons commented on the diversity of the students' creations: "Students designed the ornaments in any way their imaginations and talents could take them. We asked only that they remain true to the spirit of the original carol. To everyone's delight, the ornaments came in as many shapes and sizes as there were students. Each is a testament to the developing talent and artistry of the next generation." A total of 5,040 white lights sparkled in the tree, and at its base was the green quilted tree skirt from the previous year.

The East Garden Room featured a charming children's tree, which was decorated with 350 ornaments created by children from the chosen exemplary schools under the guidance of the Department of Education. Oversized wreaths filled the East Colonnade, which looked out into the Jacqueline Kennedy Garden,

★ OPPOSITE ★

The official White House Christmas tree, trimmed with ornaments inspired by "The Twelve Days of Christmas."

★ BELOW ★

A partridge-in-a-pear-tree ball by Shirley McCoy of Buhl, Idaho. The ornament was one of many contributed by members of the National Society of Tole and Decorative Painters.

where Mrs. Clinton maintained an exhibit of twentieth-century sculpture. Committed to recycling, the First Lady reused many of the angel decorations from 1993, a custom she would maintain while she was in the White House. Ornaments such as the winged versions of President Clinton and Socks were hung on a tree at the end of the East Colonnade. The Ground Floor Corridor was lined with white poinsettias.

In the Diplomatic Reception Room, furnished as a drawing room from the Federal period, the fireplace was flanked by trees trimmed with ornaments contributed by the National Society of Tole and Decorative Painters (now the Society of Decorative Painters).

A beautiful kissing ball of boxwood and mistletoe hung between the columns in the Cross Hall.

The greenery throughout the State Floor was accented with burgundy and gold, often in the form of natural materials such as dried hydrangeas and baby's breath dipped in gold. Mantel arrangements consisted of greenery, magnolia leaves, pine cones, and gilded berries. Trees up to twenty feet tall sported more gold hydrangea blossoms, interspersed with burgundy velvet and gold tulle ribbon. Holiday topiaries of green and mauve flowers were displayed in the Green Room. The dried hydrangeas were sug-

★ TOP ★

The Cross Hall, trimmed in holiday greenery.

★ ABOVE ★

The 1994 White House holiday tour guide featuring the partridge in a pear tree, from "The Twelve Days of Christmas."

gested by the Ralph Lauren team, but otherwise the décor bore no imprint of the famous designer except in the East Colonnade, where the tartan ribbon was a reminder of his signature look.

In the State Dining Room, garlands of greenery with accents of burgundy and gold draped the Lincoln portrait. The gingerbread house this year was an authentic replica of President Clinton's childhood home in Hope, Arkansas. Working from old photos of the green and white Tudor home, the White House pastry team fine-tuned every detail of the seventy-pound structure, right down to the green shutters, the President's German shepherd King, and a pie cooling in the window. President Clinton was both delighted and touched. "When he looked it over for the first time, he had tears in his eyes," recalls Chef Mesnier. The elaborately built confection came close to being dismantled, however. In mid-December, when the White House was mysteriously fired upon and one of the bullets penetrated a window of the State Dining Room, the bullet was nowhere to be found. Secret Service agents concluded that the bullet must be lodged in the gingerbread house and were on the verge of taking apart the chef's masterpiece when the bullet was discovered in the rug.

The mansion this year was filled with thirty-one trees, trimmed with 40,280 lights.

★ TOP ★

President Clinton admires the 1994 gingerbread house, a replica of his childhood home. Chef Mesnier created it as a surprise for the President.

★ ABOVE ★

Executive Pastry Chef Roland Mesnier and Marlene Roudebush assemble the gingerbread house replica in the China Room.

Twas the Night Before Christmas

RS. CLINTON'S THEME FOR 1995 revolved around the beloved nineteenth-century poem "A Visit from St. Nicholas," traditionally attributed to Clement C. Moore and more commonly known as "'Twas the Night before Christmas." Three groups of artisans were invited to create different decorative elements of the décor. Members of the American Institute of Architects, including architecture students, submitted ornaments with motifs inspired by the poem's phrase "all through the house"— rooftops, chimneys, windows, shutters, and the like. The American Needlepoint Guild and the Embroiderers' Guild of America made the holiday stockings, "hung by the chimney with care." And, finally, chefs and their students at culinary schools around the country made edible ornaments inspired by "visions of sugarplums."

The Fraser fir in the Blue Room was decked with ornaments made by the architects, needlepointers, and embroiderers. Once again the 3,500 ornaments on the tree demonstrated talent and imagination. The architectural items ranged from miniature White Houses to a Florida beach house to a spiral staircase with children climbing up the stairs to go to bed. A rendition of the First Lady in a kerchief and the President in a cap appeared among the tree's branches, as did numerous ornaments alluding to the mouse in the poem. The green velvet tree skirt from Mrs. Clinton's first White House Christmas was the finishing touch.

Architectural scenes were displayed in the other two parlors. The mantel in the Green Room featured a cardboard silhouette of the Washington skyline, created by architects from Commu-

★ ABOVE ★

President and Mrs. Clinton in front of the official White House Christmas tree, just moments before a holiday party in the Mansion.

★ OPPOSITE ★

An exquisite view inside of the Blue Room tree from the Truman Balcony.

nity Design Services, a program of the Washington Architectural Foundation. A row of houses in the foreground included such architectural details as Corinthian columns and Moorish arches. A miniature paper kite flew over the scene as a tribute to Benjamin Franklin, whose portrait hangs above the mantel.

The hand-painted street scene on the marble mantel in the Red Room consisted of cardboard row houses and a Santa with reindeer on a bed of cotton, the work of sixth-graders at John Eaton Elementary School in Washington, D.C. The pupils were assisted by architects and college architecture students from the Architecture in the Schools program.

In the Grand Foyer four nineteen-foot trees were adorned with the magnificent edible ornaments from many of the nation's

top culinary schools. Jean-Luc Derron, a pastry instructor at Johnson & Wales University's College of Culinary Arts in Providence, Rhode Island, made twelve oval plaques from pastillage, a dough of confectioners' sugar, gelatin, and cornstarch that dries hard enough to be sanded smooth. He and his students then used food coloring to "paint" the plaques with scenes of candles, candy canes, and other motifs from the poem. A border of chocolate marzipan was applied to create a frame for each ornament, which was then attached to a gold cord for hanging.

Also in the Grand Foyer was a kissing ball made by needlepoint artist Hyla Hurley of Washington, D.C. Based on a family tapestry that hung in the private residence, it depicted President Clinton's journey to the White House.

★ ABOVE ★

The 1995 gingerbread house, a replica of the First Lady's childhood home.

★ RIGHT ★

Chefs Franette McCulloch and Susie Morrison, and Executive Pastry Chef Roland Mesnier with the gingerbread house in the China Room. The seventy-pound confection took the pastry team five months to construct.

★ OPPOSITE ★

A skyline of the nation's capital in the Green Room. Made by architects from Community Design Services of Washington, D.C., the display features prominent structures like the Washington Monument, the Capitol, and the Smithsonian Castle.

In the Diplomatic Reception Room two trees flanking the fireplace were trimmed in ornaments made by primary and secondary art students at the nation's Blue Ribbon schools. Both trees carried out the poem's theme.

Mrs. Clinton continued her custom of displaying trees to highlight past themes. The tree in the East Garden Room was decorated with angel ornaments from 1993. "The Twelve Days of Christmas" decorations from 1994 hung on a tree in the East Foyer, where previous presidential Christmas cards were also on view.

For a second time, sculptor Zachary Oxman created an exuberant hand-cast menorah that was displayed in the West Wing lobby.

Gold and burgundy ribbons were used to trim the six trees in the East Room as well as decorations for the mantels, sconces, and doorways in the State Dining Room. This year, again as a surprise, Chef Mesnier replicated the First Lady's childhood home in Park Ridge, Illinois, while staying true to the season's theme. Two open windows offered glimpses of a bedroom where children were "snug in their beds" and a living room with "stockings hung by the chimney with care." Marzipan reindeer were outside in the snowy yard, peeping in.

★ TOP ★

Festive table settings in the oval-shaped Diplomatic Reception Room, featuring the famed panoramic Zuber wallpaper.

★ ABOVE ★

Hyla Hurley with her needlepoint kissing ball in the Grand Foyer.

★ OPPOSITE ★

The Blue Room tree, decorated with miniature chimneys, rooftops, and shutters, from "Twas the Night before Christmas."

1996
The Nutcracker

IN 1996 THE FIRST LADY REVISITED the "Nutcracker" theme for the White House decorations, first used by Jacqueline Kennedy in 1961 and then by Barbara Bush in 1990. As President and Mrs. Clinton noted in their welcome letter in the holiday booklet, the ballet "has great personal meaning for millions of Americans and especially for our family. Ever since we took our daughter Chelsea to her first performance at age two, it has been a highlight of our Christmas celebrations." In fact, Chelsea performed the role of the Favorite Aunt this season in the Washington Ballet's production.

As in the previous year, three groups were invited to make the themed ornaments: 300 ballet companies, 100 woodcraft artists, and 350 members of the American Needlepoint Guild and the Embroiderers' Guild of America.

The array of ornaments on the Blue Room tree represented characters and motifs in Tchaikovsky's classic—a pirouetting sugarplum fairy, toy soldiers, Herr Drosselmeyer with an eye patch, a Chinese man made of polymer clay, and ballet slippers, of course. The Colorado blue spruce was also adorned with exquisite Christmas stockings, embroidered and stitched with similar motifs, and draped with gold beads.

★ RIGHT ★

A needlepoint kissing ball designed and stitched by Hyla Hurley of Washington, D.C. The scene reflects the party from "The Nutcracker Suite."

★ OPPOSITE ★

The President and Mrs. Clinton in front of the official tree in the Blue Room.

The mantels in the other parlors were decorated with miniature ballet sets designed by New York artist Christopher Radko, known for his highly prized Old World-style glass ornaments. The vignette in the Red Room recreated the opening scene of "The Nutcracker Suite," with children gathered around a Christmas tree and two nutcrackers representing George Washington and Abraham Lincoln. The vignette in the Green Room portrayed the Sugarplum Fairy and her Cavalier, along with gracefully posed ballerinas. The dolls were created by the New York City Ballet's costume department under the direction of Holly Hynes and other artists and craftsmen.

The four large trees in the Grand Foyer glistened with gold ribbon, roses made of gold ribbon, and glass ornaments. But the focal point was a needlepoint kissing ball created by needlepoint artist Hyla Hurley. Her astonishing 625 stitches per inch brought to life Clara, the Prince, and other characters from the children's party in "The Nutcracker Suite." "It was the hardest work I've ever done," she said. "I wouldn't do it for anybody else or any other place." She worked three weeks straight on the piece and even kept the UPS driver waiting while she finished it.

★ ABOVE ★

Christopher Radko's mantel decorations for the Red Room. The miniature set includes motifs from the opening scene of Tchaikovsky's classic ballet, featuring a castle of red and white candy.

★ RIGHT ★

Carved and painted wood ornaments representing "Nutcracker" characters, created by Mary Myers of Virginia Beach, Virginia. The toy soldier nutcracker was designed as a tree topper.

In the State Dining Room, Chef Mesnier's magnificent gingerbread house was modeled after a Victorian-era home, with two nutcrackers standing guard in bright red and blue uniforms. Its front parlor captured the ballet's party scene, with a miniature Chelsea in a pink ballerina dress.

Mrs. Clinton again showcased themes from previous seasons. A tree with angel ornaments from 1993 stood in the East Garden Room; oversized wreaths in the East Colonnade were decorated with ornaments from "The Twelve Days of Christmas" tree of 1994; and a tree in the Library displayed ornaments from 1995.

For a third time, sculptor Zachary Oxman created a bronze menorah for the West Wing lobby. Depicting ten figures dancing and entitled "A Festival of Light III: The Celebration of Family", it later became a prop on the set of the popular TV series "The West Wing."

Committed to opening the White House to people of other faiths, Mrs. Clinton had hosted a ceremony for Muslim families in February of that year to mark the end of Ramadan. It was the first time Islamic guests had been invited to the White House for a religious event.

★ TOP ★

The 1996 gingerbread house. The scene in the front parlor recreates the party in "The Nutcracker Suite," with a miniature Chelsea dressed as a ballerina.

★ ABOVE ★

Christopher Radko highlighted the Sugarplum Fairy and her Cavalier on the mantel of the Green Room.

★ *1997* ★
Santa's Workshop

A S USUAL, PLANNING FOR THE 1997 holidays began in the spring, only months after President Clinton's inauguration for a second term. The theme "Santa's Workshop" was chosen as a way to showcase the holidays as "a time of wonder, promise and hope" when viewed through a child's eyes.

By July the White House pastry chefs had baked 250 fruitcakes, which would eventually be cut into bite-size morsels and served along with enough cookies, truffles, tartlets, and other sweets to provide 80,000 nibbles for holiday guests. Even confirmed fruitcake haters found the White House version irresistible, especially when presented as "plum pudding," as Chef Mesnier liked to do. "Ours is different," he said. "We use the best fruit in the world—dried cherries, dried figs, fabulous candied pineapple. None of that green and red stuff." Sadly, his favorite fruitcake loaf pans, loaned to the Kremlin in 1991 for a state dinner honoring President Bush, were not returned and had to be replaced with lighter-weight, less satisfactory pans.

Chef Mesnier's annual masterpiece in the State Dining Room was the talk of the town that season. In keeping with the theme, the gingerbread house was his interpretation of Santa's North Pole home and workshop, with marzipan elves busily assembling the last of the toys. On the rooftop Santa was in his sleigh holding a tiny cell phone to his ear—calling the President to ask permission for Socks to come along and help deliver gifts. "People went crazy over that cell phone," he said.

True to the theme, the White House invitation to the press preview was tied to a plate of gingerbread cookies labeled "For Santa," along with a carton of low-fat milk.

★ ABOVE ★

A needlepoint close-up of Socks the cat, as depicted by the National Needlework Association.

★ OPPOSITE ★

President and Mrs. Clinton in front of the official White House Christmas tree.

The First Lady's favorite holiday color scheme, burgundy and gold, was found throughout the State Floor in 1,464 bows, twenty-three trees, 486 feet of garland, and 224 wreaths, installed by some sixty volunteers over a four-day span. The six trees in the East Room were trimmed in gold glitter balls and burgundy ribbon.

The Fraser fir in the Blue Room was decorated with 2,352 ornaments made by special groups, as in years past. More than 100 representatives from the Council of Fashion Designers of America, including big names like Donna Karan, Ralph Lauren, Oscar de la Renta, and Vera Wang, submitted wardrobe creations for Santa and Mrs. Claus. Outfits ranged from the traditional red suit for Santa to a red couture dress, trimmed in fur, for Mrs. Claus— and even mini boots, a leopard print skirt, and a red velvet bikini.

* ABOVE *

The 1997 gingerbread house, Chef Mesnier's rendition of Santa's home and workshop. The elevator shaft at the right—its top level labeled "Up, Up and Away!"—is for lifting gifts to the roof. Santa is readying his sleigh, cell phone in hand, while Socks peeks out of Santa's bag.

* OPPOSITE *

Christopher Radko creations, Santa's Village (above) and Santa's Workshop (below) embellish parlor mantels.

"Mrs. Claus is going to start her diet right after Christmas," the First Lady joked at the press preview. Almost 200 glass artisans created ornaments with scenes of the fictionalized North Pole, and 333 members of the National Needlework Association (now the National Needle Arts Association) stitched drums, gingerbread houses, nutcrackers, snowmen, and renditions of First Cat Socks.

Mrs. Clinton again relied on Christopher Radko, known for his fine glass ornaments, to supervise a team of artisans who created mantel decorations for the parlors. In the Red Room was "Santa's Workshop," a bustling scene of Santa and his elves making toys and decorating a Christmas tree. The Green Room featured "Santa's Village," with Mrs. Claus and the elves helping the man of the hour ready his sleigh for departure.

"Santa's Office," a Christopher Radko creation, was displayed on a pier table in the Grand Foyer. Hanging from the ceiling was another needlepoint masterpiece created by Hyla Hurley, this one

a scene of Santa and his sleigh with an American flag draped over the lead reindeer.

To help the ornament artists find their creations on the State Floor, Mrs. Clinton's staff prepared handouts that categorized the ornaments by their location, with the Blue Room tree divided into north, south, east, and west quadrants, top and bottom. The names of the artists were listed alphabetically by ornament location

★ TOP ★

Grapevine angels adorned with garland and ornaments, State Dining Room.

★ ABOVE ★

Christmas trees flank the fireplace in the Diplomatic Reception Room.

★ OPPOSITE ★

George P.A. Healy's portrait of President Lincoln trimmed in greenery.

★ *1998* ★
Winter Wonderland

WITH THE HELP OF MORE THAN eighty volunteers, the White House was turned into the proverbial winter wonderland this season, despite balmy temperatures outside the Executive Mansion. In the holiday booklet's welcome letter, Mrs. Clinton described her vision for the décor: "We have so many fond memories of Chelsea's first winters. Through her eyes we relived the pleasure of playing in the first snow fall, the silver glint of skate blades on a frozen pond, breathless sled rides down a glistening slope and lopsided snowmen with carrots for noses, destined to melt in the morning sun. No matter what your age, nothing is more beautiful than the stillness of a starry winter evening—especially on Christmas Eve—when snow blankets the street and the world is calm and bright."

A visitor's journey through this winter fantasy world of gold, silver, and white began where all White House holiday tours start—in the East Garden Room, which was decorated with snowmen figures and an antique sleigh filled with presents wrapped in shiny gold and silver metallic paper. A tree symbolizing world peace was decorated with 400 ornaments that came from current and former Peace Corps volunteers and staff in more than sixty-five countries.

The Ground Floor Corridor was trimmed in fresh greenery and pine cones, a motif repeated in the Library, where pine cones from all regions of the country formed two seven-foot-tall trees that were adorned with artificial fruits and nuts.

Upstairs in the Grand Foyer, amid glittering silver and gold, white birch trees covered in white lights replaced the traditional

★ ABOVE ★

A festive President and Mrs. Clinton with the official tree.

★ OPPOSITE ★

The Grand Staircase, trimmed with a garland of pine cones, silver branches, baby's breath, and glittering balls.

★ ABOVE ★
An antique sleigh laden with gifts sits in the East Garden Room.

★ LEFT ★
Snowmen in winter gear greet visitors in the East Garden Room.

★ OPPOSITE TOP ★
The Grand Foyer filled with frosted, lighted birch trees.

★ OPPOSITE BOTTOM ★
Colette Peters' edible packages, boxes, and bows top a side table in the Grand Foyer.

evergreens. This year's kissing ball by Hyla Hurley depicted Santa in a white robe, surrounded by two polar bears and woodland animals. A pier table held an artfully arranged display of edible packages created by New York confectionary artist Colette Peters.

The edible creation was almost ruined by the President's new labrador Buddy, however. President and Mrs. Clinton, along with Chelsea, were making their annual surprise visit to the Grand Foyer to thank all the volunteers who were hurriedly putting the final touches on the decorations. This year they were accompanied by Prime Minister Jean Chretien of Canada, who happened to be in town, and Buddy. The volunteers were so excited that no one noticed Buddy making a beeline for the tantalizing confection on the pier table. The President caught him just in time! After that, re-

porters were told, Buddy was put under twenty-four-hour guard.

Ms. Peters' creations also graced the mantels of the Red Room and Green Room. Her edible sculpture in the Red Room was a North Pole scene with penguins and polar bears; the Green Room mantel featured an ice palace surrounded by an ice garden. Despite heavy demand for her fabulous cakes, Ms. Peters contributed her talents to the project full time for almost a month. "I didn't think a minute about accepting the job," she said. "It's a great honor. And it's a chance to do something of my own design."

The East Room was transformed into a glittering display of eighteen cone-shaped gold and silver faux trees, created by New York floral designer Robert Isabell and his team. The soaring trees were made of gold-dipped leaves and sprigs of white birch branches, decorated with pine cones, gilded birds, and twinkling white lights. Complementing the gold of the East Room crèche was a magnificent 600-pound gold and silver advent wreath, suspended from the ceiling and ringed with electric candles. Capricia Marshall, the White House social secretary, explained to a televis-

★ ABOVE ★

A trumpeting angel made of woven grapevine adorns a mantel in the East Room.

★ OPPOSITE TOP ★

The East Room sparkles with a gold and silver décor designed by Robert Isabell of New York. Gold-dipped leaves and white birch branches were used to make the trees.

★ OPPOSITE BOTTOM ★

Robert Isabell's 2,000-pound holiday wreath is suspended outside on the South Portico. The 1,500 bulbs were hand-dipped to achieve the intense shade of "presidential blue."

Christmas at the White House ✣ 263 ✣ The Clinton Years

★ ABOVE LEFT ★

An ice palace and garden made of royal icing topped the Green Room mantel.

★ ABOVE RIGHT ★

Entirely edible, festive polar bears and penguins are on display in the Red Room.

★ OPPOSITE TOP ★

The gingerbread house serves as an impressive centerpiece in the State Dining Room. Constructed as a castle with towers and bridges, the 150-pound structure was too large for its usual place on the console table.

★ OPPOSITE BOTTOM ★

First Lady Hillary Clinton speaks with the press about the gingerbread house.

sion audience that, with the chandelier removed for repairs, the wreath served a dual purpose: "We decided that we really needed to do something with that space. Mrs. Clinton came up with the idea [of the wreath] so that there was light in that space, something decorative and really reflective of the holiday season."

Another spectacular wreath, weighing 2,000 pounds and said to be the largest holiday wreath ever hung at the White House, was the one Mr. Isabell considered his masterpiece. Made of noble fir greenery and 1,500 blue lights, it was attached to the roof of the South Portico and suspended in front of the Truman Balcony. He and his assistants hand-dipped the bulbs into a blue gel to get just the right color—"presidential blue," as he called it. "Royal blue is not the color of the presidency," he said. "That's too dark. It has no life. And navy blue is very blackish. This is a very intense, memorable blue."

Floral volunteer Ed Gage of Nashua, New Hampshire, explained how extensively the White House decorations had evolved in his twenty-five years of service. "I remember the years when the decorations in the big house were very traditional, magnolias on the mantels, poinsettias in the hall. In the Blue Room, we used to put a wreath of wet moss, dripping all over the place. This year I hung the grand staircase with ferns, silver branches and baby's

breath greens. I said 'wow' when I saw the huge wreath in the East Room. The President and Mrs. Clinton walked through and spoke nicely to everybody. They're very gracious."

Reinforcing the year's theme, the 2,343 ornaments on the balsam fir in the Blue Room consisted of snowmen and other objects associated with the winter season. The snowmen were made by artisans selected by governors' offices in all fifty states. Members of the Knitting Guild of America made little mittens and caps for the tree, and more than 500 members of the Society of Decorative Painters created miniature wooden skis, sleds, and other ornaments suggesting winter activities.

Chef Mesnier's gingerbread house—or castle, rather—was constructed on such a grand scale that it was actually the centerpiece of the dining table. This is the only year to date that the gingerbread house has not been placed on its usual console table in the State Dining Room.

The family tree in the Yellow Oval Room was decorated with silk flowers due to President Clinton's allergies.

The menorah displayed in the West Wing this year was loaned from Gomez Mill House in Marlboro, New York, the oldest extant Jewish homestead in North America.

★ *1999* ★

Holiday Treasures

THE HOLIDAY THEME FOR 1999 WAS especially meaningful to Mrs. Clinton because it dovetailed with her Save America's Treasures program, which she had spearheaded and officially unveiled the previous year. This public-private initiative focused on rescuing priceless but deteriorating historic sites and artifacts. As Mrs. Clinton wrote in the holiday program, "One of the most powerful ways for us to imagine America's future is to preserve what we truly value of our past—our monuments, our art and documents and historic sites will tell the story of this Nation to future generations."

To promote the Save America's Treasures campaign, the First Lady embarked on a tour of some thirty historic and cultural sites, many of which donated an ornament for the White House holiday season and were showcased on a "treasures tree" in the East Entrance area. The model of Eleanor Roosevelt's Val-Kill Cottage in Hyde Park, New York, was made with one of the saws used by her head cabinetmaker to construct furniture. A miniature of Benedict Arnold's gunboat Spitfire, which was sunk during the Revolutionary War, signified the efforts made by Lake Champlain Maritime Museum in Vergennes, Vermont, to protect historic shipwreck sites. Miniature replicas also included Fort Egbert, part of Alaska's Eagle Historic District National Historic Landmark, Mission San Jose de Tumacacori in Arizona, the Ellis Island Ferry Building in New Jersey, and Ventfort Hall in Lenox, Massachusetts, an Elizabethan-style mansion listed on the National Register of Historic Places and the home of the Gilded Age Museum.

Vignettes with more handcrafted reproductions of histor-

★ ABOVE ★

A "treasures tree" in the East Foyer honors projects in the Save America's Treasures program. The replicas were made by craftsmen at the sites, which the First Lady visited in promoting the effort.

★ OPPOSITE ★

Models of historic structures decorate the mantels of the parlor in the Red Room.

ic landmarks topped the mantels in the Red Room and Green Room, as well as pier tables in the Ground Floor Corridor and Grand Foyer. Even the gingerbread "house" in the State Dining Room was a complex of architectural treasures in and around the nation's capital: the Jefferson Memorial, the Washington Monument, Mount Vernon, and the White House.

In keeping with the theme, the noble fir in the Blue Room was decorated with ornaments honoring significant events, places, people, and artifacts in American history. Dollmakers created an array of famous figures ranging from Benjamin Franklin, George Washington, and Dolley Madison to other cultural icons: a Native American, Paul Bunyan, Amelia Earhart, Charles Lindbergh, Albert Einstein, Sojourner Truth, Rosa Parks, Mother Teresa, and surprises like Rosie the Riveter and Judy Garland. Tinsmiths and other artisans, using centuries-old techniques, crafted ornaments in the shape of Colonial candlesticks, Revere lanterns, and three-cornered hats of the Revolutionary War era. At the First Lady's request, multi-colored lights were mixed with white, a departure from tradition that gave the tree extra sparkle.

★ ABOVE ★

The First Lady stands in the State Dining Room with Chef Mesnier next to his gingerbread replicas of architectural treasures around the Nation's Capitol, complete with the Potomac River.

★ OPPOSITE TOP ★

Models of historic structures decorate the mantel of the Green Room parlor.

★ OPPOSITE BOTTOM ★

The official White House Christmas tree. The handcrafted ornaments featured historic events and cultural icons.

The People's House was trimmed from top to bottom with a total of twenty-eight trees, as well as 324 wreaths and 1,120 feet of garlands fashioned with fruits, cinnamon sticks, pine cones, and ribbons that evoked an old-fashioned style of decoration. Instead of bright red, a ruby hue predominated, along with cranberry reds.

The antique crèche in the East Room was given a new deep blue setting this year but framed with the customary gold brocade curtain. To highlight the colors of the scene, the six trees in the room were trimmed with gold and white lights, gold velvet ribbons, gold pine cones, hydrangeas, and cornucopias and dusted with tinsel. The four mantels were decorated with garlands and gold ribbon, with accents of hydrangeas and pine cones of gold and glass. Wreaths suspended with gold ribbon were hung in the windows and over the four mirrors in the room.

In the East Foyer a beautiful tree of poinsettias paid tribute to Dr. Joel Poinsett for his role in giving the nation what has become a decorative treasure of the holidays. He introduced the plant into the United States around 1825 while he was serving as foreign

★ **ABOVE** ★

*Dolls representing George Washington and others decorate
wreaths in the East Colonnade.*

★ **RIGHT** ★

First Pets Socks and Buddy stand guard in the Oval Office.

★ **OPPOSITE** ★

*A 20-foot sparkling grapevine wreath designed by Robert Isabell
of New York lights up the South Portico.*

minister to Mexico.

Portraits of former Presidents and First Ladies throughout the State Floor conveyed a sense of history while artwork on the walls of the parlors highlighted modern-day masterpieces. Georgia O'Keeffe's "Bear Lake, New Mexico," the first painting by a contemporary female artist to be displayed on the State Floor, hung in the Green Room, along with "Sand Dunes at Sunset, Atlantic City," by Henry Ossawa Tanner, the first African-American artist to be included in the permanent White House collection.

A stunning highlight of the State Dining Room was the ornate Monroe plateau, displayed in its entirety, a rare occurrence. President James Monroe ordered the gilded bronze centerpiece, measuring more than fourteen feet long when its seven mirrored sections are fully extended, from France during the 1817 reconstruction of the White House.

The gingerbread house was both a history lesson and a confectionary extravaganza consisting of Washington's iconic monuments. The Jefferson Memorial had a milk chocolate miniature of the founding father behind columns of gingerbread, and Mount Vernon was trimmed in holiday décor, with tiny topiary trees full of fruits like pineapples, apples, and more, all made from marzipan.

Another of Robert Isabell's impressive wreaths, this one made of woven grapevine and twinkling white lights, hung in front of the South Portico. To usher in the new millennium, the 75,000 colored lights on the National Christmas Tree outside the White House gave way to a profusion of white lights at 10 p.m. on December 31.

★ *2000* ★

Holiday Reflections

FOR HER FINAL CHRISTMAS AT 1600 Pennsylvania Avenue, Mrs. Clinton decided to give the decorations from the previous seven seasons a grand encore. She called this fond farewell "Holiday Reflections." Ornaments, wreaths, and mantel decorations, spanning from the angels of 1993 (said to be Chelsea's favorite) to examples of America's treasures from 1999, trimmed the Executive Mansion one more time. It was a nostalgic season for the President and First Lady: "They are very, very weepy," explained Capricia Marshall, the White House social secretary.

Mindful of the talent and hard work that so many people contributed to the White House Yuletide finery each year, President and Mrs. Clinton wrote in the 2000 holiday tour guide: "As we prepare to leave this grand house, we thank all who have made the holidays so special, not only for us, but also for tens of thousands of visitors who come to share in its lively holiday splendor. We especially pay tribute to the countless artists and volunteers who have transformed the White House into a showcase rich with the creative spirit of our great nation—from the talented craftsmen who fashioned handmade ornaments for the Blue Room tree to the devoted

The Grand Foyer. The eight cone-shaped trees, designed by Robert Isabell for the entry
area, are decorated with fruit, hydrangeas, and rich burgundy ribbons.

The 2000 kissing ball, designed and stitched by Hyla Hurley of Washington, D.C. The
needlepoint design incorporates motifs from all of Mrs. Clinton's previous themes.

designers and volunteers who have decked the halls of the White House."

Sorting through some 10,000 ornaments commissioned since 1993, Chief Florist Nancy Clarke and staffers chose the cream of the crop; Mrs. Clinton then decided which individual pieces to showcase. Ribbons were pressed while glitter and paint were re-applied to some of the balls and angels. Among all the decorations—324 wreaths, 1,120 feet of garland, 1,071 bows, and 50,000 lights—the only major additions were a new gingerbread house and a burgundy velvet tablecloth in the State Dining Room.

Hanging from the ceiling in the Grand Foyer was Hyla Hurley's sixth kissing ball for Mrs. Clinton, this one celebrating all the themes from the Clintons' White House holidays. The room was also adorned with eight cone-shaped trees decorated with fruit, hydrangeas, and ribbons of rich burgundy, a color favored by Mrs. Clinton.

The official tree in the Blue Room, the traditional centerpiece

* ABOVE *

Mrs. Clinton displays the "Holiday Reflections" tour booklet and the gingerbread house at her final press preview, December 4, 2000.

* OPPOSITE *

President and Mrs. Clinton with daughter Chelsea in front of the Chihuly glass tree, December 31, 1999.

of the decorations, was a Douglas fir trimmed with 900 favorite ornaments from the past seven seasons, along with the state balls, 550 glass balls, and 11,250 white lights. The green velvet tree skirt created for Mrs. Clinton's first year in the White House draped the base of the tree for the final time. Pier tables featured art from the White House Collection of American Crafts.

Christopher Radko's 1996 interpretation of ballet dancers in a scene from "The Nutcracker" rested on the mantel in the Green Room. The Red Room's mantel brought back a sweet memory: Colette Peters' Ice Palace from 1998, freshly recreated for this season. Other rooms featured themed trees and vignettes from the various years.

Mrs. Clinton again chose to display the famous Monroe plateau in the State Dining Room. Vying for attention was the gingerbread house, a replica of the White House with cutaway views of the East Room, Blue Room, and State Dining Room. In keeping with the retrospective theme, Chef Mesnier decorated his confection with miniature versions of his past creations. But he also had

the future in mind—the reindeer atop the mansion were pulling a sleigh filled with a shiny red apple, signifying that the First Lady was now a senator-elect, soon on her way to New York.

In the East Foyer a sleigh was brimming full of items from Christmases past, including some of Ms. Hurley's previous kissing balls. Along the East Colonnade, wreaths hung in the windows, an ornament centered in each wreath to represent one of the seven holiday themes.

The White House Christmas card collection, displayed as always in the East Foyer, included the original watercolor for the Clintons' final White House card. The painting by Ray Ellis of Martha's Vineyard, Massachusetts, portrayed the Yellow Oval Room in the private residence, reflecting Mrs. Clinton's wish that the artist select a White House subject that most people had never seen. The 2000 card conveyed a nostalgic message from President and Mrs. Clinton, greetings filled with "warm and treasured memories of our special time in the White House."

Mrs. Clinton continued the wonderful traditions of the First Ladies before her, but she also left her own mark. She broadened the selection of holiday themes to include a wider range of motifs and ornament contributors than seen in prior administrations. Her legacy also includes the introduction of an effective recycling system, highlighting the décor of previous seasons. Perhaps most significant, she expanded the concept of holiday decorations to embrace many kinds of objects, from fine art to ordinary items fashioned from unusual materials.

During her tenure, approximately 150,000 people toured the mansion each year, and she invited more than 30,000 guests to private parties. Comfortable with her role as hostess, she wanted to "invite America" into the White House: "This house and its history belong to all Americans, and we have worked hard to share this national treasure with as many people as possible—not just dignitaries, politicians, or the rich and famous, but Americans from every corner of the country and every walk of life."

The Official White House Christmas Ornament

ONE ORNAMENT ON THE BLUE ROOM TREE every year also hangs on Christmas trees across the nation—the official White House Christmas ornament which is issued annually by the White House Historical Association. Purchasing the ornament not only brings a bit of White House history into the family living room but also keeps the Executive Mansion livable. Proceeds from the ornaments' sales support the nonprofit, nonpartisan organization's mission of maintaining the historical rooms of the White House as well as acquiring historical furnishings and artwork for the permanent collection.

The ornament series was proposed in 1981 by Bernard R. Meyer, the organization's executive vice president, as a way to raise additional funds. To supplement private donations, the organization has always relied on revenue from the sale of tour guides, books on the history, architecture, and furnishings of the White House, and commemorative merchandise, such as a series of presidential medals and first lady medallions.

A miniature replica of a nineteenth-century weather vane depicting the angel Gabriel was selected as the first ornament in the series, as weather vanes crowned many of the nation's historic landmarks from Mount Vernon to Independence Hall. To commemorate the 250th anniversary of George Washington's birth, the 1982 ornament replicated the Dove of Peace weather vane atop the cupola of Mount Vernon. Both ornaments were fash-

2009

1982

1983

1984

1985

1986

1989

1987

1988

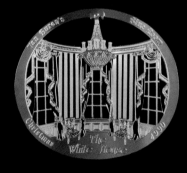

1990

1991

1992

1993

1994

ioned after real weather vanes and made of sheet copper with a green patina finish for a weathered look.

Since the inception of the series, most ornaments have paid tribute to presidential administrations in chronological order. The only president elected to two nonconsecutive terms, Grover Cleveland, has been honored with two ornaments (2007 and 2009). Occasionally, an ornament has celebrated an important anniversary in White House history—such as the bicentennial of the presidency (1989), the 200th anniversary of the construction of the White House (1992), the 200th anniversary of the White House as the home of the U.S. president (2000), and the centennial of the Roosevelt restoration of the White House (2002).

The ornaments are manufactured by ChemArt of Lincoln, Rhode Island, using a photo-etching process that produces intricate designs and involves seventeen or more steps, depending on the specialty treatments required by the design, such as casting or the application of decals or crystals. Some ornaments are engraved.

A winning design is first selected by the White House Historical Association through an annual design contest. Competitors submit designs that they have developed based on images and background information provided by the association. Except for the first two weather vanes, the ornaments have been made from polished sheets of brass that are plated with nickel and 24-karat gold. They are sold in velour-lined gift boxes and include an educational brochure with a history of the featured subject and brief reading list.

In the years since 1981, when about 5,000 ornaments were made (the sales price was $7.50), public demand for these educational and artistic collectibles has grown by leaps and bounds. According to Michael Melton, who is in charge of the ornament program, the White House Historical Association now sells more than one million ornaments annually, counting current and previous designs. It is the most popular ornament program in the world.

People from all over the world collect the ornaments and also buy them as gifts. The first family always receives an ample supply to give away.

The ornaments are sold at the White House Visitor Center as well as through the White House Historical Association's online shop (www.whitehousehistory.org). They are also resold by museum shops, many embassies in Washington, and organizations that purchase them in bulk and resell them for their own fundraisers.

2008

1995

1996

1997

1998

1999

The WHITE HOUSE

200TH ANNIVERSARY

CHRISTMAS 2000

2001

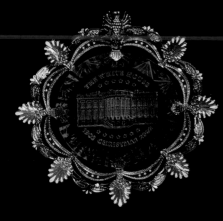

2002

2000

2003

2004

2005

2006

2007

The Bush Years

2001-2008

PLANNING FOR CHRISTMAS AT THE White House begins as early as March, so the anticipation of the season lasts almost all year. Each year, Nancy Clarke, the wonderful White House florist, would remind the Social Secretary and me that we had better get busy - and what fun that was! I would think of a theme that was special to me and run the idea by George and our girls. Then I would tell Nancy, who was always enthusiastic. She would suggest ways that we could illustrate our theme and then enlist the White House carpenters, plumbers, and electricians to help. They must have felt like Santa's elves as they built decorations, and I loved popping in on them to see the progress. Gary Williams, the White House plumber, built huge nutcrackers that stood sentinel at the White House entrance. One year, they were toy soldiers, and another year, they were two Uncle Sams holding the American flag.

For our first Christmas at the White House, I chose the theme "Home for the Holidays," because George and I are homebodies and because I love houses - dollhouses and real houses. And what a perfect theme for "The People's House!" The White House staff created replicas of presidential homes, from Mount Vernon to Lyndon Johnson's Texas ranch house, to decorate the mantels and pier tables. Little did we know when we chose "Home for the Holidays" how poignant our theme would be that Christmas of 2001, when many Americans were missing a loved one at home and all Americans were thankful for the family and friends who surround them.

Other Christmases we highlighted our animal companions - "All Creatures Great and Small," America's magnificent national parks, and children's storybooks with ornaments borrowed from my mother and father-in-law that were used for Christmas 1989.

Our last year at the White House, we celebrated "A Red, White, and Blue Christmas."

Every season, we celebrated Hanukkah at the White House with the lighting of the menorah and a kosher buffet. We borrowed magnificent menorahs from synagogues from across the country. Many of them were antiques that had made their way to the United States with families who had moved here to escape persecution. The most meaningful one to me was a small menorah that belongs to the family of Daniel Pearl, which was lit at the White House by Danny's parents, Judea and Ruth Pearl.

Every December the White House staff, including the chef, pastry chef, butlers and ushers, worked to make each reception and tour special for guests and visitors from around the country. At the last holiday party, held for the Residence staff, we thanked everyone and their families for their hard work. Then we would leave with our girls and our pets to meet the extended family at Camp David for the rest of our Christmas celebration. There we could put our feet up and rest after the many nights of receiving lines, and the White House staff could take a well-deserved holiday!

Our traditions at Camp David were a sweet and sacred part of our holiday. We attended the Camp David chapel of worship with the troops stationed at Camp. We watched and laughed at the antics of their children in the annual Christmas pageant. We took communion together at the Christmas Eve service and on Christmas Day we visited with families of the troops at the Camp David galley for Christmas Dinner.

Christmas is always a special time of year for George and me, and our days at the White House will remain some of my fondest holiday memories.

Laura Bush

ALTHOUGH MRS. BUSH CHOSE THE 2001 theme many months before the events of September 11, "Home for the Holidays" had special significance that year, as President and Mrs. Bush noted in their welcome letter for the holiday booklet: "Because this year's holiday season follows a national tragedy, both home and family have special meaning to all Americans. Gatherings of friends and family can be a tremendous source of strength and reassurance during this time. Our thoughts are with those who will be missing loved ones this year, and we pray that the blessings, the beauty, and the miracle of the holidays will bring comfort and hope to us all."

Over recent administrations, the number of Christmas trees used in the White House had been increasing, and 2001 set a record—forty-nine trees. Arranged throughout the halls, the trees were flocked with artificial snow and accented with gold birds, white lights, icicles, and tinsel for an enchanting, forest-like effect. A Fraser fir in the East Foyer was adorned with snowflakes created by third-graders attending elementary schools on Washington-area military bases.

For the Blue Room tree, Mrs. Bush invited the fifty

LAURA BUSH

When Mrs. Bush arrived at 1600 Pennsylvania Avenue, she came with much experience regarding the holidays. She had not only decorated the Governor's Mansion in Texas for six years, but also visited the White House all four years that her in-laws, President and Mrs. George H. W. Bush, resided there. As she approached her first Christmas season in the mansion, she told an interviewer, "I remember how magnificent the White House was, and I know it will be again this year, thanks to the White House staff." And like all the first ladies before her, Mrs. Bush recognized the essence of the season: "One of the things that make Christmas so special is the opportunity to do something for somebody else."

★ LEFT ★

A replica of Abraham Lincoln's home in Springfield, Illinois, made by Judith Winkelmann, hangs on the Blue Room tree.

★ OPPOSITE ★

A pair of boots tooled with the façade of Mission San José de Tumacácori near Nogales, Arizona, made by Paul Bond.

Pierre Menard Home

Ellis Grove, Illinois

Mount Pleasant
Philadelphia, Pennsylvania

LUCY

The official 2001 Blue Room tree trimmed for Mrs. Bush's theme "Home for the Holidays."

Close-up of ornaments on the official White House tree in the Blue Room. Clockwise from top left: a replica of Pierre Menard's home in Ellis Grove, Illinois by Mary Hackett; J.W. Cannon's home in Concord, North Carolina by Len Barnhardt; a close-up of the top of the official White House tree; Lucy the Elephant, in Margate, New Jersey by J. Kenneth Leap; a reproduction of Mount Pleasant in Philadelphia, Pennsylvania by Linda Brubaker.

state governors to designate local artisans to handcraft ornaments representing a special historic home or other type of structure in their region, using primarily shades of white. The result was 200 inventive creations of all shapes, sizes, and styles, made of diverse and, in some cases, unexpected materials: a cut-paper sculpture of the Biltmore Estate in Asheville, North Carolina; the façade of an Arizona mission tooled into a tiny pair of leather boots; and a fabric version of the Pierre Menard Home in Ellis Grove, Illinois. The stately concolor fir was accented with silver and gold balls, crystal snowflakes, white glass pine cones, and glass icicles, then dusted with artificial snow—all beautiful complements to its soft, silvery-blue foliage.

In keeping with the theme, mantels and pier tables throughout the mansion were filled with miniature replicas of former presidents' private homes. Executive Residence staff used the original floor plans of nineteen houses to create these scale models, an effort that involved electricians, plumbers, and carpenters. Forty-two representatives from the floral industry volunteered

JAMES MADISON
"MONTPELIER"
Montpelier Station, Virginia

THOMAS JEFFERSON
"MONTICELLO"
Charlottesville, Virginia

ANDREW JACKSON
"THE HERMITAGE"

★ ABOVE ★

Replica of Lyndon B. Johnson's presidential homestead, below the portrait of Mamie Eisenhower. The ranch located in Johnson City, Texas, was the westernmost of the presidential homes represented.

★ OPPOSITE ★

Replicas of presidential homesteads. Clockwise from top left: Montpelier, in Orange, Virginia, the home of James Madison; Thomas Jefferson's home, Monticello in Charlottesville, Virginia; Ulysses S. Grant's home in Galena, Illinois; The Hermitage, home of Andrew Jackson in Nashville, Tennessee; Woodrow Wilson's birthplace in Staunton, Virginia; Abraham Lincoln's home in Springfield, Illinois.

their time and talents to install the decorations.

In addition to the displays of historic homes, rooms throughout the State Floor featured floral arrangements and other decorations. In the Green Room, two topiaries of crystal fruit flanked the sofa, and peach-colored poinsettias and fresh limes were placed on side tables. In the Red Room, two small tables were decorated with red poinsettias; and the traditional cranberry tree, surrounded by holly, rested in its usual place atop the marble-top center table.

In the State Dining Room, a vignette of miniature carolers, all dressed in white and standing amid snowy evergreens, occupied the center of the dining table. White House Chief Florist Nancy Clarke and her staff painted the carolers' faces by hand, while volunteers stitched their outfits. Another highlight of the room was Chef Mesnier's gingerbread masterpiece, modeled this year on the original White House of 1800. Like the other presidential homes on display, the gingerbread house was reproduced to scale using blueprints made especially for Chef Mesnier by engineers in the Usher's Office. Even the marzipan carolers, "serenading"

the White House, were attired for the period. Several special residents were featured this year: Spot, Barney, and India ("Willie"), the White House pets.

On a landing of the Grand Staircase was a replica of the Calvin Coolidge Homestead, on loan from the Vermont Division for Historic Preservation. The railing of the staircase was trimmed with garlands of mixed greenery tied with white velvet ribbon.

This year marked the first time that a menorah-lighting ceremony had been held in the residence portion of the White House

On December 10 in the Booksellers Area, President and Mrs. Bush joined members of their staff, staffers' children, and Jewish leaders in lighting the second candle of a century-old lamp borrowed from the collection of the Jewish Museum in New York. The guests were then invited upstairs for a kosher buffet in the East Room. The Bushes held a White House Hanukkah party every year thereafter.

In a break with tradition, the Bushes chose a biblical inscription for their holiday card, two verses from Psalm 27. It was the

LEFT

Situated in Kinderhook, New York, Lindenwald was the retirement home of President Martin Van Buren. This replica created by White House staff was displayed in the Red Room.

BELOW

The mantel in the Green Room displayed a replica of Peacefield in Quincy, Massachusetts. The mansion was home to four generations of Adamses, including two presidents: John Adams and his son John Quincy Adams.

OPPOSITE

Mount Vernon, the home of our founding father and first President George Washington, was most prominently placed in the Grand Foyer. He was noted for stating of his Virginia home that "no estate in America is more pleasantly situated than this."

JOHN ADAMS AND
JOHN QUINCY ADAMS
"PEACEFIELD"
Quincy, Massachusetts

★ ABOVE ★

The cranberry tree, a Red Room annual tradition.

★ OPPOSITE TOP ★

The gingerbread house placed in the State Dining Room was a replica of the White House when John Adams became President. President Bush's pets Spot, Barney, and India the cat were placed on the White House grounds along with carolers, Santa, and his reindeer. The home was constructed with more than 80 pounds of chocolate and 20 pounds of marzipan, and took more than three weeks to build.

★ OPPOSITE BOTTOM ★

White House volunteers set up the Blue Room trimmed in keeping with Mrs. Bush's theme "Home for the Holidays."

★ PRECEDING PAGES ★

The East Room and Cross Hall were filled with flocked trees. 2001 was a record-breaking year when 49 trees filled the Executive Mansion.

first official White House card to include a Bible verse, a practice that the presidential couple continued for their remaining years at 1600 Pennsylvania Avenue.

Public tours of the White House, which were canceled in the wake of the terrorist attacks, did not resume for the holiday season at the recommendation of the Secret Service. So that citizens would still feel a part of the White House holiday magic, the First Lady provided descriptive interviews for television and had a video tour played at the White House Visitors Center. Here additional replicas of presidential homes were on display: Dwight D. Eisenhower's boyhood home in Abilene, Kansas; Harry S. Truman's residence in Lamar, Missouri; and Herbert S. Hoover's home in West Branch, Iowa.

Andi Ball, Mrs. Bush's chief of staff, remembers 2001 as her favorite White House Christmas. "It was delightful and enchanting," she says. "All the rooms and hallways were a fairyland of white, shimmering snow, glittering trees, twinkling lights, and lovely decorations. All who saw the decorations that year were totally wowed! And with the events of the previous four months, ending the year with this beautiful White House with the theme 'Home for Holidays' was extraordinarily special."

★ *2002* ★

All Creatures Great and Small

ANIMALS HAVE BEEN A PART OF every White House administration—from horses to dogs to more exotic species. As the trend has evolved from functional barnyard animals to treasured, furry housemates, these animals have become goodwill ambassadors of sorts, often revealing a more intimate side of the First Family.

Inspired by her affection for animals, especially her family's own pets, Mrs. Bush chose a line from a beloved nineteenth-century hymn for children as the theme for the 2002 season. She felt that it would "illustrate the endearing role of dogs, cats, birds, horses, sheep and even alligators and raccoons in White House history."

Twenty-five charming papier-mâché sculptures of presidential pets, past and present, were on display, ranging from beloved ponies to sheep that once grazed the White House lawn to a playful pair of marauding raccoons. White House staffers hand-painted these lifelike figures, accurate down to every spot, stripe, whisker, or hoof. The team of in-house artisans included White House calligrapher Debra Brown, who noted, "We write beautiful letters all day long, and this is a wonderful departure to be able to use our

★ OPPOSITE ★

President and Mrs. Bush pose with Millie, the beloved English springer spaniel of President and Mrs. George H.W. Bush, and her puppy, Spot, below the portrait of Barbara Bush. Spot is the only pet to have lived in the White House during two different administrations.

★ RIGHT ★

One of the ornaments that hung on the 2002 official White House tree was a paper birdhouse ornament by Catherine McClung of Whitmore Lake, Michigan.

★ ABOVE ★

*Barney and red ornaments by the official White House
Christmas tree during the filming of the Barney Cam video, a
popular new tradition launched by First Lady Laura Bush.*

★ RIGHT ★

*The 2002 holiday tour booklet "All Creatures Great and
Small," illustrated by Cheryl Barnes.*

★ OPPOSITE ★

The 2002 official Christmas tree, Blue Room.

hands in a different way and create more of a three-dimensional
figure. It's just a nice change."

Andi Ball, the First Lady's chief of staff, looks back on 2002
as "a very fun year." She says that children and adults alike "were
very entertained with the stories of White House pets, and they
especially loved the papier-mâché figures of the raccoons and alligators. There was a bit of history in the decorations!"

A prominent place in the Grand Foyer was devoted to likenesses of the Bushes' pets—Spot, an English springer spaniel and
the offspring of Barbara Bush's Millie; Barney, a Scottish terrier and
something of a family mascot; and the black cat India ("Willie").

The noble fir in the Blue Room was trimmed with ornaments representing native birds, created by artisans from across

India "Willie", Spot, and Barney, the current residents of the White House, greet visitors in the Grand Foyer.

Nancy Clarke paints a "Barney" replica in the White House flower shop.

the country. From puffins to owls to bluebirds to mockingbirds—even a pair of nesting birds sporting Santa caps—these beautiful creations were nestled among red balls, gold beads, and sparkling garlands and lights. The tree was draped with a red velvet tree skirt made from more than twenty yards of fabric.

Chief Florist Nancy Clarke created a grid of the tree with a key to each ornament's location. Ornament makers who visited the White House could go to the Usher's Office and pick up a booklet containing the grid so they could see where their ornaments were placed on the Blue Room tree.

A majestic American bald eagle, the symbol of our nation, graced the center of the great mahogany table in the State Dining Room. Volunteers crafted the figure from gold-dipped hydrangea leaves. Another bald eagle, this one in the East Room, was made of chocolate. To make this impressive creation, the White House pastry staff stacked together handmade "feathers" of chocolate and marzipan, resulting in a bird five feet tall and with a sixty-inch wingspan.

This patriotic motif also appeared in President and Mrs. Bush's official Christmas card, which featured Zhen-Huan Lu's oil painting of the mansion's most famous piano, the Steinway

ALLIGATOR
President John Q. Adams

A sculpture of Liberty, the beloved golden retriever of President and Mrs. Ford, displayed beneath the portrait of her mistress, Betty Ford. Rob Roy, the regal white collie that belonged to Calvin and Grace Coolidge, stands proud in the Ground Floor Corridor. Mrs. Coolidge included her in her official portrait, which hangs in the China Room. Macaroni, Caroline Kennedy's beloved pony, stands on a pier table outside the State Dining Room.

Nelson, the famous horse that led us to victory in the American Revolution, points to his master George Washington in the East Room. A replica of the alligator that John Quincy Adams reportedly kept in an East Room bathtub. The "pet" was a gift of the Marquis de Lafayette.

piano. Typically kept in the East Room but shown in the Grand Foyer, the piano is much admired for the massive American eagles forming its legs. "I liked the eagles," said the artist, "because they symbolized the spirit and patriotism of this country, especially after 9/11."

Throughout the mansion, red velvet ribbon, red glass balls, red icicles, and red pepper berries accented traditional garlands and wreaths. Massive displays of the traditional Christmas plant, the poinsettia, emphasized the color palette.

The Green Room was decorated with topiaries of gold and green fruit, as well as bright-red poinsettias and fresh green pears. The Red Room was lush with garlands and topiaries made of pomegranates, pears, and magnolia leaves, and the annual cranberry tree surrounded by holly.

The Oval Office was full of holiday cheer this year, with a Christmas tree covered in iced and ornately decorated gingerbread animals, including replicas of Barney and Spot, made by the White House chocolate shop. President Bush was known for snatching cookies right off the tree and eating them and would offer them to anyone else in the room, recalls Chef Mesnier. "I was often the first one there every morning to replace the cookies dai-

★ **ABOVE** ★

Volunteers put the finishing touches on the State Dining Room centerpiece, a magnificent golden eagle.

★ **RIGHT** ★

Barney and Spot have their holiday portrait taken.

★ **OPPOSITE TOP** ★

The stunning 2002 gingerbread house designed according to Mrs. Bush's theme, with marzipan creations of pets that have belonged to the presidents and their families.

★ **OPPOSITE BOTTOM** ★

A chocolate eagle, truffle tree, and pastries on display with Pastry Chef Roland Mesnier and the pastry shop personnel in the East Room.

A close-up of the President's Oval Office Christmas tree, featuring gingerbread ornaments including a replica of Spot.

Poinsettia trees highlight the Cross Hall.

ly," he says. Gingerbread cookies are a longtime Bush family tradition as First Lady Barbara Bush is known for her gingerbread. "A lot of our friends remember going to the Bushes' house where you got to take a cookie off the tree and then [Barbara Bush] would put them in little sacks," remembers Laura Bush. "[George] loves her gingerbread cookies. And when we first moved into the Texas Governor's Mansion, there would be gingerbread cookies in the reception rooms on the tree." Gingerbread cookies were also in the Oval Office during President George H.W. Bush's term as President.

With access to the White House still restricted, a small creature saved the day for would-be holiday visitors. The Bushes' little terrier Barney, wearing a tiny video camera on his dog collar, taped a "tour" of the mansion's decorations as he scurried around the White House. The result was a four-and-a-half-minute video, available for online viewing at the White House website. Conceived as a way to share the decorations at the People's House with the people, the Barney Cam video was an immediate hit, resulting in 24 million views on the day it was launched. Due to its popularity, the Barney Cam was an annual holiday feature for the remainder of the Bush administration. With Barney always in the starring role, the videos developed more defined plotlines and even introduced celebrities in cameo roles.

★ 2003 ★
A Season of Stories

★ OPPOSITE ★

The official holiday portrait of President and Mrs. Bush, Blue Room.

★ BELOW ★

Barbara Bush presides over H.A. and Margaret Rey's "Curious George," a vignette of the Man with the Yellow Hat and the mischievous monkey himself.

FOR LAURA BUSH, A FORMER LIBRARIAN and a driving force behind the Texas Book Festival and later the National Book Festival, the Christmas theme of 2003 was very appealing and perhaps inevitable. Like Barbara Bush's literacy theme of 1989, "A Storybook Christmas," "A Season of Stories" brought to life characters and scenes from classic children's tales once again. In fact, the Blue Room tree was decorated with fifty-nine of the ornaments from 1989, borrowed from the George H.W. Bush Presidential Library.

It was with some initial hesitation that Mrs. Bush reused her mother-in-law's storybook theme: "I felt like it was an idea that she had already done, but then I realized that families love to hand down decorations. And it was really perfect to borrow these ornaments from Barbara and Jenna's grandparents to put on the big tree."

Barbara Bush's literary-themed figures, each about two feet tall, filled the Fraser fir in the Blue Room. The fictional characters ranged from Rapunzel to Peter Pan to the pig Wilbur from "Charlotte's Web." Sixty-two big painted wooden letters of the alphabet were interspersed with red and gold glass ornaments. At the base of the tree, forming a kind of literary "tree skirt," were 350 books loved by readers of all ages.

National Park Service employees pull the official tree through the Grand Foyer toward the Blue Room.

The 2003 official White House tree in the Blue Room.

A close-up of a Blue Room tree decoration depicting Mrs. Piggle Wiggle, and books underneath the official White House tree.

A close-up of a Blue Room tree ornament, Scrooge, a character from the classic "A Christmas Carol."

The Queen of Hearts presides on top of the tree.

Fifteen new vignettes—composed of forty-three storybook characters from classic tales as well as recent favorites—stood on mantels and pier tables. Mrs. Bush selected favorites from her own childhood, from books she read to children as a school librarian, and from those her twin daughters, Barbara and Jenna, enjoyed when they were young. Starting months ahead of the holidays, Chief Florist Nancy Clarke and her staff turned the White House floral shop into the proverbial Santa's workshop as they dressed plastic dolls in costumes to match storybook pictures provided by Mrs. Bush. After spraying the dolls with gesso to give them a papier-mâché look, the floral staff hand-painted the dolls, making each one unique.

A Candyland motif went hand in hand with the storybook theme. In the Green Room, topiaries made of sugarplums, gumdrops, and rock candies flanked the sofa, and a garland full of bright-colored candies cascaded down the mantel. The mantel in the Red Room was draped with a garland made of red candy apples and popcorn balls.

The East Room was perhaps the most elaborately decorated space on the State Floor. In addition to four trees trimmed with red and white glass ornaments and candy canes, more literary figures were placed on the mantels. The centerpiece on the dessert table was inspired by Roald Dahl's "Charlie and the Chocolate Factory." To build the chocolatier's factory and bubblegum ma-

★ ABOVE ★

A close-up of the garlands in the East Room.

★ OPPOSITE ★

The Green Room mantel was packed full of gumdrops, sugared candy, and more.

★ LEFT ★
Volunteers strategize the placement of thousands of ornament balls and start the process of trimming 1600 Pennsylvania Avenue on the State Floor.

★ BELOW ★
Characters from Lewis Carroll's "Alice in Wonderland" form the centerpiece for the State Dining Room.

★ OPPOSITE TOP ★
Dr. Seuss' "Cat in the Hat" on a table in the Cross Hall.

★ OPPOSITE BOTTOM ★
The Hardy Boys & Nancy Drew on display in the East Room.

★ ABOVE ★

"Charlie and the Chocolate Factory" was on the center of the dessert table in the East Room, created by Executive Pastry Chef Roland Mesnier. Charlie, Willie Wonka, Violet Beauregarde, and Oompa-Loompas were all represented.

★ LEFT ★

"Make Way for Ducklings" characters were displayed in the Ground Floor Corridor on a pier table.

★ OPPOSITE ★

J.K. Rowling's "Harry Potter and the Sorcerer's Stone" was depicted on a mantel in the East Room, as were Meg, Jo, Beth, Amy, and Marmee from "Little Women."

LITTLE WOMEN
Louisa May Alcott

First Lady Laura Bush and Executive Pastry Chef Roland Mesnier display the gingerbread house for the press on December 4, 2003.

The 2003 gingerbread house, a replica of the White House. Tiny marzipan figures represent favorite characters from "Winnie the Pooh," "The Three Little Pigs," "The Very Hungry Caterpillar," and "The Secret Garden." The open window on the top floor recreates a room from "Goodnight Moon."

Twelve-foot-tall nutcracker figures, from E. T. A. Hoffman's "The Nutcracker and the Mouse King," stand guard in the Grand Foyer. Larry Forrest of the National Parks Service, assembled the statues from multiple components and used a lift to apply the finishing touches to the topmost parts.

chine, White House pastry chefs used fifty pounds of chocolate, ten pounds of bubblegum, and ten pounds of lollipops, in addition to parts from a hardware store.

A giant sleigh filled with a selection of Mrs. Bush's favorite children's stories graced the East Garden Room. The red wreaths lining the hallway of the East Colonnade were studded with crabapples and hung with large red velvet bows.

Ultimately, it took 245 wreaths, 251 bows, 660 feet of garland, nineteen trees, more than 70,000 lights, and 675 balls to create the season's festive décor. But perhaps the real highlight of the season was the reopening of the White House doors for holiday tours, despite new restrictions.

2004

A Season of Merriment and Melody

THE BEST-LOVED SONGS OF THE Christmas season—from "Jingle Bells" to "Frosty the Snowman"—inspired the holiday décor in 2004, and scenes that captured the mood of these songs enlivened every room of the mansion. Mrs. Bush selected thirteen holiday melodies that she and President Bush had grown up with, including her personal favorite, "I Saw Mommy Kissing Santa Claus," to depict in vignettes on mantels and pier tables.

The decorations in the Grand Foyer and Cross Hall captured the mood of the ever-popular tune "White Christmas," written by Irving Berlin in 1940. Flocked trees glittered with snowflakes, crystals, balls, icicles, and gold and white lights, creating the winter wonderland effect that was so favored by Nancy Reagan. Vignettes were nestled in fluffy "snowdrifts" and among miniature evergreens. A total of forty-one flocked Christmas trees were located throughout the mansion, double the number of trees from the previous year.

The noble fir in the Blue Room was decorated with 350 musical instruments painted by members of the Society of Decorative Painters. The organization distributed small replicas of musical instruments and asked their members to paint them in jewel colors with decorative stroke work to reflect Mrs. Bush's holiday theme. A total of 750 ornaments were

★ **OPPOSITE** ★

A vignette in the Grand Foyer depicts the popular holiday tune "White Christmas" with a festive pair, miniature packages, and frosted trees.

★ **BELOW** ★

This piano was one of 350 ornaments placed on the Blue Room tree, painted by Scottie Foster of the Society of Decorative Painters.

I Saw Mommy Kissing Santa Claus

submitted from members of chapters in all fifty states, from which 350 were chosen by the Society. A complete symphony of tiny pianos, violins, drums, trumpets, harps, and more adorned the tree, accented by glass balls and beads.

Each room on the State Floor had its own look and special signature touches. The Green Room was adorned with Della Robbia garlands and topiaries made of iced fruit. For the Red Room, gold leaves surrounded tiny drums and red crystal eggs on the mantels. Gold topiaries in vermeil containers and the cranberry topiary added the final touch to this perfectly colored holiday room. The

★ ABOVE ★

"I Saw Mommy Kissing Santa Claus" depicted in the Ground Floor Corridor.

★ OPPOSITE TOP ★

A vignette in the East Room interprets the popular holiday tune "Frosty the Snowman."

★ OPPOSITE BOTTOM ★

A small village on display with "Here Comes Santa Claus" as the theme in the Ground Floor Corridor.

wreaths in the windows of the East Colonnade were also covered in iced Della Robbia fruit.

The State Dining Room featured embossed red velvet and taffeta, embellished with crystal and silk. A dramatic arrangement of white flowers in a large vermeil vase complemented the gilded candelabra, glittering chandelier, and elegant wall sconces. Each sconce was decorated with greenery and decorative musical instruments. A long silk garland, fashioned with gold magnolia leaves, draped over the mantel and pooled gracefully onto the floor.

The new White House Executive Pastry Chef, Thaddeus DuBois, debuted his rendition of the traditional gingerbread

★ ABOVE ★

Carolers in their carriage sing "Jingle Bells" in the Cross Hall.

★ OPPOSITE ★

Tabletop vignettes of holiday songs, created by the residence staff, greet visitors in the Ground Floor Corridor. (top) Andi Ball, Chief of Staff to First Lady Laura Bush, stands next to "Blue Christmas." (bottom) "Up On the Housetop."

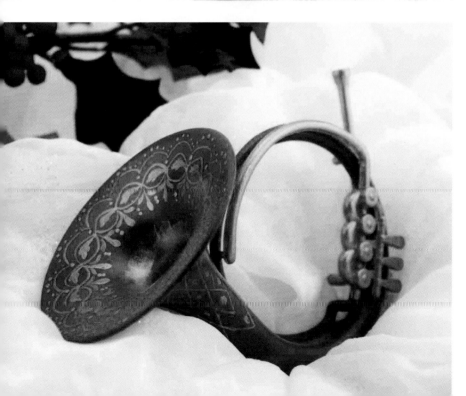

★ ABOVE ★

Contributions to the Blue Room tree by the Society of Decorative Painters for the theme "A Season of Merriment and Melody." Clockwise from top left: a close-up of a bell ornament created by Sheridian Sylvester; red, black, and gold maracas by Deborah Ann Roberts; a tambourine by Jan O'Quinn; a blue French horn with gold strokes by Louise E. Kramer; a red harp painted by Patricia Ann Moore.

★ OPPOSITE ★

The official White House Christmas tree, Blue Room.

★ LEFT ★

A Marine Band pianist plays
the Steinway grand piano in the
Grand Foyer amongst sparkling
Christmas trees.

house—a magnificent scale replica of the White House based on actual blueprints. Tiny marzipan figures included the Marine Band on the roof of the mansion, carolers on the lawn, and, of course, Barney and Willie. For guests attending holiday parties and receptions, Chef DuBois and his staff had been working for more than two months to whip up some 24,000 cookies and other sweets.

A measure of normalcy had returned to the White House, and an estimated 44,000 visitors had reservations to tour the mansion during the holidays, with an additional 6,500 guests invited to attend receptions. The Barney Cam was also up and running, allowing cyber visitors an insider's view of the decorated rooms.

★ ABOVE ★

"All I Want for Christmas is My Two Front Teeth"
displayed in the Ground Floor Corridor.

★ OPPOSITE TOP ★

Executive Pastry Chef Thaddeus DuBois and the White
House pastry shop created a wonderful rendition of the south
view of the mansion covered in holiday melodies, the Marine
Band, and the First Pets.

★ OPPOSITE BOTTOM ★

A close-up of the Marine Band, also known as the
"President's Own," lining the roof of the cookie replica
of the White House.

All Things Bright and Beautiful

A S IN 2002, THE CHILDREN'S HYMN "All Things Bright and Beautiful" provided the annual theme. In their holiday program the Bushes explained that the theme was chosen "to highlight the beauty to be found in nature" and to emphasize "the many ways that plants, trees, fruit and flowers can be the stars of holiday decorating."

The decorations this year had a fresher, simpler, more natural look. As Mrs. Bush noted in the press preview, "We used natural, real flowers and fruits and garlands to show how beautiful nature is and how many things we can use from our own gardens or woods." She added, "Every year I think it's the prettiest year, but this year I really do think it's the prettiest year."

The Fraser fir in the Blue Room was breathtaking, trimmed stylishly with fresh white lilies, clear crystal balls, and beaded glass garlands. The real flowers, however, posed a special challenge for the White House floral shop in keeping everything fresh and beautiful. So the lilies in the less accessible and less visible places—at the top and the back of the tree—were freeze-dried, with fresh ones elsewhere, allowing for weekly replacement. First the pollen

★ OPPOSITE ★

The Blue Room set for a Christmas Party.

★ BELOW ★

Mrs. Bush with First Pets Barney and Miss Beazley.

was extracted from the lilies; then each flower's stem was placed in its own water-filled glass tube, which was secured to the tree. A tree skirt made of fresh moss wrapped the bottom of the tree, completing the natural look.

The décor was boldly accented with colors of tangerine, lime green, and hot pink.

Boxwood wreaths accented with gold and lime green ribbon hung in the windows along the East Colonnade. At the end of the hall was a bay topiary tree with white lights, real pears, and a partridge ornament at the very top. Official Christmas cards from the permanent White House collection were displayed in the East Foyer, along with the original art used for the Bushes' 2005 card,

an oil painting of the South Portico. Painted by third-generation artist James Browning Wyeth, it featured the Andrew Jackson magnolia tree laden with snow.

Lining the halls of the Ground Floor Corridor were myrtle topiaries interspersed with animal topiaries made of ivy and moss, along with clusters of sweet-scented paperwhites. The animal topiaries resembled bears, swans, and the Presidential Scotties Barney and Miss Beazley.

The Library was decked with traditional holiday garlands made with greenery and bright green pears. An arrangement of orange Rilona amaryllis was prominently displayed on the center table.

* ABOVE *

Boxwood garland and tulips frame the Grand Foyer mirror for the 2005 holiday season.

* RIGHT *

A painting by Jamie Wyeth that portrays a wintry White House with Barney, Miss Beazley, and even Willie the cat, is displayed in the East Room during the press preview. The painting was the model for this year's White House Christmas card.

* OPPOSITE *

A close-up of the lilies on the Blue Room tree.

In the Cross Hall, large "trees" of white azaleas stood between the columns, a counterpoint to the graceful pink and orange tulips on the pier tables. Boxwood garlands, studded with twinkling lights, silver and gold crystals, and amber glass balls, draped the doorway, while garlands tied with lime-green and gold ribbon cascaded down the Grand Staircase.

The State Dining Room featured a striking buffet table covered in a lime-green taffeta tablecloth with a vivid orange overlay. At each end of the table stood 5-foot-tall topiaries, made of alternating layers of lemon leaves and tangerines. At the center of the table was a mass of orange French tulips.

Chef DuBois' majestic gingerbread house was a replica of the White House, its architectural details rendered with the intricate piping of white icing. Lights were even visible through frosty windows, made with clear, poured sugar. The marzipan figures of Barney, Miss Beazley, and Willie —all black against the snowy

★ ABOVE ★

Scottie-shaped gingerbread ornaments trim the tree in the Oval Office.

★ OPPOSITE TOP ★

First Pets Barney and Miss Beazly run along the Ground Floor of the White House in topiary form.

★ OPPOSITE BOTTOM ★

Winter white tulips stand tall in the Vermeil Room. The mantel is trimmed with a boxwood garland. Official portraits of several First Ladies, inlcuding Elizabeth Shoumatoff's rendering of Lady Bird Johnson above the mantel, hung in this room.

Christmas trees were decorated with roses and the traditional scene of the crèche is featured prominently. The focal point of the decor for "All Things Bright and Beautiful" in this room was the historic table covered in a lime green taffeta cloth with a matching overlay.

Hot pink tulips and green pears in silver pedestals stand in line on the center table creating a natural centerpiece for the East Room.

The press pool samples holiday food in the State Dining Room during the press preview of the White House Christmas decorations, November 30, 2005.

★ ABOVE ★

Topiaries of hot pink roses in vermeil cache pots in the East Room.

★ OPPOSITE TOP ★

The gingerbread house, created by Pastry Chef Thaddeus DuBois, is seen on display in the State Dining Room.

★ OPPOSITE BOTTOM ★

The 2005 family tree, trimmed with the Bushes' personal ornaments. The Yellow Oval Room, part of the private residence, is seldom seen by the public.

lawn, made their appearance.

In the Yellow Oval Room of the private residence Barney and Miss Beazley also appeared on the family tree as ornaments, along with the collection of personal ornaments, many from Mrs. Bush's family and her own childhood. Because daughters Barbara and Jenna were born on November 25, Mrs. Bush received many Christmas ornaments as baby gifts, which she always hung on the tree.

This year's holiday magic was achieved with a total of 63 volunteers, 18 Christmas trees, 580 feet of garland, 204 wreaths, and 4,638 shiny red ornament balls. For the 9,500 guests who were invited to holiday receptions, the kitchen staff prepared not only 30,000 Christmas cookies and other goodies but also 2,100 pounds of sweet potatoes! Some 45,000 visitors made reservations to tour the Executive Mansion over the holidays.

Deck the Halls and Welcome All

RETURNING TO A MORE CONVENTIONAL theme for 2006, Mrs. Bush was inspired by the dramatic color of the Red Room, not only because red is traditional in a holiday setting, but also because the room has long been used by First Ladies as a place for welcoming guests. Hues of scarlet, crimson, and fuchsia accented the lush greenery and more than 260 festive evergreen wreaths graced the windows and walls, most trimmed with red ribbon, and 4,638 red balls adorned trees and 1,089 feet of greenery.

Iridescent glass ornaments were suspended from red bows on the Douglas fir in the Blue Room, along with glass icicles, varying sizes of snowflakes, and mirrored ornaments that caught reflections of the tree lights. Strands of crystal beads were draped over the tree's branches, which were sprinkled with artificial snow. The tree skirt was made of green moss.

Among the other sixteen Christmas trees, one in the East Wing lobby and another just outside the Oval Office were trimmed with 250 ornaments made by North Carolina artisans working through an economic development project. The First Lady ordered the hand-blown red glass balls and "Carolina snowflakes"

★ **OPPOSITE** ★

A wreath in the window of the Blue Room that overlooks the Washington Monument. As twilight falls over Washington, D.C., the decorations in the Blue Room remain ever bright. 269 wreaths were displayed at the White House in 2006.

★ **BELOW** ★

A close-up of the Blue Room tree trimmed for the holiday theme, "Deck the Halls and Welcome All."

(woven from reeds dyed red, green, and walnut-brown) from the Home of the Perfect Christmas Tree program in Spruce Pine, a community hard hit by the loss of manufacturing jobs. Despite much red tape and some initial concerns that the White House order would appear to be a product endorsement, Mrs. Bush was committed to the idea. Anita McBride, the First Lady's Chief of Staff, observed that Mrs. Bush "just cut through all that and did the right thing. . . . . It is . . . another one of those indications of what a platform she has, in big ways and in small ways."

Festive decorations resembling trees were placed throughout the State Floor. Twelve-foot-tall red poinsettia topiaries filled the Cross Hall and the Grand Foyer, while both spherical and conical topiaries fashioned from shiny red balls stood in

★ OPPOSITE ★

The 2006 Christmas holiday decorations looking down the Cross Hall. The doorways in the Cross Hall were outlined with boughs of evergreen garland and trimmed with glass ornaments, painted in red, green, and silver.

★ ABOVE ★

The official Blue Room tree, as seen through the Cross Hall doorway opening.

the East Colonnade, their bases made to look like big toy drums.

Garlands studded with red and silver balls draped doorways and mantels. The Red Room, of course, had its cranberry tree, which fit perfectly with this year's color scheme.

In the State Dining Room, tables were topped with red-on-red tablecloths. The centerpiece on the dining table was a snowy forest scene, and on the smaller tables, mint julep cups were filled

★ ABOVE LEFT ★

A twelve-foot-tall nutcracker statue with a lollipop welcomes visitors at the East Entrance. Crafted by the White House Executive Residence staff, the nutcracker is weighted down with cleverly concealed sandbags.

★ ABOVE RIGHT ★

Ivy topiaries of Barney, Miss Beazley, and India "Willie" with bright red bows accent a pier table beneath the portrait of First Lady Betty Ford by Felix de Cossio in the Ground Floor Corridor.

★ RIGHT ★

Volunteers create an ornament tree of red balls for the East Colonnade. Over 4,638 red balls were used to trim the White House in 2006.

★ OPPOSITE TOP ★

A patriotic view down the Cross Hall into the State Dining Room.

★ OPPOSITE BOTTOM ★

The Red Room with holiday decor.

★ PRECEDING PAGES ★

The East Colonnade is lined with wreaths and accented with red glass ornaments. This year, more than 269 wreaths were hung in the White House.

★ RIGHT ★

The gingerbread house is carried inside from the North Portico entrance, under the careful watch of Pastry Chef Roland Mesnier.

★ BELOW ★

Mrs. Bush and Pastry Chef Roland Mesnier discuss the gingerbread White House with the press in the State Dining Room, November 30, 2006. The house consists of more than 300 pounds of dark chocolate and gingerbread and has over 800 snowflakes made from hand-piped icing.

★ ABOVE ★

The Christmas holiday decorations in the State Dining Room.

★ RIGHT ★

The table is set for a 2006 holiday dinner.

with more of the red and silver balls.

Mrs. Bush did not want to see the end of the tradition of the gingerbread house following the departure of Chef DuBois from the White House. So Chef Roland Mesnier temporarily emerged from retirement for a command performance and created another of his culinary works of pastry art—the largest ever. The confection represented the south side of the White House, and in keeping with the theme, the windows were all marked with red bows. Over 800 snowflakes made of hand-piped icing dotted the miniature structure. A sleigh on the roof pulled marzipan versions of Barney and Miss Beazley while a figure of First Cat India "Willie" sat curled in the snow beneath a birdhouse.

Holiday in the National Parks

F OR 2007, MRS. BUSH CHOSE A THEME near and dear to her heart—"Holiday in the National Parks." As the honorary chair of the National Park Foundation and an enthusiastic hiker of the parks each summer, she had a keen interest in educating schoolchildren about the nation's park system. When a child once asked her to name her favorite national park, she replied, "Of course I love the White House, but I think I'd have to say the Grand Canyon." Mrs. Bush was alluding to the fact that the 82 acres surrounding the White House constitute President's Park, a unit of the national park system.

To highlight the history and diversity of the country's 391 national parks (which include national seashores, rivers, trails, monuments, battlefields, cemeteries, historic sites, and others), Mrs. Bush's staff sent each park a simple gold ball and asked the park officials to select a local artisan to create an ornament emblematic of that site.

The balls on the Fraser fir in the Blue Room depicted park scenes ranging from the White House itself to Shiloh National Military Park to the nation's most recent national park: the site in Pennsylvania where Flight 93 went down on September 11. Large gold stars and amber lights accented each one-of-a-kind ornament, creating a dramatic gold effect.

At a reception hosted by Mrs. Bush, each of the art-

★ OPPOSITE ★

The official White House Christmas tree with ornaments honoring the National Parks, Blue Room.

★ BELOW ★

First Lady Laura Bush next to the official tree during a press preview.

ists were able to see the exact placement of his or her ornament on the tree. Anita McBride, the First Lady's Chief of Staff, explained: "We gave them a little booklet with a chart showing where their ornament was. They stood with Mrs. Bush and took pictures on their side of the tree. It made for a most memorable event."

Golden hues unified other areas of the State Floor, with the color gold signifying the precious treasure represented by the national parks. Doorways and mantels were draped with garlands of greenery laced with gold-painted pine cones, gold leaves, and gold lights. White House carpenters and florists crafted replicas of park structures and natural features to display in hallways and on pier tables.

In the Grand Foyer, a three-foot model of the Statue of Liberty was prominently placed on the pier table in front of the grand mirror. In the Cross Hall, flocked trees with gold lights featured birds, golden butterflies, and other creatures from the great outdoors.

★ ABOVE ★

A close-up of the 2007 Blue Room tree ornaments highlighting the National Parks waiting to be placed on the tree.

★ OPPOSITE ★

Blue Room tree ornaments highlighting the National Parks hanging on the tree. (top left) Flight 93 National Memorial by Ginny Barnett. (top right) Padre Island National Seashore by Kay Barnebay. (middle left) The White House and President's Park by Margaret Huddy. (middle right) Appomattox Court House by Susan Book. (bottom left) Assateague Island National Seashore by Scott Oatman. (bottom right) Salem Maritime National Historic Site by Racket Shreve.

The niches of the hall framed two striking oil paintings by Pennsylvania artist Adrian Martinez, each depicting a scenic view in Grand Canyon National Park and in Zion National Park. After the White House carpenters fabricated a shell of plywood and canvas that fit perfectly into each niche, the artist tackled the challenging work—physically and mentally—of painting the scenes on concave surfaces, which meant working on ladders and scaffolds as well as on his knees. "The fact that the surface was curved gave me considerably more trouble than I had anticipated, but after they were completed, this shape added a delightful space element to the viewing experience," Martinez said.

In the East Room, the White House crèche was flanked by two sixteen-foot trees trimmed with glass ornaments and gold globes, gold birds, gold leaves, and more gold lights.

Bright pink tulips spread holiday cheer in the Green Room, where the mantel was draped with a garland of greenery accented with gold glass acorns and pine cones. Ornamental birds and bird nests filled miniature Christmas trees on side tables.

★ LEFT ★

Beneath Gilbert Stuart's portrait of George Washington is a garland packed with gilded leaves and pine cones in the Diplomatic Reception Room.

★ BELOW ★

A model of The Alamo in San Antonio, Texas on the Ground Floor Corridor.

★ OPPOSITE ★

Cape Hatteras Lighthouse of Hatteras Island, North Carolina, the nation's tallest lighthouse, stands in the East Garden Room. The White House carpenters constructed it with a functioning light.

★ **ABOVE AND LEFT** ★

The Palm Room held complementary displays depicting the National Seashores which represented "from sea to shining sea," including a unique tree made entirely of seashells.

★ **OPPOSITE TOP** ★

A chocolate reproduction of Mount Rushmore, Ground Floor Corridor.

★ **OPPOSITE BOTTOM** ★

A close-up of ornaments hanging on the First Family's Christmas tree in the private residence.

Gold also predominated in the State Dining Room. Sconces were adorned with mixed greenery, gold ribbons, and gold pine cones while the gilded Monroe plateau formed the spectacular centerpiece for the dining table, which was covered with an embossed gold tablecloth. In preparing food for holiday parties, White House Executive Chef Cristeta "Cris" Comerford made sure that beef tenderloin was on the menu—"It's President Bush's favorite dish," she said.

The room's showstopper was this year's gingerbread house, a to-scale replica of the south view of the White House, its lawn inhabited by tiny bears, coyotes, elk, moose, raccoons, and other wildlife found in the national parks. Created by new White House Pastry Chef, William "Bill" Yosses, it was covered entirely in white chocolate, making it not only quite realistic but also the heaviest gingerbread house yet! And, of course, on the rooftop were the Bush pets. In addition to this masterpiece, Chef Yosses and his assistants had to keep the dessert table laden with treats. "During the holidays we have to use the White House bowling alley for extra space," he noted.

★ ABOVE ★

President Bush completes a cookie in the Vermeil Room, where the pastry team has temporarily set up shop while getting ready for the holiday parties at 1600 Pennsylvania Avenue. Executive Pastry Chef Yosses said, "It was a fun, memorable moment for everyone when the President came in."

★ OPPOSITE TOP ★

Executive Chef Cris Comerford during the press preview detailing the holiday menu. Over 10,000 handmade tamales and 1,000 pounds of shrimp were served.

★ OPPOSITE BOTTOM ★

The Monroe plateau in all its glory of gold was perfect for Mrs. Bush's theme, "Holiday in the National Parks," which used the color of gold as a unifying element.

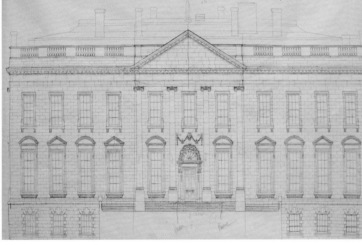

Executive Pastry Chef Bill Yosses (middle) and assistants Chef Chris Phillips and Chef Susie Morrison assemble the white chocolate White House, China Room.

Prepared by the White House engineers, this blueprint was made to ensure that the gingerbread house was accurately built to scale of the actual White House.

The white chocolate gingerbread house featured a rooftop sleigh with Barney and Miss Beazley, and even a chocolate "mousse."

The 2007 edition of the Barney Cam reinforced the season's theme, weaving a plot in which Barney dreams of himself and Miss Beazley as Junior Park Rangers. British Prime Minister Tony Blair even makes a cameo appearance, congratulating the two Scotties on their achievement and quipping, "It's always good to see the Scots doing well." The video closes with President Bush reminding Barney that the grounds of the White House are a national park.

This theme was reiterated in the East Wing reception area, where wall panels displayed photographs of former presidents and their families celebrating the holidays at the White House and visiting other national parks.

2008

A Red, White and Blue Christmas

WITH THE INAUGURATION OF A new president just around the corner, a patriotic red, white and blue décor was a fitting way for the Bushes to celebrate their final Christmas at 1600 Pennsylvania Avenue. At last it was time for a theme that Mrs. Bush had often considered. It was also a theme that Americans had suggested in letters to the White House. "For as long as I've been Mrs. Bush's chief of staff, she's mentioned this red-white-and-blue idea," said Anita McBride. "But then other great ideas would always come up. This finally seemed like the right year for it."

The holiday booklet described the significance of this theme: "The colors of Old Glory have come to represent the ideals Americans hold dear. Red symbolizes bravery, white represents purity, and blue signifies perseverance and justice."

Many decorations were recycled from previous seasons. For the East Wing entrance, the White House carpenters and florists transformed the towering nutcracker statues from 2006 into two Uncle Sams, each holding an American flag and dressed in a patriotic suit of red, white and blue. Inside, in the East Garden Room, a life-size figure of Santa, suited in the stars and stripes of the American flag, sat in the familiar red sleigh filled with presents.

The replicas of former presidents' homes from 2001 were displayed on tables in the Ground Floor Corridor and the East Garden Room, while ornaments from that year's Blue Room fir adorned the tree in the East Reception Room. Clusters of shiny

★ OPPOSITE ★

The official 2008 White House tree trimmed with ornaments from across the country.

★ BELOW ★

Uncle Sam, 13 feet tall, greets guests outside the entrance to the East Wing.

red glass balls, reminiscent of 2006, accented the mantel garland in the Diplomatic Reception Room.

More patriotic symbols and the colors of Old Glory filled the State Floor. Garlands draping the arches, door frames, mantels, and presidential portraits were entwined with red and blue glass beads as well as red, white and blue ribbon printed with an American flag design.

In the East Room two fourteen-foot trees glistened with shiny red, silver and blue balls and stars. Garland of greenery with red and blue beads and silver stars draped all four mantels and a

★ ABOVE ★

The State Dining Room, trimmed for Mrs. Bush's final holiday theme.

★ OPPOSITE TOP ★

A mantel trimmed in snow, pinecones, and red, white and blue glass ornaments in the East Room.

★ OPPOSITE BOTTOM ★

The snow-filled Cross Hall trimmed in keeping with the theme "A Red, White and Blue Christmas."

★ ABOVE ★

First Lady Laura Bush looks at the ornaments for the Blue Room tree along with volunteers.

★ LEFT ★

Giovanna McBride, daughter of the First Lady's Chief of Staff, Anita McBride, helps the summer interns mail out uniform ornaments to all members of Congress.

★ OPPOSITE ★

Close-ups of the 2008 Christmas ornaments honoring the White House Christmas theme, "A Red, White and Blue Christmas." Senator Kay Bailey Hutchison's ornament was painted by Texas legend James Avery. California Congressman Duncan Hunter selected artist Mark Martensen to represent his district. Maryland's Senator Ben Cardin selected artist Nina Orlando. South Dakota Congresswoman Stephanie Sandlin selected artist Carol Green. South Carolina's Congressman Henry Brown selected artist Carol Gardener. Kentucky Congressman Ed Whitfield selected artisan Maggie Smith, who depicted Lewis and Clark on the ornament for her district.

pair of vermeil urns on each mantel held a burst of red tulips. The majestic centerpiece for the table was a series of topiaries, each in a hand-painted drum of red, white and blue with shiny red and silver balls clustered at the base.

The State Dining Room was likewise full of patriotic cheer. Miniature silver flutes, toy drums, and little drummer boys were tucked into the garland draped over Lincoln's portrait, and more flutes, toy drums, and red bows decorated the sconces. As in the East Room, the centerpiece consisted of topiaries anchored in red drums. The highlight of the room, as always, was the magnificent gingerbread house, a model of the south side of the mansion. At

★ ABOVE ★

The annual gingerbread house was a replica of the White House's North Portico. Taking more than two months to make, the all-gingerbread foundation (125 pounds of gingerbread in all) was completely covered by more than 350 pounds of white chocolate, and was the heaviest ever to be made.

★ OPPOSITE TOP ★

Cookies fashioned after the Old Guard Fife and Drum Corps were incorporated in honor of Mrs. Bush's holiday theme.

★ OPPOSITE BOTTOM ★

Replicas of the Bush family pets Barney, Miss Beazley, and India "Willie" were placed in a sleigh on the roof of the white chocolate gingerbread house.

Jolly Saint Nick in his sleigh with toys, including a teddy bear in honor of President Theodore Roosevelt, greeted visitors in the East Garden Room. Silver eagles, carved by Texas craftsmen, held snow-filled wreaths lining the East Colonnade.

★ RIGHT ★

First Lady Laura Bush with Chief of Staff Anita McBride going over the final details of the holiday decor.

★ OPPOSITE TOP ★

A striped poinsettia tree in the Palm Room.

★ OPPOSITE BOTTOM ★

The replicas of the presidential homes from 2001 were placed on pier tables throughout the Ground Floor Corridor. Two red drums flank the doors at the opening to the Palm Room.

★ LEFT ★

A special "Harley Davidson" Christmas tree in the office of the Chief of Staff to the President, Josh Bolten.

★ OPPOSITE TOP ★

The President's Christmas tree in the Oval Office, filled with red, white and blue gingerbread cookies and some of the ornaments from the previous year's "Holiday in the National Parks" Blue Room tree.

★ OPPOSITE BOTTOM ★

A close-up of ornaments on the President's Oval Office tree.

the front steps were miniature figures of a fife and drum corps from the era of the American Revolution.

The Green Room shone with elegant silver decor. Two topiaries made with silver balls flanked the sofa, and the mantel's garland was laden with silver eagles and stars. Silver urns were filled with vibrant red roses. In the Red Room, the garland that festooned the mantel was covered in glittering red, blue and silver bells and large silver stars. Arrangements of red roses and red

poinsettias graced side tables.

The official tree in the Blue Room was a Fraser fir, trimmed with ornaments made by artists from all over the United States. Mrs. Bush's staff sent a large silver ball to all the 535 members of Congress, along with a request to choose a local artist to embellish the holiday ball. The result was 369 magnificent ornaments that ran the gamut in terms of styles and artistic media. Paint, fabric, beading, and other materials were used to depict the key features

of every region, such as local foods, historic buildings, natural re-
sources, or famous personages. According to the First Lady's Chief
of Staff, Anita McBride, it was important to Mrs. Bush that every
state and congressional district be represented on the tree. "The
idea was so wonderfully characteristic of Mrs. Bush and showed
just how wide her arms reach in embracing everybody and the
entire country," said Mrs. McBride.

★ ABOVE ★

The Marine Band in their festive red coats in the Grand Foyer, 2008.

★ OPPOSITE ★

*The First Family in the Red Room. From left to right: Henry Hager, Jenna Bush Hager,
President Bush with Barney, Mrs. Bush with Miss Beazley, and Barbara Bush with First
Cat India "Willie."*

During her years in the White House, Mrs. Bush selected many wonderful holiday themes, carefully chosen from a store of imaginative ideas that reflected her experience as a librarian. At a time when access to the People's House became restricted, she reached out to share it in other ways. The holiday seasons under her tenure will also be remembered for the creation of the wildly successful Barney Cam as well as the tradition of hosting Hanukkah celebrations with a kosher kitchen. Jeanne L. Phillips, former Ambassador and friend of First Lady Laura Bush, may have characterized it best: "Christmases at The White House with Laura Bush will be remembered for their imagination, their beauty, their whimsy and most of all, their classic elegance that will stand the test of time. For Mrs. Bush, Christmas at the White House was intended to be a magical experience for her guests and, in fact, it always was."

At her last press preview, the First Lady described her fond feelings for the White House: "It's been a privilege to live here and to be steward of all the fabulous things that are in this house: the beautiful art, the historical furniture, the beautiful building itself."

"Peace on earth, good will to men,"

the angels said. "Peace on earth, good will to men,"

may we all repeat to our children and those we love,

in villages and cities, this Christmas Eve,

wherever men may gather.

— Jacqueline Kennedy

NATIONAL CHRISTMAS TREE ASSOCIATION GRAND CHAMPIONS

YEAR	SPECIES	STATE	GROWER
1966	Balsam Fir	Wisconsin	Howard Pierce
1967	Blue Spruce	Ohio	Gordon Anderson
1968	White Pine	Indiana	Don Goodwin
1969	Blue Spruce	Ohio	Roy R. Pierce
1970	White Spruce	Wisconsin	Calvin J. Frelk
1971	Fraser Fir	North Carolina	Kermit Johnson
1972	Noble Fir	Washington	Alvin Hofert
1973	Fraser Fir	North Carolina	Homer and Bruner Sides
1974	Concolor Fir	Michigan	Ed Cole
1975	Douglas Fir	New York	Guy Cockburn
1976	Balsam Fir	Wisconsin	Ken Guenter
1977	Noble Fir	Washington	Alvin Hofert
1978	Veitch Fir	New York	Guy Cockburn
1979	Douglas Fir	West Virginia	Eric and Gloria Sundback
1980	Douglas Fir	Indiana	Harry Eby
1981	Douglas Fir	Pennsylvania	Eric and Gloria Sundback
1982	Fraser Fir	North Carolina	Hal and Sarah Johnson
1983	Noble Fir	Washington	Ken Scholz
1984	Fraser Fir	North Carolina	Hal and Sarah Johnson
1985	Blue Spruce	Michigan	Stephen Vander Weide
1986	Fraser Fir	Washington	Ron and Dorothy Palmer, Charles and Dorothy Burton
1987	Fraser Fir	West Virginia	Eric and Gloria Sundback
1988	Balsam Fir	Wisconsin	Irv and Alyce Daggett
1989	Fraser Fir	Pennsylvania	Duane, Meade, and Bradley Berkey
1990	Fraser Fir	North Carolina	R. Bruce and Michael Lacey
1991	Noble Fir	Oregon	Gary and Audrey Sander
1992	Grand Fir	Oregon	Bob Kintigh
1993	Fraser Fir	North Carolina	Wayne Ayers
1994	Blue Spruce	Missouri	Lynn and Myron Schmidt
1995	Fraser Fir	North Carolina	Ron Hudler and Danny Dollar
1996	Blue Spruce	Ohio	Kenneth Scheetz
1997	Fraser Fir	North Carolina	Sanford Fishel
1998	Balsam Fir	Wisconsin	James and Diane Chapman
1999	Noble Fir	Washington	Ed and Cindy Hedlund
2000	Douglas Fir	Pennsylvania	Paul and Sharon Shealer
2001	Concolor Fir	Pennsylvania	Janice, Darryl, and Aimee Bowersox
2002	Noble Fir	Washington	Ed and Cindy Hedlund
2003	Fraser Fir	Wisconsin	Jim and Diane Chapman
2004	Noble Fir	Washington	John and Carol Tillman
2005	Fraser Fir	North Carolina	Earl, Buddy, and Betsy Deal
2006	Douglas Fir	Pennsylvania	Francis Botek
2007	Fraser Fir	North Carolina	Joe Freeman
2008	Fraser Fir	North Carolina	Jessie Davis and Russell Estes

ACKNOWLEDGMENTS

This book would never have been put together were it not for my amazing husband, Bryan.
I am most grateful for his love and support.

And to my wonderful parents Sandy and Mike Boswell, who taught me that I could do anything - thank you!

I am also thankful to the following First Ladies for their enthusiasm and participation in this book:

First Lady Barbara Bush
First Lady Laura Bush
First Lady Rosalynn Carter
First Lady Hillary Clinton
First Lady Betty Ford
First Lady Nancy Reagan

In addition, thank you to Letitia Baldrige, Tricia Nixon Cox, and Lynda Johnson Robb
for their heartfelt reflections of the Kennedy, Nixon, and Johnson years.

Christmas at the White House would never have been completed (or started) without the following individuals. I am
appreciative of their tireless dedication to the project, and most importantly, for their friendship.

Paul Dickerson
Dan Hanson
Nancy Ann Hunt
Anita McBride
Roland Mesnier
Eric O'Keefe
Jeanne L. Phillips
Wren Powell
Kimberlee Rawson
Jodie Steck

This book is the result of the help of so many kind individuals
for which I am grateful.

Bess Abell
Amanda Aulds
Andi Ball
Jack Bangs
John Boop
Dee Boswell
George Bush Presidential Library, Mary Finch, and Bonnie Burlbaw
The Office of First Lady Laura Bush
Jimmy Carter Presidential Library, Polly Nodine, Sara Saunders

William J. Clinton Presidential Library, John Keller
Colonial Williamsburg, Jan Gillian
Cris Comerford
Laurie Firestone
Gerald R. Ford Presidential Library and Museum,
James W. Draper, Kenneth G. Hafeli, Nancy E. Mirshah
Debbie Francis
Sally Geymuller
Shannon Graham
The Harmon Family and Meadow Acres Farm
Faye Haskins, DC Public Library
The Rutherford B. Hayes Presidential Center, Nancy Kleinhenz
Hyla Hurley
Lyndon Baines Johnson Presidential Library and Museum,
Anne Wheeler, Morgan Blue, Kristen Lambert
John F. Kennedy Presidential Library and Museum,
Colleen A. Cooney, Ethan Hawkley, Keiko Makishima
Cathie Lechareas
Alex Leckerling
Capricia Marshall
Mark Mahorsky
Sara McIntosh
Melissa Montgomery
Chris Mulder
Nancy Myers
The National Christmas Tree Growers Association, Rick Dungey
The National Needle Arts Association, Patty Parrish
Louis Nichole
The Olmsted Family
Olmsted-Kirk Paper
Ronald Reagan Presidential Foundation and Library, Kimberlee Lico
William Seale
Rebecca Sherman
Society of Decorative Painters, Cheryl Capps, Teri Mott
Billye Turner
Tish Visinsky
Charity Wallace
The White House Historical Association,
William Bushong, Hillary Crehan, Maria Downs, Brenda Fike
The White House, Office of the Curator, Lydia Tederick
Lucy Winchester
Pat and Bubba Wood
Bill Yosses

PHOTOGRAPHY CREDITS

Courtesy of the Albright-Knox Art Gallery, Buffalo, New York, Photo by Tom Loonan:
Page 29

AP Photo, Henry Burroughs:
Page 58

AP Photo by Ron Edmonds:
Page 265

Courtesy of the Brandywine River Museum:
Page 161

George Bush Presidential Library and Museum:
Pages 111, 192, 194, 195, 197, 198, 199, 200, 201, 202, 203, 204, 205, 206, 209, 210, 211, 212, 213, 214, 215, 216, 217, 219, 220, 221

Courtesy of the George W. Bush Presidential Library, photos by Joyce N. Boghosian:
Pages 53, 54, 369, 371, 376, 377

Courtesy of the George W. Bush Presidential Library, photos by David Bohrer:
Pages 30, 190

Courtesy of the George W. Bush Presidential Library, photos by Shealah Craighead: Pages 8, 56, 85, 86, 114, 282, 284, 337, 338, 339, 340, 341, 342, 343, 344, 345, 346, 347, 348, 350, 351, 352, 353, 354-355, 357, 359, 363, 364, 365, 366, 367, 368, 370, 372, 374, 375, 378, 379, 380, 381, 382, 383

Courtesy of the George W. Bush Presidential Library, photos by Eric Draper:
Pages 309, 310, 336

Courtesy of the George W. Bush Presidential Library, photos by Chris Greenberg:
Pages 112, 360, 361, 362, 367, 371, 373, 375

Courtesy of the George W. Bush Presidential Library, photos by Tina Hager: Pages 289, 290, 291, 292, 293, 295, 298, 299, 301, 302, 303, 304, 305, 306, 307, 308-309, 332-333

Courtesy of the George W. Bush Presidential Library, photos by Hewitt
Page 349

Courtesy of the George W. Bush Presidential Library, photos by Moreen Ishikawa:
Pages 14, 300

Courtesy of the George W. Bush Presidential Library, photo by Paul Morse:
Page 88

Courtesy of the George W. Bush Presidential Library, photos by Susan Sterner:
Pages 112, 286, 287, 288, 294, 296, 297, 307, 311, 312, 314, 315, 316, 317, 318, 319, 320, 321, 322, 324, 325, 326, 327, 328-329, 331, 334, 335

Jimmy Carter Library, photo by Mary Anne Fackelman:
Page 116

Jimmy Carter Library, photos by Bill Fitz-Patrick:
Pages 118, 120, 121, 122, 123, 125, 130, 131, 132, 133, 134

Jimmy Carter Library, photo by Jack Kightlinger:
Page 124

Jimmy Carter Library, photos by Karl Schumacher:
Pages 126, 127, 128, 129

William J. Clinton Presidential Library, photos by Ralph Alswang:
Pages 239, 249, 258, 261, 262, 263, 270

William J. Clinton Presidential Library, photos by Sharon Farmer:
Pages 228, 246, 259, 271, 272, 274, 277

William J. Clinton Presidential Library, photos by Barbara Kinney:
Pages 235, 248

William J. Clinton Presidential Library, photos by Bob McNeely:
Pages 241, 244

William J. Clinton Presidential Library, photos by David Scull:
Pages 268, 276

Condé Nest Publications, photo by Horst/House and Garden, ©1967:
Page 42

Courtesy of Paul Dickerson:
Page 138

Courtesy of Gerald R. Ford Library:
Page 93

Gerald R. Ford Library, photos by Bill Fitz-Patrick:
Pages 99, 100, 103, 108

Gerald R. Ford Library, photos by Karl Schumacher:
Pages 90, 92, 94, 95, 97, 102, 103, 104, 105, 106, 107, 109

Courtesy of Scottie Foster:
Page 323

Courtesy of Jenalee Frazier:
Page 231

Courtesy of Sue Harmon:
Page 55

Courtesy of Rutherford B. Hayes Presidential Center:
Page 67

Courtesy of the Herbert Hoover Presidential Library-Museum:
Page 70

Courtesy of Hyla Hurley:
Pages 207, 208, 211, 244, 247, 273, 275

NOTES

JACQUELINE KENNEDY

1961

19   the usual site: Office of the Curator, The White House, e-mail communication, Mar. 18, 2009.

20   The tree was decorated by: Mitchell Owens, "Paul Leonard Dies at 70; Decorated Famed Interiors," *New York Times,* Nov. 3, 2002.

20   Mrs. Mellon was a longtime friend: She also redesigned the Rose Garden and the East Garden, which was dedicated as the Jacqueline Kennedy Garden by Lady Bird Johnson in 1965. The famous life portrait of Thomas Jefferson by Rembrandt Peale was given to the White House by the Mellons. The painting hangs in the Blue Room.

20   the tinsel had not yet been draped: W. B. Ragsdale Jr., "Christmas Excitement for Caroline," *Indiana Evening Gazette,* Dec. 14, 1961.

20   "were bought this year": Marie Smith, "Christmas Magic Comes to White House," *Washington Post,* Dec. 14, 1961; Maxine Cheshire, "Costly White House Ornaments," *Washington Post,* Dec. 15, 1974. It is unknown which, if any, decorations remained with the White House. Decorations given to Mrs. Kennedy by the Mellons left the White House with her in 1963. A very few, such as two raffia birds, are housed at the John F. Kennedy Presidential Library but are not on display.

20   Ten other trees: Ibid.

21   There were also trees upstairs: Letitia Baldrige, e-mail communication, Mar. 26, 2009.

21   To the White House grounds superintendent: Dennis Tompkins and Pam Helmsing, "Behind the Scenes of the White House Christmas Trees," *American Christmas Tree Journal,* Jan. 2002, pp. 30–32.

21   "in the manner of an American country home": Quoted in Smith, "Christmas Magic Comes to White House."

21   "less colorful and lavish": Ibid.

21   the last Eisenhower Christmas: In 1960 the State Floor was decorated with more than a dozen trees of varying sizes, all trimmed with "tinsel, baubles and lights." "Eisenhowers Host Staff, Employees at White House," *Daily Capital News* (Jefferson City, Mo.), Dec. 23, 1960.

21   instituted a third type of party: "Christmas with the Kennedys," *Redbook* 120 (Dec. 1962): 54.

1962

23   grown in New England: Office of the Curator, The White House, e-mail communication, Mar. 18, 2009.

23   an exhibit of figures: Mrs. Howard had exhibited some of her collection as a Christmas centerpiece at Tiffany & Company in New York while Letitia Baldrige was working there as public relations director. Noelle Mercanton, "Table Settings by Leading Hostesses Here Are on Exhibition," *New York Times,* Oct. 24, 1958.

23   "Since thousands go through": Letitia Baldrige to Mrs. Howell H. Howard, Oct. 1, 1962, White House Social Files, Box 120, Christmas Decorations, John F. Kennedy Presidential Library.

24   "The President and I": Jacqueline Kennedy to Mrs. Howell H. Howard, Dec. 14, 1962, White House Social Files, Box 120, Christmas Party Only, Kennedy Library.

24   unsent Christmas card: Mary Evans Seeley, *Season's Greetings from the White House: The Collection of Presidential Christmas Cards, Messages and Gifts* (Tampa, Fla.: A Presidential Christmas, 2007), p. 97. Some thirty of the cards were signed but were not discovered until 1985; this is considered the rarest of the official White House Christmas cards.

26   "An ancient tale tells us": Jacqueline Kennedy, "A Christmas Message," *Look* 27, no. 27 (Dec. 31, 1963): 14. "The Story of the Presidents at Christmas" was written by Fletcher Knebel.

THE WHITE HOUSE CRÈCHE (1962–1965)

28   This was arranged: Grace (Mrs. Calvin) Coolidge, "What Christmas Means to Me," *Hartford Courant,* Dec. 21, 1930.

28   she arranged a manger scene: "Yuletide Joys in Washington," *Prescott Evening Courier,* Dec. 20, 1929.

28   on an electrically lighted miniature stage: "Crèche for White House Tree," *New York Times,* Dec. 13, 1955.

28   a Nativity scene in three sections: "Eisenhowers Host Staff, Employes [*sic*] at White House," *Daily Capital News* (Jefferson City, Mo.), Dec. 23, 1960.

28   a tradition that reached its pinnacle: Linn Howard and Mary Jane Pool, *The Angel Tree: A Christmas Celebration* (New York: Harry N. Abrams, 1993), p. 59.

28   sculpted of terra cotta and polychromed: Ibid., p. 66.

29   a three-foot-high table: "The White House Crèche," *Chicago Tribune,* Dec. 15, 1963; "The Crèche in the White House," *Ladies Home Journal* 83 (Dec. 1966): 98–99; Marie Smith, "White House Is Sparkling in Yule Décor," *Washington Post,* Dec. 13, 1962.

29   white azaleas, roses, and carnations: Daisy Cleland, "First Lady and the Children Will Leave for Florida," *Washington Star,* Dec. 13, 1962.

29   In 1972, in memory of her friend: Joe Gerace, Albright-Knox Art Gallery, personal communication, Mar. 11, 2009. By 1964 Mrs. Howard had already donated most of her crèche collection to the Metropolitan Museum of Art in New York, where some 150 figures are on view each year during the holiday season in the museum's Medieval Sculpture Hall.

LADY BIRD JOHNSON

1963

35   the black mourning crepe: Seeley, *Season's Greetings,* p. 104.

35   Untrimmed trees: Marjorie Hunter, "Johnsons to Spend Christmas at Ranch in Texas," *New York Times,* Dec. 19, 1963.

35   Having learned of Mrs. Kennedy's plans: "The White House Creche," *Chicago Tribune,* Dec. 15, 1963.

35   With fires burning: Isabelle Shelton, "President Is a Genial Host," *Washington Star,* Dec. 24, 1963.

35   When the rooms began to fill: Isabelle Shelton, interview by Anne Ritchie, Nov. 11, 1992, Washington, D.C. *Women in Journalism,* WPCF Oral History Project (Washington, D.C.: Washington Press Club Foundation, 1993).

35   "I walked the well-lit hall": Quoted in Jane Jarboe Russell, *Lady Bird: A Biography of Mrs. Johnson* (Lanham, Md.: Taylor Trade Publishing, 2004), p. 235.

1964

37   "Christmas for us": Lady Bird Johnson, "Christmas Story," typescript, final draft for Christmas issue of *Redbook,* p. 2, photocopy, author's files.

37   In faithfulness to the style: Bell Abell, personal communication, Feb. 2009.

37   Dan Arje: "Dan Arje, 69, Dies; Fashion Display Artist," *New York Times,* Mar. 24, 1993.

37   contributed his time: Bonwit Teller billed the White House for materials used in the decorations, which amounted to "a couple of hundred dollars." Maxine Cheshire, "Costly White House Ornaments," *Washington Post,* Dec. 15, 1974.

37   3,000 small ornaments: "White House Decorations Up; Season's First Party Today," *New York Times,* Dec. 16, 1964.

37   960 bee lights: "Bee lights" are mentioned frequently in press releases of the 1960s and 1970s; this early term for miniature lights was common in the window display industry. The tiny glass hand-blown bulbs were sharply pointed at the end, like a bee's stinger. They were also called "wheat lights" because they came from the manufacturer bundled like a shock of wheat, with all of the bulbs at one end fanning out. First imported from Italy and then Japan, miniature lights were introduced to U.S. consumers in the mid-1950s and marketed as "fairy," "midget," and "firefly" lights. Thanks to Michael Jekot and the National Association of Display Industries for this information.

37   figures made from burned wood: Daisy Cleland, "Christmas Comes to White House," *Washington Star,* Dec. 16, 1964.

37 When Mr. Arje purchased: Transcript of Message Left by Bess Abell about Gingerbread Cookies on the White House Christmas Tree, Oct. 23, 2000, LBJ Library.

37 gingerbread cookies in the shape of camels: The cookies were made by Vera Reis of New York. Smith, "Christmas Radiance at the White House," p. 192.

38 added to the lower branches: Lynda J. Robb, personal communication, Feb. 11, 2009.

38 "such a hit with children": Bess Abell to Mrs. Vera Ries, Oct. 29, 1965, Social Files, Box 1751, LJB Library. The purpose of Mrs. Abell's letter was to request another batch of cookies for the 1965. Mrs. Ries made a batch each subsequent year of the Johnson administration. Transcript of Message Left by Bess Abell about Gingerbread Cookies.

39 "a touch of tradition": Ellen Kay Blunt, "White House Dons Fiesta Yule Air," *Washington Post,* Dec. 17, 1964.

39 Bowls of holly: Cleland, "Christmas Comes to White House."

1965

41 Grown in West Virginia: West Virginia was the home state of L. Walter Fix, president of the National Christmas Tree Growers' Association. Marie Smith, "Prize Fir Hits Yule Big Time," *Washington Post,* Dec. 10, 1966.

41 3,000 small ornaments: Office of the Press Secretary to Mrs. Johnson, "Christmas Decorations at the White House," press release, Dec. 14, 1965, LBJ Library; "Yule Lights Glow," *Washington Post,* Dec. 14, 1965.

41 Della Robbia garland: Della Robbia is a type of floral design that combines flowers, fruits, greenery, and often ribbons. The design is copied from patterns of fruit and flower garlands created in the fifteenth century by the della Robbias, a family of sculptors in Florence, Italy.

1966

43 After a holiday party: Scottie Fitzgerald Smith, "Christmas Radiance at the White House," *House and Garden* 132, no. 6 (Dec. 1967): 192.

43 twenty-foot, 600-pound balsam fir: Howard Pierce, "Diary of a Trip to the White House," *American Christmas Tree Journal,* Feb. 1967, p. 33.

44 they were given a tour: Smith, "Prize Fir Hits Yule Big Time."

44 "I doubt that the Blue Room": Pierce, "Diary of a Trip to the White House," p. 33.

44 a new, contemporary-style crèche: Office of the Press Secretary to Mrs. Johnson, "Facts on Christmas Decorations at the White House," press release, Dec. 12, 1966, LBJ Library. Thanks to Karol Bartlett, Special Collections Librarian, Morse Institute Library, Natick, Massachusetts, for providing Katherine M. (Mrs. Harold B.) Bryant's full name.

44 Gothic arches: Frances Lide, "New Crèche Is Contemporary: Nativity Scene Dominates East Room Christmas Decorations," *Washington Star,* Dec. 12, 1966.

45 "Sister" Parish and Albert Hadley: Born Dorothy May Kinnicutt, Sister Parish (Mrs. Henry Parish II) is credited with originating American country style in the 1960s. She served as a consultant to Jacqueline Kennedy in the redecoration of the White House and was also a member of the committee that helped Mrs. Kennedy furnish the White House with authentic period pieces.

In 1962 she and Albert Hadley established the interior decorating firm Parish-Hadley Associates in New York. Mrs. Kennedy's use of a leading society decorator to revamp the White House set a precedent that was followed by Nancy Reagan and Barbara Bush, who hired Ted Graber of Hollywood and Mark Hampton of New York, respectively, to redecorate the private quarters. Eric Pace, "Sister Parish, Grande Dame of American Interior Decorating, Is Dead at 84," *New York Times,* Sept. 10, 1994; Elaine Rice Bachmann, "Circa 1961: The Kennedy White House Interiors," *White House History,* no. 14 (Winter 2004): 16.

45 The Grand Foyer featured: Office of the Press Secretary to Mrs. Johnson, "Facts on Christmas Decorations at the White House."

1967

47 Ohio blue spruce: Office of the Press Secretary to Mrs. Johnson, "Fact Sheet on Christmas Decorations," press release, Dec. 12, 1967, LBJ Library.

47 "This is a lovely Christmas gift": Quoted in Isabelle Shelton, "Johnsons Hail Gift of Crèche," *Washington Star,* Dec. 16, 1967.

47 ". . . we opened presents": Mrs. Lyndon B. Johnson, "For McCall's Christmas Issue," typescript, 1968, p. 1, LBJ Library. Published as "Christmas Memories from the White House," *McCall's,* vol. 96 (Dec. 1968): 80–81.

1968

49 The 5,000 other ornaments: "Yule Tree Lighted," *Daily Oklahoman,* Dec. 17, 1968.

49 "They are for good luck": Richard Lebherz, "At Christmastime The White House," *The Post* (Frederick, Md.), Dec. 21, 1968.

49 garlands of pine boughs: Isabelle Shelton, "The White House Is Decked with Christmas" *Washington Star,* Dec. 17, 1968.

49 A six-foot reproduction: Lebherz, "At Christmastime The White House."

50 "In the case of the large tree": Ibid.

51 For her birthday: Lynda J. Robb, e-mail communication, Jan. 14, 2009.

THE OFFICIAL WHITE HOUSE CHRISTMAS TREE

52 purchased or donated: Office of the Curator, The White House, e-mail communication, Mar. 18, 2009. In 1940, for example, the twenty-foot tree in the East Room was harvested in northern Michigan and given to the Roosevelts by the Fort Brady Civilian Conservation Corps. Drew Pearson and Robert S. Allen, "White House Christmas Tree Now Lighted Electrically," *St. Petersburg Times,* Dec. 25, 1940.

52 the Chequamegon National Forest: "News from Northern Counties: News Briefs," *Capital Times* (Madison, Wis.), Dec. 19, 1966. Howard Pierce later wrote, "I wish I could believe the pleasant fabrication I've read repeatedly that I raised the tree (in one instance that I had sheared it six times), and even that it was the identical tree that won the contest!" Howard Pierce, "Diary of a Trip to the White House," *American Christmas Tree Journal,* Feb. 1967, p. 33. Little did he realize the importance this contest would assume in the future. According to his daughter, Cindy Hanson, "He was bemoaning the fact that it was his busiest time of year to have to deliver that tree." "The First in a First-Class Tradition," *American Christmas Tree Journal* 49, no. 5 (Oct. 2005): 18.

52 the front yard of another Mayville resident: Office of the Press Secretary to Mrs. Ford, press release, Dec. 3, 1974, Sheila Weidenfeld Files, Box 35, Christmas 1974—White House Tree, Ford Library; Mardee Cole, personal communication, Mar. 20, 2009.

52 a Michigan congressman's aide: "White House Christmas Tree Shakes Off Brush with Auto," *Los Angeles Times,* Dec. 6, 1974.

52 bought a twenty-one-foot balsam fir: "White House Tree Delivered," *Anderson (Ind.) Herald,* Dec. 5, 1976.

52 specific requirements: Rick Dungey, National Christmas Tree Association, e-mail communication, Mar. 9, 2009.

52 a full two feet: James F. Clarity and Warren Weaver, "Briefing: Jellybean Scoops," *New York Times,* Dec. 27, 1984.

55 "Winning Grand Champion status": Dungey, e-mail communication, Mar. 9, 2009.

55 White House staffers: They included Irvin Williams, White House chief horticulturist; Mrs. Johnson's press secretary, Liz Carpenter; and staffers Marta Ross and Kristin Anderson.

55 Mrs. Ford was busy: "White House Tree Delivered"; Jack Bangs, personal communication, Mar. 4, 2009.

55 followed the tree: "White House Trees through the Years," *American Christmas Tree Journal* 49, no. 5 (Oct. 2005): 19.

55 Its presentation to the first lady: In years past, the tree was delivered on the first Wednesday or Thursday of December. Now delivery typically occurs on the first Monday after Thanksgiving. But this varies according to the first lady's schedule and the start of holiday parties. Rick Dungey, National Christmas Tree Association, e-mail communication, Apr. 27, 2009.

55 consists of a drum: Tompkins and Helmsing, "Behind the Scenes of the White House Christmas Trees."

55 holds about fifteen gallons: Office of the Curator, The White House, e-mail communication, May 14, 2009.

PATRICIA NIXON

61 "You can't overdo": Quoted in Lucia Mouat, "A Special Aura in U.S. Capital," *Christian Science Monitor,* Dec. 20, 1969.

61 "Few presidential couples": "Christmas at the Nixons'," *Time,* Dec. 26, 1969, p. 6.

61 which increased from one-third: Margaret Truman, *First Ladies* (New York: Random House, 1995), p. 198.

1969

61 "so people going by": Quoted in Trude Feldman, "Pat Nixon Is Ready for Christmas in 1971," *Van Nuys News,* Dec. 29, 1970.

61 Working with the First Lady: Marie Smith, "White House Christmas Décor Represents All States in Union," *Charleston Gazette,* Dec. 16, 1969.

61 "an American flower Christmas tree": "White House Glitters for Christmas and Reunion," *New York Times,* Dec. 13, 1971.

61 "People like to walk around": Quoted in "Christmas at the White House: Mrs. Richard Nixon Talks about the Decorations and the Celebrations," *House and Garden,* Dec. 1971, p. 63.

61 Saks contributed Mr. Callahan's time: Cheshire, "Costly White House Ornaments."

61 Two matching gold wall sconces: Marie Smith,

"White House Glitters for Christmas," *Des Moines Register,* Dec. 19, 1969. Mrs. Kennedy hung portraits of Daniel Webster and Martin Van Buren where the sconces had been mounted on the wall.

62 Impressed by the rich, colorful décor: Isabelle Shelton, "Christmas Finery Fills White House with Color Profusion," *Washington Star,* Dec. 16, 1969.

62 for the first time in more than twenty-five years: Ibid.

65 "splendid and sophisticated" ornaments: Marian Burros, "Chatty Visit with the First Lady," *Washington Star,* Dec. 14, 1969.

65 In keeping with another Nixon tradition: Feldman, "Pat Nixon Is Ready for Christmas."

65 "so filled with history": Quoted in "White House Aglow with Yule Finery," *Los Angeles Times,* Dec. 15, 1970.

1970

69 "we have to choose things": Quoted in "Christmas at the White House: Mrs. Richard Nixon Talks about the Decorations and the Celebrations," *House and Garden* 140 (Dec. 1971): 64.

70 his executive secretary's son: George Akerson Jr., one of George Akerson's three sons, loaned the fire engine to the White House for exhibit, then donated it to the Hoover Presidential Library in January of 1971. His brothers, Charles and Fred, also gave the library their fire engines, which were slightly different models. It is presumed that all ten children received one of these toys from President Hoover at the 1930 staff party, but this has never been confirmed. Marcus E. Eckhardt, Assistant Curator, Herbert Hoover Presidential Library and Museum, e-mail communication, May 5, 2009.

71 At the request of her parents: Nancy Kleinhenz, Rutherford B. Hayes Presidential Center, e-mail communication, Feb. 27, 2009.

1971

73 designed the flower arrangements: J. Liddon Pennock's first project for the Nixon White House was the creation of the lighted outdoor pavilion for the outdoor dinner dance hosted by Julie Eisenhower and Tricia Nixon during the visit of Prince Charles and Princess Anne of Great Britain in July of 1970. Maxine Cheshire, "Pat Nixon Vetoes 'Nylon Stockings' on New Drapes," *Anderson (Ind.) Daily Bulletin,* Dec. 23, 1971.

73 they were duplicates: Isabelle Shelton, "Firefly Lights and Velvet Cardinals," *Washington Star,* Dec. 14, 1971.

73 Designed by Helen Murat: A Chicago native and a dress designer, Helen Murat founded the House of Murat, which specialized in musical Christmas ornaments. Neiman Marcus, Lord & Taylor, Saks Fifth Avenue, and Macy's were among her customers. "Helen Mura, 96, Dress Designer, Made White House Ornaments," *Chicago Tribune,* Apr. 16, 2003.

73 It was Mrs. Nixon's specific request: Norma Schuelke, "Look What's on the White House Christmas Tree: Florida—Along with the Other 49 States," *Palm Beach Times,* Nov. 26, 1971.

74 to create a bell shape: Shelton, "Firefly Lights and Velvet Cardinals."

1972

77 she had always liked Della Robbia wreaths: Isabelle Shelton, "White House Never So Beautiful," *Washington Star,* Dec. 12, 1972. Mrs. Nixon purchased her gift wreaths from Boys Republic in California.

The wreath program got its start in 1923, and the teens continue to make the wreaths, which have numbered more than 50,000 in recent years.

79 The red velour "clashed too much": Helen Thomas, "President, Pat Sharing Joys of Christmas with Visitors," *Lebanon (Penn.) Daily News,* Dec. 19, 1972.

79 She also pointed out: "White House Decorated with 'Nature's Bounty,'" *Anniston (Ala.) Star,* Dec. 12, 1972.

79 a miniature Christmas tree: Helen Thomas, "First Family Prepares for Holidays," *Modesto Bee,* Dec. 17, 1972. At the time, Henry Kissinger was President Nixon's National Security Advisor; he became Secretary of State in September of 1973.

1973

81 As their Christmas gift: Seeley, *Season's Greetings,* p. 128.

81 in the midst of an energy crisis: The federal energy administrator had recently announced his intention to ban all outdoor lighting, but not indoor Christmas tree lights. Sarah Booth Conroy, "Christmas Decorating Minus Electricity," *Washington Post,* Dec. 16, 1973.

81 The Norwegian blue spruces: Isabelle Shelton, "Christmas Tree Omen," *Washington Star,* Dec. 15, 1973.

81 installed in 1970 at Mrs. Nixon's request: Julie Nixon Eisenhower, *Pat Nixon: The Untold Story* (New York: Simon & Schuster, 1986), pp. 304–305.

81 only one large light at the top: This low-key tree topper was markedly different from the controversial "atomic" peace symbol that crowned the tree in 1972. Consisting of four circles lighted with 120 bulbs and a bright, 500-watt bulb at the center (a design that suggested electrons traveling around a nucleus), the decoration was criticized for being nontraditional and secular. One newspaper editor urged the public to demand that the peace symbol be replaced by a star. A spokesman for the National Park Service told reporters that the tree had not been topped by a star since 1962 and that its topmost ornaments had included "representations of ice cream cones, teardrops, snowflakes and pointed objects with flowers." The peace symbol was the creation of a GE lighting designer. Donald Sanders, "Atomic Symbol on Yule Tree Stirs Dispute," *Colorado Springs Gazette-Telegraph,* Dec. 14, 1972.

82 dimming the interior lighting: Shelton, "Christmas Tree Omen."

82 "an omen, a sign of very good luck": Quoted in Helen Thomas, "Nest in White House," *St. Petersburg Times,* Dec. 15, 1973.

83 "I suppose of all the places": Quoted in "Christmas at the White House," p. 68.

THE WHITE HOUSE CRÈCHE (1967–PRESENT)

84 Marisa Piccoli Catello: It was from Eugenio Catello, Marisa Catello's father, that Loretta Howard purchased a large part of her collection in 1956. Loretta H. Howard to Betty C. Monkman, Office of the Curator, Nov. 18, 1978, Records of the First Lady's Office, 1977–1981, Gretchen Poston's Social Files, 1977–1981, Box 32; Christmas Planning [1], Carter Library.

84 "except that it was for the White House": Quoted in Isabelle Shelton, "Johnsons Hail Gift of Crèche," *Washington Star,* Dec. 16, 1967.

84 consisted of thirty-nine pieces: This total number is based on a list of crèche objects provided by the Office of the Curator at the White House. Press

releases and newspaper articles from 1967 gave the number as thirty, which did not count all the animals and accessories.

84 depicted riding horses: "New Yule Creche for White House," *Washington Post,* Nov. 15, 1967; Smith, "Christmas Radiance at the White House," p. 192.

84 stage designer Donald Oenslager: Office of the Press Secretary to Mrs. Johnson, press release, Dec. 13, 1967, Social Files, Box 1751, LBJ Library.

84 "It's taken almost as much work": Quoted in Smith, "Christmas Radiance at the White House."

84 Mrs. Johnson hosted a reception: Shelton, "Johnsons Hail Gift of Crèche."

84 Ten more figures: Howard to Monkman, Nov. 18, 1978.

87 "I was never very happy": Mrs. Charles W. Engelhard to Mrs. Gerald R. Ford, Jan. 27, 1976, Maria Downs Files, Box 28, Christmas—White House Crèche, Ford Library.

87 "some fundamental changes": Maria Downs to Mrs. Ford, Feb. 10, 1976, ibid., Ford Library.

87 Whenever a holiday event was scheduled: Office of the Curator, The White House, e-mail communication, May 7, 2009.

87 The new eleven-foot-high vertical setting: Howard to Monkman, Nov. 18, 1978; Gretchen Poston to Mrs. Carter, Dec. 12, 1978, "Press Preview," Records of the First Lady's Office, Subject Files, 1977–1981, Box 34, HO16, Holidays/Christmas–New Year, Oct. 12, 1978–Dec. 31, 1979, Carter Library.

87 given a new look: "Holiday Treasures at the White House 1999," holiday tour booklet, author's collection.

87 The new aesthetic and architectural elements: Office of the Curator, May 7, 2009.

87 "She traveled all over to find it": Telephone interview with Bess Abell, Feb., 2009.

Betty Ford

93 "It could be considered a goldfish bowl": "There's No Gilded Cage for Betty," *Time,* Dec. 1, 1975, p. 22.

93 for the first time, unmarried guests: "Betty Ford's Folksy White House," *U.S. and News and World Report,* Dec. 30, 1974.

93 the kind of old-fashioned Christmas: Edward Gottlieb & Associates to Florists' Transworld Delivery, "Patchwork Designs Highlight 'Old Fashioned Christmas' at White House; Florists from 24 States Donate Services," press release, Dec. 13, 1974, Box 35, Christmas 1974, Ford Library.

1974

93 In TV interviews: "White House Has Old-Fashioned Christmas," typescript, p. 10, Dec. 10, 1974, Sheila Weidenfeld Files; Box 3, Ford Library.

93 the number of official Christmas parties: Internal White House memo. The following year, the press reported that, as an economy move, the White House had dropped the fish course at official dinners and had borrowed antique duck decoys to use as centerpieces instead of fresh flowers. "Gerald Fords Pay for Own Meals," *Prescott Courier,* Feb. 11, 1975. The idea of duck decoys, however, came from designer Jack Banks, who had been asked by Mrs. Ford to create informal centerpieces that would highlight Americana and stimulate conservation among the guests. Jack Banks, personal communication, Mar. 4, 2009.

93 approved of one small extravagance: "White House Has Old-Fashioned Christmas," p. 11.

93 symbolizing thrift and recyling: Maxine Cheshire,

"A Theme of Thrift, Simplicity for the White House Tree," *Washington Post,* Dec. 10, 1974; Dorothy McCardle, "Patching Up the Christmas Tree," *Washington Post,* Dec. 11, 1974.

93 "When she became the First Lady": Maria Downs, e-mail communication, Mar. 6, 2009.

94 550 different patchwork ornaments: Office of the Press Secretary to Mrs. Ford, untitled press release, Dec. 10, 1974, Ford Library.

94 Washington florist William Dove: J. Liddon Pennock, who had designed the holiday decorations for the Nixons, was suggested to the Fords, but they decided to "simplify" the décor for a warmer look. Cheshire, "A Theme of Thrift, Simplicity."

94 an old necktie of President Ford's: Celine Mahler, personal communication, Feb. 13, 2009.

94 "I have always loved handicrafts": Untitled typescript, Dec. 10, 1974, Sheila Weidenfeld Files; Box 3, Ford Library. Despite the emphasis on money-saving decorations, the cost of the patchwork ornaments totaled $1,600. Mrs. Ford said she was "taken aback" but considered it money well spent because she wanted to put the craftspeople to work. Cheshire, "Costly White House Ornaments.".

94 a Pennsylvania toymaker: The toymaker was Bill Mueller Wooden Toys, Inc., of Telford, Pennsylvania. Mrs. Ford later distributed the toys to underprivileged children. McCardle, "Patching Up the Christmas Tree."

94 Natural-wood baskets: Some of the baskets were made by Cherokees from North Carolina and loaned to the White House by the Department of the Interior. Others were made by a resident of Luray, Virginia.

95 an award-winning patchwork quilt: Made by Iris Fitzsimmons of Abilene, Texas, the quilt was a 1971 winner at the Texas State Fair. The quilt in the Red Room was loaned by Miriam Cassell of Sea Cliff, New York; the quilts in the East Room and the Green Room were from the collection of Mrs. Mahler, founder of the Quilter's Workshop in Bayside, New York.

95 Designed by Charles Smith: "Members Fill White House with Christmas Spirit," *FTD News,* Jan. 1975; Kathryn Elliott, "White House Decorations for Your Home," *Washington Star,* Dec. 15, 1974.

95 while Secret Service agents: Celine Mahler, personal communication, Feb. 13, 2009.

95 For the third year in a row: Edward Gottlieb & Associates to Florist Wire Services, "Christmas Decorations at White House To Be Fashioned by Intercity Florist Groups," press release, Nov. 12, 1974, Sheila Weidenfeld Files, Box 36, Christmas 1974: White House Decorations, Ford Library.

1975

97 Seventy Colonial Williamsburg employees: Jan Gilliam, Manager of Exhibit Planning and Associate Curator of Toys, Museums of Colonial Williamsburg, e-mail communication, Mar. 3, 2009.

97 3,000 ornaments. Office of the Press Secretary to Mrs. Ford, untitled press release, Dec. 15, 1975, Sheila Weidenfeld Files, Box 36, Christmas 1975: White House Decorations, Ford Library. Unless otherwise noted, information for 1975 comes from this press release.

97 Strings of red peppers: Kathryn Elliott, "Heritage Christmas at the White House and Decorations That Can Be Used at Home," *Washington Star,* Dec.

14, 1975.

99 Mrs. Ford made a red cloth bird: Laurie Johnson, "150 Tree Trimmers Feted by Mrs. Ford," *New York Times,* Dec. 16, 1975.

99 "It was an honor": Jane Hanson, personal communication, Dec. 7, 2008.

103 three-foot painted wooden Santa: "Santa Clause [sic]," Ford Library.

105 "In our increasingly synthetic world": Beatrix T. Rumford to Sheila Weidenfeld, Sept. 11, 1975, Sheila Weidenfeld Files, Box 36, Christmas 1975: White House Decorations, Ford Library.

105 "to top Williamsburg": Maria Downs to Mrs. Ford, Feb. 10, 1976, Maria Downs Files, Ford Library.

1976

107 "what Christmas is all about": "Betty Ford Shows Off Family's Last White House Yule Tree," *The Register* (Danville, Va.), Dec. 10, 1976.

107 The tree's 2,500 flower ornaments: Office of the Press Secretary to Mrs. Ford, press release, Dec. 9, 1976, Sheila Weidenfeld Files, Box 36, Christmas 1976: White House Decorations, Ford Library. Unless otherwise noted, information for 1976 comes from this press release as well as project notes provided by Jack Bangs.

107 some of these gifts: "Betty Ford Shows Off Family's Last White House Yule Tree."

108 "to complement the house": Quoted in Sarah Booth Conroy, "The White House Christmas Tree," *Washington Post,* undated clipping, author's files. Jack Bangs had also served as the designer for White House state dinners hosted by the Fords. Mrs. Ford had noticed a feature article about his work in *House Beautiful* while she was recovering from surgery in the fall of 1974. Jack Bangs, personal communication, Mar. 4, 2009.

108 "the love that goes into the White House Christmas tree": Quoted in Jean Jones, "A Dream Come True," *[Auburn Citizen],* undated clipping, author's files.

109 "Both the President and Mrs. Ford": Quoted in "Betty Ford's Folksy White House," p. 12.

109 Some historians have noted: Alvin Rosenbaum, *A White House Christmas.* (Washington D.C.: The Preservation Press, 1992) p. 161.

THE GINGERBREAD HOUSE

111 three gingerbread houses: One was from a pastry chef in New Jersey. Another, decorated with candies, came from a New York restaurant that had sent it on behalf of German-American children living in the Yorkville neighborhood of New York. The gingerbread houses, along with books, were among the few gifts that the Kennedy children were allowed to keep. Carl Sferrazza Anthony, *The Kennedy White House: Family Life and Pictures, 1961–1963* (New York: Simon & Schuster, 2002), p. 206; Marie Smith, "Kennedy Children Get Gifts Galore," *Evening Independent* (St. Petersburg, Fla.), Jan. 3, 1963.

111 Assistant Chef Hans Raffert fashioned: Hugh Sidey, "The White House Becomes a Home," *Time,* Dec. 31, 1973, p. 11.

111 completely edible concoction: Sheila Tate to Jim Rosebush and Muffie Brandon, "Scenario for Press Preview of Decorations," undated memo, Christmas at the White House 1981, OA 7176, Press Preview, Dec. 12, 1981, Reagan Library.

111 The gingerbread house took twelve hours: Amalie Adler Ascher, "Trimmings at the White House Reflect the Somber Times," *The Sun,* Dec., 16, 1979,

H4, Records of the First Lady's Office, Gretchen Poston's Administrative Files, 1977–1981, Box 54, Press Clips: Christmas 1979.

111 "Any available social aide": Stephen Bauer, *At Ease in the White House: Social Life as Seen by a Presidential Military Aide,* rev. ed. (Lanham, Md.: Taylor Trade Publishing, 2004), p. 94.

111 guarded by two Marines: "Helen Hayes and Amy Carter Share Stage at the White House," *New York Times,* Dec. 15, 1977.

113 took a week to make: "Christmas at the White House 1982," holiday tour booklet, author's collection.

113 For twenty-three years: Newspaper articles from the early 1970s sometimes give credit to Executive Pastry Chef Heinz Bender for the gingerbread houses; despite Chef Bender's official title, they were actually made by Chef Raffert from 1969 until he retired in the third year of the George H. W. Bush administration. Roland Mesnier, "My White House Years," *White House History* no. 20 (Spring 2007): 43.

113 the shims and supports: Candy Sagon, "Christmas at the White House: All the President's Gingerbread Men; Tarts & Truffles & Tales of Baking 80,000 Sweets," *Washington Post,* Dec 17, 1997.

113 came up with a technique: Interview with Roland Mesnier, Fairfax Station, Virginia, Mar. 12, 2009.

113 most difficult of the year: The White House, "The Working White House Today: The Tradition Continues" *Inside the White House,* online newsletter, Fall 1997, http://clinton2.nara.gov/WH/kids/inside/html/trad2.html.

113 "building the gingerbread house": Interview with Mesnier, Mar. 12, 2009.

113 almost met with disaster: Ibid.

ROSALYNN CARTER

119 "commercialism has cost the nation": Quoted in "Christmas Spirit Loss Lamented by Mrs. Carter," *Los Angeles Times,* Dec. 13, 1977; "Carters' Christmas: A Busy Time of Year," *Wisconsin State Journal,* Dec. 16, 1977.

119 "It's very, very important": Quoted in "Home-Style Christmas at the White House," *U.S. News & World Report,* Dec. 16, 1977, p. 59.

119 decisions about decorations: Rosenbaum, *A White House Christmas,* p. 163.

119 "The President was as involved": Quoted in ibid.

1977

119 classic American Christmas: "Christmas in White House Decked with Boughs of Holly," *Pasadena Star-News,* Dec. 14, 1977; various clippings in Press Clips—Christmas 1977, Records of the First Lady's Office, Gretchen Poston's Administrative Office Files, 1977–1981, Box 54, Carter Library.

119 active in mental health reform: A member of NAMH's board of directors, Mrs. Carter had used her position as first lady of Georgia to focus attention on mental health issues. She also served as an active honorary chair of the President's Commission on Mental Health, which President Carter established in 1977.

119 The project involved: Peg Barry, Director of Public Information, National Association for Retarded Citizens, news release, Dec. 13, 1978 [1977], Records of the First Lady's Office, Mary Hoyt's Press Releases and Speeches Files, 1977–1981, Christmas 1977, Box 3, Carter Library.

119 wanted the decorations to reveal: Ann Anderson to

Mrs. Carter, Re: Talking Points for Press Preview of Tree, Dec. 12, 1977, Records of the First Lady's Office, ibid.

119 Amy's favorite was a worm: "Carters' Christmas: A Busy Time of Year."

120 "homey, simple and traditional". Quoted in "Carter Tree Lighted," *Press-Courier* (Oxnard, Calif.), Dec. 15, 1977.

120 baskets of poinsettias: "Christmas in White House Decked with Boughs of Holly."

120 the Carters entertained 5,000 guests: Terence Smith, "Thousands Pack White House in Holidays," *New York Times,* Dec. 19, 1978.

120 Heinz Bender baked seventy-five fruitcakes: Marian Burros, "White House Fruit Cake Has Rum," *Winnipeg Free Press,* Dec. 8, 1977.

120 "she likes the way they work": "Make It Pink, With Ruffles," *Salinas Journal,* Dec. 2, 1977.

120 "A manufacturer, eager to please": "No Chain Saw for Amy," *Daily Mail* (Hagerstown, Md.), Dec. 10, 1977.

121 The Carters returned them all: Rosalynn Carter, *First Lady from Plains* (Boston: Houghton Mifflin, 1984), p. 171.

1978

123 In the course of redecorating: Gretchen Poston to Mrs. Carter, "Background on Christmas Decorations," Records of the First Lady's Office, Subject Files, 1977–1981, Box 34, HO 16, Holidays/ Christmas-New Year 10/23/78 to 12/31/79; "Old-Fashioned Christmas at the White House," *U.S. News & World Report,* Dec. 25, 1978/ Jan.1, 1979, pp. 72–73.

123 hand-colored steel engraving: The engraving was a reproduction of a wood engraving that had appeared in a March 1877 issue of *Harper's Weekly.* As a reference, the unknown artist used a photograph "by L. E. Walker." This was most likely Lewis Emory Walker, who held the position of Government Photographer in the Office of the Supervising Architect of the Treasury Department from 1857 until his death in 1880. Renowned for his architectural photographs, he set up the first government photography lab in Washington, D.C., and photographed the construction of the Capitol. Robert G. Lewis, e-mail communication, Feb. 19, 2009.

123 they continued to use: Seeley, *Season's Greetings,* pp. 146–147.

123 "Jimmy, Amy and I invite you": "The White House Christmas Tree 1978," holiday tour booklet, author's collection.

124 the help of museum representatives: The museum staffers included Director H. J. Swinney.

124 Each item on the tree: Paula to Mary/Betty/Vikki, "Re: Dec. 6 Arrival of Tree, Decorations, and other Christmasy Things," Dec. 4, 1978, Records of the First Lady's Office; Gretchen Poston's Administrative Office Files, 1977–1981, Box 54, Press Clips—Christmas, 1978, Carter Library.

125 coinciding with an exhibit: The name of the exhibit, "Teddy and the Bear," alluded to the lore surrounding the origin of the popular toy: President Theodore Roosevelt's refusal to shoot a helpless bear.

125 not yet open to the public: The White House was the only location outside the Rochester area where pieces from the museum's collection had been displayed at this time. Although Margaret Woodbury Strong laid the groundwork for the Rochester museum before her death in 1969, the

task of cataloging and arranging her collection of 300,000 objects, including 27,000 dolls, took more than a decade. The museum officially opened its doors in 1982. Lauren Sodano, Collections Manager, Strong National Museum of Play, personal communication, Feb. 24, 2009; Susan Martin, "300,000 Eclectic Items in New Museum," *The New Mexican* (Santa Fe), Oct. 12, 1982.

125 The museum toys were valued: "White House Decorators Recreate Christmas Past." *FTD News,* Mar. 1979, p. 54.

125 "It reminds me": Quoted in "White House Done Up in Old-Fashioned Yule Finery," *Salina (Kans.) Journal,* Dec. 13, 1978.

1979

127 "caroling in July": Quoted in Quoted in Sarah Booth Conroy, "Trimming the Tree at the White House," *Washington Post,* Dec. 9, 1979.

127 "It's a special time of year": Quoted in "A Subdued Christmas at the White House" *U.S. News & World Report,* p. 56.

127 holiday parties would be more subdued: "On with the Season," *Washington Post,* Dec. 11, 1979, clipping, Records of the First Lady's Office, Gretchen Poston's Administrative Office Files 1977–1981, Box: 54, Press Clips, Christmas 1979, Carter Library.

127 "ornaments that represented the handwork": Quoted in Conroy, "Trimming the Tree at the White House."

127 a design team of ten fine arts students: The fine arts students worked under the direction of Professors Rona Slade and William Christenberry. Ceramics students were supervised by Professor Robert Epstein. "The White House Christmas Tree 1979," holiday tour booklet, author's collection.

127 500 ornaments in mixed media: "Corcoran School of Art Decorates the 1979 White House Christmas Tree," press release, Dec. 10, 1979, Records of the First Lady's Office, Mary Hoyt's Press Release and Speeches Files, 1977–1981, Box 10, "Christmas at the White House, 1979," Carter Library.

127 One thousand artificial red apples: Ascher, "Trimmings at the White House Reflect Somber Times."

128 life-size ceramic objects: Sarah Booth Conroy, "On with the Season," *Washington Post,* Dec. 11, 1979.

128 "Even with careful preseason planning": Dottie Temple and Stan Finegold, *Flowers, White House Style,* (New York: Simon & Schuster, 2002), p. 162.

128 solar collector windows: Conroy, "On with the Season."

128 installation of solar panels: "A Possibility, Not a Novelty," *Time,* July 2, 1979, p. 17.

1980

131 Mrs. Carter sought out the decorating talents: The First Lady had seen an article in the December 1979 issue of *Good Housekeeping* about Louis Nichole's home furnishings and Christmas decorations, particularly his wreaths. Soon after the magazine hit the stands, Mr. Nichole picked up his phone and heard a voice say, "This is Rosalynn Carter from the White House." Thinking it was an aunt known for being the family comic, he said, "Aunt Marge, that's the worst imitation of Rosalynn Carter I've ever heard." Louis Nichole, e-mail communication, Mar. 8, 2009.

131 "The inside of the rose": Quoted in Sarah Booth

Conroy, "White House Color," *Washington Post,* Dec. 22, 1980, Records of the First Lady's Office, Gretchen Poston's Administrative Office Files 1977–1981, Box 54, Press Clips—Christmas 1980, Carter Library.

131 She described the theme: Gretchen Poston to Mrs. Carter, "Press Preview of Christmas Decorations, Monday, December 15, 1980, 2:00 P.M.," Dec. 12, 1980, Records of the First Lady' Office, Mary Hoyt's Press Releases and Speeches Files 1977–1981, Box 12, Christmas, 1980, Carter Library.

131 the "roses and lace" tree: In 1992 the Jimmy Carter Library and Museum, with the assistance of Louis Nichole, recreated the 1980 Blue Room tree for a holiday display. Since that time, it has been an annual attraction, featuring dolls, toys, and ornaments that that closely resemble the originals. Jimmy Carter Library and Museum, "1980 White House Christmas Tree Recreated at the Jimmy Carter Presidential Library," news release, Dec. 13, 2005.

132 The designer and his extended family: Louis Nichole, e-mail communication, Mar. 10, 2009; www.louisnichole.com.

132 10,000 real miniature bricks: Jim Abrams, Real Good Toys, Montpelier, Vt., personal communication, Feb. 23, 2009. The following year, the dollhouse company produced "The First Lady," a special-edition kit for a sixteen-room dollhouse that was a replica of the one created for the White House. The house measured five feet by three feet by two feet.

132 To give the decorations the antique look: Louis Nichole, e-mail communication, Mar. 26, 2009.

133 No one ever complained: Louis Nichole, e-mail communication, Mar. 10, 2009.

133 Mr. Nichole designed a party dress: One of Mr. Nichole's assistants, Elizabeth Eisloeffel, made the gown in addition to the gowns of the dolls on the tree. Elizabeth Eisloeffel, personal communication, Feb. 23, 2080.

134 The centerpieces in the State Dining Room: Conroy, "White House Color"; Poston to Carter, "Press Preview," Dec. 12, 1980.

134 250 fruitcakes and 12,000 cookies: Conroy, "White House Color."

134 When he was hired: Interview with Roland Mesnier, Dallas, Texas, Dec. 5, 2008.

135 "one of the happiest times": "Remarks of Former First Lady Rosalynn Carter at the National Press Club, Washington, D.C., Dec. 5, 2001," news release, Carter Center, Atlanta.

135 one of her many projects: She also developed another type of booklet, called "The White House . . . It's Your House Too," which answered children's most common questions about the mansion and provided a pictorial tour. Carter, *First Lady from Plains,* p. 170.

CANDLELIGHT TOURS

136 1.5 million people: David Montgomery, "Fuzzy Reception at the White House," *Washington Post,* Dec. 18, 2002.

136 estimated 125,000 to 160,000 people: David Montgomery, "Christmas at the People's House (Restrictions May Apply)," *Washington Post,* Dec. 18, 2008.

136 President and Mrs. Nixon announced: "The Washington Record," *New York Times,* Dec. 25, 1969.

136 "a big hit": Quoted in "Candlelight Tours of White House," *Oakland Tribune,* Dec. 6, 1970.

136 a tradition was born: During the Nixon years, one

candlelight tour had to be canceled—on December 28, 1972, which President Nixon proclaimed a national day of mourning following the death of Harry S. Truman. The regular daytime tours were canceled as well. "America Mourns Truman Death," *St. Petersburg Times,* Dec. 27, 1972.

136 the addition of Christmas music: Helen Thomas, "Nixons Open Home to Thousands," *Bennington Banner,* Dec. 28, 1970.

137 To enhance the ambience: Eisenhower, *Pat Nixon,* p. 264; Bonnie Angelo, "The Woman in the Cloth Coat," *Time,* July 5, 1993.

137 "We've always tried": Quoted in "Christmas at the White House: Mrs. Richard Nixon Talks about the Decorations and the Celebrations," *House and Garden* 140 (Dec. 1971): 63.

137 The staff will dim the electric lights: Hugh Sidey, "The White House Becomes a Home," *Time,* Dec. 31, 1973, p. 11.

137 "Fires burned in the Red": Eisenhower, *Pat Nixon,* p. 303.

137 began during Mrs. Nixon's tenure: Betty Monkman, e-mail communication, May 11, 2009.

137 teakwood that is believed to be part: Office of the Curator, The White House, e-mail communication, May 14, 2009. President Eisenhower received the shipment of teak from Prime Minister U Nu in 1956. "Burma Sends Ike 10 Tons of Teak," *Times Record* (Troy, N.Y.), Mar. 20, 1956.

137 the custom of burning fires: Office of the Curator, e-mail communication. May 14, 2009.

137 A regular daytime tour: Until 2001, from Tuesday through Saturday, the White House Visitor Center would distribute up to 6,000 free tour tickets each day. Tickets were available starting at 7:30 a.m. and were usually gone in a few hours. They were valid only for tours that same day.

137 "Candlelight tours are often very crowded": The White House, Public Events Calendar, http://clinton4.nara.gov/WH/Tours/special_events.html#candle.

137 a National Park Service ranger estimated: Pamela Constable, "Waiting at the White House Is No Holiday; Visitors Endure Outside Cold to Be Able to See Inside Glow," *Washington Post,* Dec. 29, 1998.

137 as many as 1,200 people: Montgomery, "Christmas at the People's House."

NANCY REAGAN
1981

143 "Christmas is my favorite season": "A Christmas Potpourri, White House Style," *New York Times,* Dec. 23, 1981; "Christmas at the White House," *Ladies' Home Journal,* Dec. 1981, p. 78.

143 every last detail: Muffie Brandon to Mrs. Reagan's Staff, "Re: Christmas Plans," July 8, 1981, Mabel (Muffie) Brandon Files, 1981–1984, OA 7169, Christmas 1981, Reagan Library.

143 "I don't like a white tree": Quoted in Helen Thomas, "Christmas," AP wire story, Dec. 13, 1982, Sheila Tate Files, 1981–1982, OA 6222, Reagan Library.

143 "The basic concept": Muffie Brandon to Peter McCoy, Joe Canzeri, and Michael Deaver, "Re: Christmas at the White House," Nov. 6, 1981, Mabel (Muffie) Brandon Files, 1981–1984, OA 7169, Christmas at the White House, Binder 1/7, Reagan Library.

144 800 animal ornaments: Sarah Booth Conroy, "Dreaming of a White (House) Christmas," *Washington Post,* Dec. 6, 1981. The eight artists

were Ivan Barnett, Stevens, Pennsylvania; Gladys Boalt, Stormville, New York; David Claggett, Christiana, Pennsylvania; Ruth Ann Greenhill, Milford, Connecticut; Eleanor Meadowcroft, Salem, Massachusetts; Sally Sundstrom and Arlene Lawson, Baltimore; Nancy Thomas, Yorktown, Virginia. They were selected by Marie DiManno, who was familiar with their work as manager of the museum's gift shop.

144 white crocheted snowflakes: The snowflake ornaments were made by Central Pennsylvania Village Crafts in State College, Pennsylvania. Ibid.

146 paper-folding expert: Michael Small became well known for designing origami Christmas trees, such as "Paper Magic on Fifth Avenue" for Japan Airlines and "The Origami Holiday Tree" for the American Museum of Natural History. The Friends of the Origami Center of America is now known as Origami USA. J. Michael Elliott, "Michael Shall, 45, American Expert on Origami," *New York Times,* Feb. 16, 1995.

146 more than the usual number of trees: Tompkins and Helmsing, "Behind the Scenes of the White House Christmas Trees."

146 a handmade Victorian dollhouse: "Christmas at the White House 1981," holiday tour booklet, author's collection.

146 some of the magnolia leaves: Conroy, "Dreaming of a White (House) Christmas."

147 the plants had to be relocated: Dottie Temple and Stan Finegold, *Flowers, White House Style,* (New York: Simon & Schuster, 2002), p. 162.

147 a class of New Jersey fifth-graders: Making shell wreaths was an annual project for Thomas Levin's fifth-grade class at Cape May Elementary School in Cape May, New Jersey. After a visit to Colonial Williamsburg, Levin assigned each student the task of making two wreaths—a family wreath and another for a public place, determined by a class vote. In 1981 Levin's class voted to send their wreaths to the White House. Class members received an invitation to view their handiwork at the White House. "Distinctly December Classroom: Golden Wreaths at the White House," *Instructor,* Nov./Dec. 1982, clipping, First Lady Press Office: Records, 1981–1989, OA 8997, Reagan Library; "Christmas Decorations for the White House, Background on Shell Wreaths," attached to Cape May City Elementary School to Ms. Brandon, Nov. 27, 1981, Mabel (Muffie) Brandon Files, 1981–1984, OA 7169; Reagan Library.

1982

149 "I love an old-fashioned theme": "Christmas at the White House 1982," holiday tour booklet, author's collection.

149 between twenty and twenty-five years old: Office of the First Lady's Press Secretary, "Notice to the Press: Background on Presentation of the White House Christmas Tree, December 9, 1982," press release, Dec. 13, 1982, First Lady Press Office: Records, 1981–1989, OA 8550, Reagan Library.

149 "The residents of Second Genesis": Sidney Shankman and Alan M. Rochlin to Mrs. Ronald W. Reagan, Dec. 15, 1982, First Lady Press Office: Records, 1981–1989, OA 8997, December 1982—Christmas Ornament, Reagan Library.

150 "We wish the Christmas tree": Muffie Brandon to Donald Adams, Director, Greenfield Village and Henry Ford Museum, Mabel (Muffie) Brandon Files, 1981–1984, OA 7176, Christmas Decorations, Reagan Library.

151 "quite magical": Quoted in "The Social Season in High Gear," *Washington Times,* Dec. 15, 1982.

151 Fir trees decorated with clip-on candles: Sheila Tate to Jim Rosebush and Muffie Brandon, "Scenario for the Press Preview of Decorations, December 8, 1982," Sheila Tate Files, 1981–1982, OA 6222, Reagan Library.

1983

153 1,200 antique toys and artifacts: "Christmas at the White House 1983," holiday tour booklet, author's collection.

1984

161 Mrs. Reagan was so taken: Ingrid Jacobson, "Saturday's Child, Natural Look at the White House," *Washington Post,* Dec. 14, 1984.

161 2,800 ornaments: "Christmas at the White House 1984," holiday tour booklet, author's collection.

165 "I think this year is prettier": Quoted in Helen Thomas, Dec. 10, 1984, untitled AP wire story, Reagan Library. The nine-week-old black sheepdog, Lucky, was a gift to the Reagans from March of Dimes poster child Kristen Ellis. Lucky made his formal debut at the unveiling of the Christmas décor. Helen Thomas, "The 'First Puppy' Catches on," *Syracuse Herald-American,* Dec. 11, 1984.

165 a child named Amie Garrison: "Press Preview of Christmas," Dec. 10, 1984, Gahl Hodges Files, 1983–1984, OA 12293, Reagan Library; "NFL Running Back Plays Santa for White House," *Casa Grande (Ariz.) Dispatch,* Dec. 11, 1984.

1985

167 1,500 ornaments: "Christmas at the White House 1985," holiday tour booklet, author's collection.

169 "For our tribute": Temple, *Flowers, White House Style,* p. 164. Stuffed toy bears were being made in Germany some years before a cartoonist satirized President Theodore Roosevelt's refusal to shoot a bear on a hunting trip in 1902. But because the incident gave rise to the term "Teddy's bear" and the domestic manufacture of these toys, 1902 is often viewed as the birth of the teddy bear in the United States. Anniversaries keyed to other important years in teddy bear history are also celebrated.

169 cone-shaped boxwood topiaries: Ibid., p. 176.

1986

175 Fifteen soft-sculpture scenes: "A Mother Goose Christmas 1986," holiday tour booklet, author's collection.

1987

179 The song "Toyland": "A Musical Christmas 1987," holiday tour booklet, author's collection.

1988

185 As she felt "very sentimental": Michael Kilian, "A 'Very Sentimental' Season Opens as the Reagans Prepare to Depart," *Chicago Tribune,* Dec. 13, 1988.

185 300 wooden candles: "Old-Fashioned Christmas 1988: The White House," holiday tour booklet, author's collection.

186 "I felt as if I needed to put on a coat": Interview with Mesnier, Dec. 5, 2008.

186 "That was one of my greatest memories": Interview with Anita McBride, Chief of Staff to the First Lady and Assistant to the President, Washington, D.C., Aug. 16, 2008.

187 "The last Reagan Christmas": Telephone interview with William Seale, Editor, *White House History,* Dec. 23, 2009.

187 fully decorated trees: For example, the China-themed tree is decorated with fortune cookies, fans, and a lion's head at the top; the Germany tree, with gingerbread men and gingerbread houses; the Italy tree, with grape clusters, crosses, and angels. The highlighted countries vary each year, and the trees also include decorations given to the Reagans as gifts.

THE CRANBERRY TREE

188 Christine Heineman: Kathryn Elliott, "Heritage Christmas at the White House and Decorations That Can Be Used at Home," *Washington Star,* Dec. 13, 1975. At the time, Mrs. Heinemann was a frequent lecturer on the garden club circuit, having served as a judge at the New York Flower Show for almost two decades. Barbara Ormsby, "Presidential Table Setter Shows Talent," *Delaware County Daily Times,* May 4, 1976.

188 "Red was a favorite color": Telephone interview with Myrtle Elmore, Mar. 7, 2009.

BARBARA BUSH

195 started planning for the holidays: Janice McDaniel, "White House Holiday Tour Time," *Washington Post,* Dec. 28, 1989.

195 "I thought Nancy Clarke": Barbara Bush, *Barbara Bush: A Memoir* (New York: Scribner, 1994).

1989

195 "The huge official tree": "A White House Christmas 1989," holiday tour booklet, author's collection. Unless otherwise noted, information for 1989 comes from this source.

195 "Millie cannot steal this show": Quoted in "State-Grown Tree Arrives at Capital," *Indiana (Penn.) Gazette,* Dec. 7, 1989.

199 "There's sort of a little message": Quoted in Donnie Radcliffe, "Decking the White House Halls," *Washington Post,* Dec. 12, 1989.

199 "Bad weather gave us": Bush, *Barbara Bush,* p. 317.

1990

201 "where magic can be most truly felt": "A White House Christmas 1990," holiday tour booklet, author's collection.

201 Mrs. Bush gave the press corps: Helen Thomas, "Barbara Bush, Millie Unveil Christmas Decorations," *Bryan (Tex.) Times,* Dec. 11, 1990.

203 forty-seven trees: Frank J. Murray, "White House Shows Spirit," *Washington Times,* Dec. 12, 1990.

203 "The heart of the season": "A White House Christmas 1990," holiday tour booklet, author's collection.

1991

207 The Bushes had admired: Radcliffe, "Decking the White House Halls."

207 the Saintly Stitchers got to work: The Saintly Stitchers group was formed in 1983 to stitch kneelers for the church. Lida Browder, who spearheaded the project for the Bush crèche, required every participant to stitch two kneelers first. Betty Ewing, "Saintly Stitchers Fill Bushes' Nativity Scene with Love, Humor," *Houston Chronicle,* Dec. 8, 1989; "To Our Beloved President and First Lady," photocopy of presentation letter, author's collection.

207 "the most beautiful thing": Quoted in Radcliffe, "Decking the White House Halls."

208 1,370 needlepoint ornaments: "A White House Christmas 1991," holiday tour booklet, author's collection.

208 106 patterns: Donnie Radcliffe, "The First Lady's Yuletide House Tour," *Washington Post,* Dec. 10, 1991.

211 "There are a lot of white-haired" Quoted in ibid.

211 At the base of the tree: Anne Gowen, "White House Is Jolly for Its Season of Holly," *Washington Times,* Dec. 10, 1991.

213 personal eighty-piece crèche: "A White House Christmas 1991." Consisting of forty-five pieces when it was first presented in 1989, the crèche had presumably acquired additional figures over the two-year period.

213 "a needlepoint world of enchantment": Ibid.

213 It was estimated: Radcliffe, "The First Lady's Yuletide House Tour."

1992

217 For Mrs. Bush's final Christmas: "Christmas, The White House 1992," holiday tour booklet, author's collection. Unless otherwise noted, information for 1992 comes from this source.

217 Given free rein by Mrs. Bush: Interview with Mesnier, Dec. 5, 2008.

219 elves sledding through white frosting: Anne Gowen, "White House Christmas One Last Time for Bushes," *Washington Times,* Dec. 8, 1992.

219 "Millie is the only": Interview with Mesnier, Dec. 5, 2008.

221 to come home to find: Comments by Barbara Bush at Genesis Women's Shelter of Dallas event, May 3, 2006.

221 "First of all, forty people": Quoted in Myrna Blyth, "Christmas at the White House," *Ladies Home Journal,* Dec. 1991, p. 152.

THE HOLIDAY TOUR BOOKLET

222 seasonal decorations for the first time: In 1970 First Lady Pat Nixon asked the White House Visitor Office to prepare foreign-language brochures about the history of the Executive Mansion, with descriptive background on its major rooms. The English text was translated into French, German, Italian, Japanese, Russian, and Spanish for the large number of visitors from other countries. However, the booklet was general, not specific to the Christmas décor. "6-Language Brochures," *Washington Post,* Dec. 1, 1970.

222 with the help of the Colonial Williamsburg staff: Sheila Weidenfeld, personal communication, Apr. 16, 2009.

222 "The President and I wish you": "A White House Christmas 1975," The White House, Washington, D.C., mailer, author's collection.

HILLARY CLINTON

First Lady Dolley Madison: Carl Sferrazza Anthony, Introduction to *An Invitation to the White House: At Home with History,* by Hillary Rodham Clinton (New York: Simon & Schuster, 2000), p. 2.

1993

231 "Being the type who's relieved": Hillary Rodham Clinton, "'Twas the Night before Christmas and All Through the Clinton White House," *Seattle Times,* Dec. 4, 1995.

231 work on the decorations: Capricia Marshall, e-mail communication, Apr. 19, 2009.

231 Year of the American Craft: In the last weeks of his presidency, George H. W. Bush had signed a proclamation entitled "Year of the American Craft: A Celebration of the Creative Work of the Hand, 1993."

231 White House crafts collection: Known as the White House Collection of American Crafts, the works were exhibited in 1995 at the Smithsonian's National Museum of American Art and subsequently at various presidential libraries. The collection was also featured in Michael Moore, *The White House Collection of American Crafts* (New York: Harry N. Abrams, 1995). Selected works are on view at the Clinton Presidential Library, where the collection is housed.

231 As one visitor observed: Marian Burros, "Holidays at the Clintons': Crafts and Plenty of Cats," *New York Times,* Dec. 7, 1993.

231 in the West Wing lobby: Zachary J. Oxman, personal communication, Mar. 12, 2009. Oxman's sculpture portrayed the nine candles of the Hanukkah menorah being held aloft by joyful men dancing in tailcoats. Rita Reif, "Making Art, Making a Living," *New York Times,* Dec. 23, 1993.

231 the first display of a menorah: Burros, "Holidays at the Clintons'."

232 "Some are quite elegant": "White House Christmas: Cozy, Funky," *St. Petersburg Times,* Dec. 7, 1993.

232 There were two angels: Jura Koncius: "Deck the White House Halls," *Washington Post,* Dec. 9, 1993.

233 A green velvet tree skirt: "Holidays at the White House 1993," holiday tour booklet, author's collection. Unless otherwise noted, information for 1993 comes from this source.

233 Twenty-one additional trees: Anne Gowen, "White House Trades Fancy for Folksy This Year," *Washington Times,* Dec. 7, 1993.

233 One of the six largest: David MacDonald, "Wheat Decorates White House Tree," *Winnipeg Free Press,* Dec. 8, 1993.

1994

237 Designers from Polo/Ralph Lauren Creative Services: "White House Halls Decked Out in Familiar Theme," *Washington Times,* Dec. 7, 1994.

237 The Colorado blue spruce: "Holidays at the White House 1994," holiday tour booklet, author's collection.

238 The dried hydrangeas were suggested: Donnie Radcliffe, "1600 Tinselvania Avenue," *Washington Post,* Dec. 6, 1994.

239 "When he looked it over": Interview with Mesnier, Dec. 5, 2008.

1995

241 Three groups of artisans: "Holidays at the White House 1995," holiday tour booklet, author's collection.

241 Architectural scenes were displayed: Patricia Dane Rogers, "Expressions of the Season: And All Through the White House," *Washington Post,* Nov 30, 1995.

242 Jean-Luc Derron: Linda Beaulieu, "Ornaments You Can Eat!" *Casa Grande (Ariz.) Dispatch,* Dec. 6, 1995.

1996

247 "has great personal meaning": "The Nutcracker: Holidays at the White House 1996," holiday tour booklet, author's collection.

247 Chelsea performed the role: "Point Well Taken: Chelsea Clinton Dances Her Annual *Nutcracker,*"

People, Dec. 23, 1996. She had attended the Washington School of Ballet since 1993.

247 the array of ornaments: Sarah Booth Conroy, "Decking the White House, Artfully," *Washington Post,* Dec 9, 1996.

248 "It was the hardest work I've ever done": Quoted in ibid.

249 became a prop on the set: Zachary Oxman, personal communication, Mar. 14, 2009.

249 It was the first time: "At the White House, the First Islamic Observance," *Philadelphia Inquirer,* Feb. 22, 1996.

1997

251 "a time of wonder, promise and hope": "Santa's Workshop: Holidays at the White House 1997," holiday tour booklet, author's collection.

251 had baked 250 fruitcakes: Candy Sagon, "Christmas at the White House: All the President's Gingerbread Men," *Washington Post,* Dec. 17, 1997. In addition to the fruitcakes, this season Chef Mesnier and his assistant, Franette McCulloch, turned out 2,500 gingerbread cookies; a total of 20,000 brownies, macaroons, pecan diamonds, hazelnut butter crescents, sables, German leckerle, linzer cookies, and fruit bars; 70 loaves of panettone; 280 cakes (pumpkin, applesauce, passion fruit, and coconut); 250 buche de Noel logs; and thousands of other assorted confections—chocolate truffles; raspberry tartlets, mini-savarins, blackberry and raspberry mousses, and petits fours. The individual servings of sweets totaled 40,000.

251 presented as "plum pudding": Roland Mesnier, *Dessert University* (New York: Simon & Schuster, 2004), p. 388.

251 "Ours is different": Quoted in Sagon, "Christmas at the White House."

251 "People went crazy": Interview with Mesnier, Dec. 5, 2008.

251 the White House invitation: Jura Koncius, "White House: Tree-Trimming Time," *Washington Post,* Dec. 11, 1997.

252 in 1,464 bows: Ibid.

252 Outfits ranged: Ann Geracimos, "White House Decorates as 'Santa's Workshop'," *Washington Times,* Dec. 4, 1997; Kimberly Stevens, "For a Jolly Old Elf," *New York Times,* Dec. 7, 1997.

255 "Mrs. Claus is going to start her diet": Quoted in "23 Trees Are Up, 300,000 Christmas Cards to Go," *Philadelphia Inquirer,* Dec. 5, 1997.

1998

259 "We have so many fond memories": "Winter Wonderland: Holidays at the White House 1998," holiday tour booklet, author's collection.

260 making their annual surprise visit: Capricia Marshall, e-mail communication, Apr. 19, 2009.

262 "I didn't think a minute": Marian Burros, "Holiday Decorations Fit for the White House," *New York Times,* Dec. 3, 1998.

264 "We decided that we really needed": *The White House Christmas [1998],* Home & Garden Television, Scripps Howard Broadcasting Company, 1998; http://www.hgtv.com/videos/white-house-christmas-1998/31305.html (21:53). The half-hour special, featuring Kitty Bartholomew as host, premiered on the HGTV channel on Dec. 20, 1998. It has become a popular annual program.

264 weighing 2,000 pounds: Elisabeth Bumiller, "A Star Floral Designer's Flights of Fancy," *New York Times,* Dec. 22, 1998.

264 "Royal blue is not the color": Quoted in ibid.

264 "I remember the years": Quoted in Sarah Booth Conroy, "The White House's Holiday Corps de Décor," *Washington Post,* Dec 14, 1998.

265 the 2,343 ornaments: Ibid.

265 decorated with silk flowers: Ibid.

1999

267 unveiled the previous year: Save America's Treasures, "National Trust for Historic Preservation Joins Forces with the White House to Preserve the Best of Our Past for the New Millennium," news release, Feb. 11, 1998. This public-private partnership involved the White House Millennium Council, the National Park Service, and the National Trust for Historic Preservation.

267 "One of the most powerful ways": "Holiday Treasures at the White House 1999," holiday tour booklet, author's collection.

267 thirty historic and cultural sites Jennifer Maddox, "'Holiday Treasures' Theme of White House Decorations," *Topeka Capital-Journal,* Dec.18, 1999.

267 used by her head cabinetmaker: David C. Caccaro, personal communication, Mar. 20, 2009.

268 created an array of famous figures: Ann Geracimos, "Holiday Treasures Fill White House with Cheer," *Washington Times,* Dec. 7, 1999.

268 multi-colored lights: *The White House Christmas [1999],* Home & Garden Television, Scripps Howard Broadcasting Company, 1999; http://www.hgtv.com/videos/white-house-christmas-1998/31305.html.

269 twenty-eight trees: Maddox, "'Holiday Treasures' Theme."

269 Instead of bright red: Geracimos, "Holiday Treasures Fill White House."

271 the first painting: "Holiday Treasures at the White House 1999."

271 the 75,000 colored lights: Coralie Carlson, "Minnesotans Help Deck the White House Halls," *Minneapolis Star Tribune,* Dec. 9, 1999.

2000

273 said to be Chelsea's favorite: Jura Koncius, "Signs of the Season at 1600 Pennsylvania Avenue," *Washington Post,* Dec. 7, 2000.

273 "They are very, very weepy": Quoted in "It Takes a Village to Put on a White House Christmas: 'Tis the Season for Parties—and More Parties—as the Clintons Celebrate Their Last Christmas at 1600 Pennsylvania Avenue," *Christian Science Monitor,* Dec. 7, 2000.

273 "As we prepare to leave": "Holiday Reflections at the White House 2000," holiday tour booklet, author's collection.

275 some 10,000 ornaments: Koncius, "Signs of the Season."

275 324 wreaths: "Holiday Reflections at the White House 2000."

275 the only major additions: Koncius, "Signs of the Season."

276 an ornament centered in each wreath: *The White House Christmas [2000],* Home & Garden Television, Scripps Howard Broadcasting Company, 2000; http://www.hgtv.com/videos/white-house-christmas-2000/31222.html.

276 reflecting Mrs. Clinton's wish: Seeley, *Season's Greetings,* p. 208.

276 "warm and treasured memories": Quoted in ibid.

276 "This house and its history": Clinton, *An Invitation to the White House,* p. 175.

THE OFFICIAL WHITE HOUSE ORNAMENT

278 nonprofit, nonpartisan organization's mission: The White House Historical Association was chartered on November 3, 1961, to "increase the nation's knowledge and appreciation of the White House" through guide books, films, and other educational materials. "White House Gets Cultural Society: Mrs. Kennedy Credited for Plan to Educate Tourists," *New York Times,* Nov. 4, 1961. Much of the impetus behind its creation came from First Lady Jacqueline Kennedy, who was disappointed by her first White House tour as a child. After "shuffling through" the mansion too fast to learn anything about its history, she realized "there wasn't even a booklet you could buy." Quoted in Bachmann, "Circa 1961: The Kennedy White House Interiors," p. 8.

278 a way to raise additional funds: White House Historical Association, "A History of the White House Historical Association's White House Holiday Ornament Program: A Conversation with Michael Melton," press release, n.d.

280 ChemArt of Lincoln: Katie Haugney, "Company Melds Chemistry, Art," *Providence Business News,* July 10–16, 2006; Lee Rush, ChemArt Company, e-mail communication, Apr. 17, 2009.

280 Some ornaments are engraved: The 1994 ornament, a replica of peace medal minted in 1801 for Thomas Jefferson, was engraved with the message "Peace and Friendship"; about 200 of the ornaments were produced with *friendship* misspelled before the mistake was discovered. Andrea Brown, "At Age 9, He's a Stickler for Spelling, Not One to Let 'Freindship Get Away, Nicholas Betz Calls Error to Attention of Manufacturer," *Colorado Springs Gazette,* Nov. 15, 2004.

280 about 5,000 ornaments were made: Jim Shea, "Collect 'Em All," *Hartford Courant,* Dec. 13, 2005.

280 According to Michael Melton: Susan Guynn, "Ornaments Every Year: One Woman's Love of the Presidential Residence Gave Rise to a Collection of Ornaments," *Frederick News-Post,* Dec. 17, 2006.

280 most popular ornament program: Haughey, "Company Melds Chemistry, Art."

280 President Bill Clinton gave: Jennifer Batog, "White House Offers Ornaments of History," *Los Angeles Times,* Dec. 7, 1997.

LAURA BUSH

287 "I remember how magnificent": Quoted in Susan Kelliher Ungaro, "Why Traditions Matter," *Family Circle,* Dec. 18, 2001, p. 104.

287 "One of the things": Quoted in ibid., p. 105.

2001

287 "Because this year's holiday season": "Home for the Holidays: The White House 2001," holiday tour booklet, author's collection.

291 engineers in the Usher's Office: Interview with Roland Mesnier, Fairfax Station, Virginia, Mar. 12, 2009.

292 on loan from the Vermont Division: William E. Jenney, President Calvin Coolidge State Historic Site, e-mail communication, Apr. 3, 2009. The model was made by Vermont folk artist Barbara McKenna in the late 1990s.

292 in the Booksellers Area: Elisabeth Bumiller, "White House Letter; A New, Inclusive Era of the Holiday Party," *New York Times,* Dec. 17, 2001.

292 the first official White House card: Seeley, *Season's Greetings,* p. 215.

297 All the rooms and hallways: Andi Ball, e-mail communication, May 1, 2009.

2002

299 hymn for children: "All creatures great and small" is a line from "All Things Bright and Beautiful," written by the Dublin-born hymn writer Cecil Frances Alexander (1823–1895) and published in her 1848 collection entitled *Hymns for Little Children.*

299 "illustrate the endearing role": "All Creatures Great and Small: Holidays at the White House 2002," holiday tour booklet, author's collection.

299 "We write beautiful letters": *The White House Christmas 2002,* Home & Garden Television, Scripps Howard Broadcasting Company, 2002; http://www.hgtv.com/videos/white-house-christmas-2002/31224.html.

305 Steinway concert grand piano: The full-size concert "state" piano is unique. It was designed by Eric Gugler (an architect selected by President Roosevelt to redesign the West Wing) in 1938 when the Steinway Company offered to donate a new piano to the White House to replace a piano the company had made in 1903. The piano's Honduran mahogany case stands on three large eagle legs carved by the sculptor Albert Stewart. Gold-leaf scenes painted by Dunbar Beck form a band around the case. Betty C. Monkman, *The White House: Its Historic Furnishings and First Families* (Washington, D.C.: White House Historical Association; New York: Abbeville Press, 2000), pp. 215–218.

305 "I liked the eagles": Quoted in Seeley, *Season's Greetings,* p. 226.

309 Conceived as a way: Barney Cam was the brainchild of Jeanie Mamo, head of Media Affairs at the White House. Production was handled by Jimmy Orr, director of the White House website (www.whitehouse.gov) and Bob DeServi, a White House communications adviser. First Lady Laura Bush announced the Barney Cam during a tour for reporters on Dec. 6, 2002. Elisabeth Bumiller, "Bush's Terrier Will Tape White House Video Tour," *New York Times,* Dec. 6, 2002.

309 24 million views: "White House 'Barney-cam' Is Online Hit," *USA Today,* Feb. 19, 2002.

311 Gingerbread cookies are a long time: "Why Traditions Matter," *Family Circle,* December 18, 2001.

2003

311 fifty-nine of the ornaments from 1989: Weldon Svoboda, George Bush Presidential Library and Museum, e-mail communication, Mar. 17, 2009. The fifty-nine ornaments consisted of sixty-one pieces.

311 "I felt like it was an idea": Office of the First Lady, "Interview of First Lady Laura Bush with ABC's Claire Shipman on Good Morning America," transcript, Dec. 4, 2003; http://georgewbush-whitehouse.archives.gov/news/releases/2003/12/20031204-17.html.

311 about two feet tall: Office of the First Lady, "Interview of First Lady Laura Bush with NBC's Norah O'Donnell on the Today Show," transcript, Dec. 4, 2003; http://georgewbush-whitehouse.archives.gov/news/releases/2003/12/20031204-13.html.

313 dressed plastic dolls in costumes: *White House Christmas 2003,* Home & Garden Television, Scripps Networks, Inc., 2003; www.hgtv.com/videos/white-house-christmas-2003/31225.html.

321 it took 245 wreaths: Office of the First Lady, "White House 2003 Holiday Theme Is 'A Season of Stories,'" press release, Dec. 4, 2003; the ornaments from 1989: "A Season of Stories: Holidays at the White House 2003," holiday tour booklet, author's collection.

2004

323 her personal favorite: *White House Christmas 2004,* Home & Garden Television, Scripps Networks, Inc., 2004; http://www.hgtv.com/videos/white-house-christmas-2004/31226.html.

323 350 musical ornaments: Office of the First Lady, "White House 2004 Holiday Theme Is 'A Season of Merriment and Melody,'" press release, Dec. 2, 2004.

323 The organization distributed: Theresa Campbell, "Villager's Ornament to Get Presidential Display," *Villages Daily Sun,* http://www.thevillagesdailysun.com/articles/2008/12/09/news/news01.txt.

324 iced Della Robbia fruit: "A Season of Merriment and Melody: Holidays at the White House 2004," holiday tour booklet, author's collection.

334 24,000 cookies: Michael Collins, "White House: A Musical Wonderland," *Frederick News-Post,* Dec. 12, 2006.

334 estimated 44,000 visitors: Richard Rainey, "First Lady Makes Sure Festive Decor, Holiday Tunes Brighten White House," *Los Angeles Times,* Dec. 3, 2004.

2005

337 "to highlight the beauty": "All Things Bright and Beautiful: Holidays at the White House 2005," holiday tour booklet, author's collection.

337 "We used natural, real flowers": Quoted in Marian Burros, "Holiday Décor at the White House Takes a Subtler Turn," *New York Times,* Dec. 1, 2005.

337 "Every year I think: Quoted in Maria Recio, "Dreaming of a Fresh, Funky White House Christmas," *Fort Worth Star-Telegram,* Dec. 15, 2005.

345 because daughters Barbara and Jenna: Ungaro, "Why Traditions Matter."

345 This year's holiday magic: Office of the First Lady, "Fact Sheet: White House Holiday Decorations," press release, Nov. 30, 2005; http://georgewbush-whitehouse.archives.gov/news/releases/2005/11/20051130-4.html.

2006

347 inspired by the dramatic color: Office of the First Lady, "Interview of the First Lady by ABC," transcript, Nov. 30, 2006; http://georgewbush-whitehouse.archives.gov/news/releases/2006/11/20061130-8.html.

347 scarlet, crimson, and fuchsia: Office of the First Lady, "White House 2006 Holiday Theme Is 'Deck the Halls and Welcome All,'" press release, Nov. 30, 2006; http://georgewbush-whitehouse.archives.gov/news/releases/2006/11/20061130-7.html.

347 260 festive evergreen wreaths: Office of the First Lady, "Fact Sheet: White House Holiday Decorations," press release, Nov. 30, 2006; http://georgewbush-whitehouse.archives.gov/news/releases/2006/11/20061130-5.html.

347 hand-blown red glass balls: Monte Mitchell, "Perfect Gift: Locally Made Ornaments Go to White House, Give Mitchell County a Holiday Bonus," *Winston-Salem Journal,* Dec. 1, 2006. The ornaments were made by glass artist Virgil Jones and basket artist Billie Ruth Sudduth and her assistants.

349 "just cut through all that": Interview with McBride, Aug. 26, 2008.

357 command performance: "Deck the Halls and Welcome All: Holidays at the White House 2006," holiday tour booklet, author's collection.

2007

359 "Of course I love the White House": Quoted in Brooke Donald, "First Lady Laura Bush Visits Charleston Navy Yard," *Boston Globe,* Apr. 25, 2006.

359 the 82 acres surrounding the White House: "Holiday in the National Parks: Christmas at the White House 2007," holiday tour booklet, author's collection.

360 "We gave them a little booklet": Interview with McBride, Aug. 26, 2008.

360 signifying the precious treasure: *White House Christmas 2007,* Home & Garden Television, Scripps Networks, LLC, 2007; http://www.hgtv.com/videos/white-house-christmas-2007/31228.html.

363 "The fact that the surface was curved": Adrian Martinez, e-mail communication, Apr. 3, 2009.

370 "It's President Bush's favorite dish": Interview with Cristeta Comerford, White House Executive Chef, Washington, D.C., Aug. 26, 2008.

372 "During the holidays": Interview with William "Bill" Yosses, White House Executive Pastry Chef, Washington, D.C., Aug. 26, 2008.

372 "It's always good to see": The White House, President George W. Bush, "Barney Cam VI: Holiday in the National Parks," transcript, http://georgewbush-whitehouse.archives.gov/holiday/2007/barneycam.html.

2008

373 "For as long as I've been": Interview with McBride, Aug. 26, 2008.

373 "The colors of Old Glory": "A Red, White and Blue Christmas: Holidays at the White House 2008," holiday tour booklet, author's collection.

384 "The idea was so wonderfully characteristic": Interview with McBride, Aug. 26, 2008.

385 "Christmases at the White House": Conversation with Jeanne L. Phillips, April 29, 2009.

385 "It's been a privilege": Quoted in Marian Burros, "For First Lady, White House Nostalgia," *New York Times,* Dec. 3, 2008.

387 "An ancient tale tells us": Jacqueline Kennedy, "A Christmas Message," *Look* 27, no. 27 (Dec. 31, 1963): 14. "The Story of the Presidents at Christmas" was written by Fletcher Knebel.

INDEX

This book was printed and bound in the United States of America.

This book was produced with 100% wind generated sources of power,
earth-friendly soy ink, and recycled paper which contains 10% recovered
fiber content, certified by the Forest Stewardship Council.

Williamson Printing Company, Dallas, Texas, is an ISO 14001:2004 certified printer.

A portion of the proceeds will be donated to the White House Historical Association.

FIFE&
DRUM
PRESS

fifeanddrumpress.com